SECTION I:
The Behavior Modifier

ISSUES IN EVALUATING BEHAVIOR MODIFICATION

PROCEEDINGS OF THE FIRST DRAKE CONFERENCE
ON PROFESSIONAL ISSUES IN
BEHAVIOR ANALYSIS (1st : 1974 : Drake University)
MARCH 1974

EDITED AND INTRODUCED BY

DR. W. SCOTT WOOD

RESEARCH PRESS
2612 NORTH MATTIS AVENUE
CHAMPAIGN ILLINOIS
61820

ISBN 0-87822-150-6

This project (Issues in Evaluating Behavior Modification) was supported in part by SRS Grant No. 56-P-35177/7-01 from the Social and Rehabilitation Service, Rehabilitation Services Administration—Developmental Disabilities.

Preparation of "Quality Control in the Behavior Analysis Approach to Project Follow Through" was supported in part by a Grant from the U. S. Office of Education, Department of Health, Education, and Welfare. However, the opinions expressed herein do not necessarily reflect the position or policy of the U. S. Office of Education, and no official endorsement by the U. S. Office of Education should be inferred.

The development and refinement of the treatment, training and evaluation models described in "Achievement Place: The Training and Certification of Teaching Parents" were supported by grants MH16609, MH13644, and MH20030 from the Center for Studies of Crime and Delinquency, National Institute of Mental Health to the Bureau of Child Research and Department of Human Development, University of Kansas, Lawrence, Kansas.

CONTENTS

SECTION III   ACCOUNTABILITY AND ETHICS

CONTRIBUTORS

W. Stewart Agras
Department of Psychiatry
Stanford University Medical Center

Beth Sulzer-Azaroff
Mansfield Training Center
University of Massachusetts

Curtis J. Braukmann
Achievement Place Research Project
University of Kansas

Don Bushell, Jr.
Department of Human Development
University of Kansas

Dean L. Fixsen
Achievement Place Research Project
University of Kansas

Robert P. Hawkins
Department of Psychology
West Virginia University

Donald A. Jackson
Project Follow Through
Department of Human Development
University of Kansas

Kathryn A. Kirigin
Achievement Place Research Project
University of Kansas

Jon E. Krapfl
Department of Psychology
West Virginia University

Jack L. Michael
Department of Psychology
Western Michigan University

Elaine A. Phillips
Achievement Place Research Project
Bureau of Child Research
University of Kansas

Elery L. Phillips
Achievement Place Research Project
Bureau of Child Research
University of Karsas

Todd R. Risley
Department of Human Development
University of Kansas

Stephanie B. Stolz
National Institute of Mental Health

Jack Thaw
Mansfield Training Center
University of Massachusetts

Carol Thomas
Mansfield Training Center
University of Massachusetts

Lynn C. Weis
Project Follow Through
Department of Human Development
University of Kansas

Montrose M. Wolf
Achievement Place Research Project
University of Kansas

W. Scott Wood
Department of Psychology
Drake University

RESPONDENTS

Jon S. Bailey
Department of Psychology
Florida State University

Stephen C. Bitgood
Department of Psychology
Jacksonville State University

Julian D. Ford
Department of Psychology
State University of New York
Stony Brook

Dale A. General
Department of Psychology
North Texas University

Bill L. Hopkins
Kansas Center for Mental
Retardation and Human Development
University of Kansas

William R. Hutchison
Department of Psychology
State University of New York
Stony Brook

Kenneth E. Lloyd
Department of Psychology
Drake University

Margaret E. Lloyd
Department of Psychology
Drake University

Richard W. Malott
Department of Psychology
Western Michigan University

Garry L. Martin
Department of Psychology
University of Manitoba

William A. Myerson
Department of Psychology
West Virginia University

J. Grayson Osborne
Department of Psychology
Utah State University

Stephen I. Sulzbacher
Child Development and
Retardation Center
University of Washington

Jayme S. Whitehead
Center for Human Development
Drake University

ACKNOWLEDGMENTS

This is the first publication of the proceedings of the Drake Conference on Professional Issues in Behavior Analysis. These conferences will provide a continuing forum for the discussion of issues in the field of applied behavior analysis that are related to the professional development of that discipline.

We, the Psychology Department at Drake University, wish to acknowledge several people whose interest and support not only made the conference possible, but who have provided us with support and encouragement in many other ways as well. We are particularly indebted to Jon E. Krapfl, West Virginia University, who was the first director of the applied behavior analysis program at Drake University. Without his planning and administrative judgment, it is unlikely that our training program, let alone the conference, would ever have occurred. We also wish to acknowledge the continuing support of the Dean of Liberal Arts, Dr. Leland P. Johnson, who has helped us to develop a graduate program that makes such a conference a vital part of our students' education. We also appreciate the support of Mr. William M. Ferguson, Regional Developmental Disabilities Consultant, whose interest and support led us to seek the grant which made the conference possible.

Two people were especially important in the coordination and organization of the conference program. Mrs. Anne Connolly, the conference coordinator, played an essential role in all aspects of the conference, from the financial planning to helping prepare the manuscripts for publication. Mrs. Sandi Martin, the department and conference secretary, also contributed much time and effort toward the organization of the conference activities.

Finally, we must acknowledge the contributions of Jack L. Michael, Western Michigan University, who served as the conference chairman. The field of behavior analysis would unquestionably exist and function as an important social resource without Jack, but it probably would have taken longer to emerge and it certainly would be a lot duller

INTRODUCTION

There are two ways to view the rapidly expanding field of behavior modification: in terms of its increasing membership, or in terms of its theoretical features and their growing influence on other disciplines. From either perspective, behavior modification is growing, with many more "behavior modifiers" and many more "behavior modification programs" than there were a decade ago. However, this situation has produced a certain amount of concern both within and outside the field because this growth has been, to a large extent, unassessed.

In the past behavior modifiers were essentially of two groups: applied researchers investigating human behavior with the methods and logic of the basic operant conditioning laboratory (the applied behavior analysts); and clinical psychologists utilizing learning theory in their treatment of clients (behavior therapists). Although somewhat dissimilar, the goals and methods of both groups were clearly understood by their respective members, each having its own professional organization and journals. In addition, they shared the commitment to objective control in dealing with human behavior that distinguished their perspective on human nature (and how to change it) from all others. However, the number of members in either group was not especially large. Also, the kinds of problems that the two groups dealt with were relatively circumscribed. The applied behavior analysts tended toward involvement with populations whose behavioral handicaps were so severe as to seemingly justify the explicit manipulation of rewards and punishment that was the hallmark of the early applied behavior analysis research. And while the behavior therapists usually dealt with less behaviorally deficit populations, the consent nature of the client-therapist relationship permitted considerable experimentation in treatment without arousing much public concern.

Today, however, both groups have considerably expanded membership and have begun research and intervention programs with more socially visible and controversial client populations. In addition, various proposals for social programs based on deliberate behavioral control, by B. F. Skinner and others, have had the result of bringing the field of behavior modification under the scrutiny of various professional and lay groups who are concerned about the personal and political implications of large-scale social programs explicitly designed to control human behavior.

It was this situation of increasing numbers of behavior modifiers and increasing public concern about the growth of behavioral control methods in society that prompted this conference on the topic of the evaluation of behavior analysis programs and personnel. Those within the field were especially concerned about the quality of training that the growing numbers of behavior modifiers were receiving, since it was apparent that people were beginning to identify themselves (or be identified by others) as behavior modifiers who had backgrounds ranging from MA's and Ph.D.'s in behavior modification (from the applied behavior analysis or behavior therapist orientation) to those who had attended an in-service workshop on behavior modification or at least knew somebody who had attended one. Thus additional support for the conference came from social agencies at federal, state and private levels that were concerned about their ability to distinguish and evaluate behavior modifiers and their programs, both with respect to their effectiveness and their ethics.

However timely the conference, the issues were not simple. The original conversations and preliminary meetings which preceded the conference tended to focus on licensing or certification procedures for behavior modifiers. In fact, some behavior therapists already had acted upon such an approach. The applied behavior analysts, being somewhat more research and less clinically oriented, were generally opposed to such a strategy, even though a growing number of applied behavior analysts were themselves more involved with treatment than they were with applied research per se. However, although licensing was a topic which surfaced frequently at the conference, there were a number of other issues discussed that were only indirectly related to that particular problem (or solution) and were of equal or greater importance regarding the professional development of the field. These are the issues that provide the organization of the following chapters.

The first section focuses on the question of the definition of a behavior modifier. Throughout the preceding discussion, I have maintained the distinction between the applied behavior analyst and behavior therapist; several conference speakers made further contributions to the issue of identifying the behavior modifier more precisely.

A second key area elaborated on by a group of conference speakers and respondents was the problem of evaluating behavior analysis procedures and programs. Earlier applied behavior analysis research followed a relatively standard (and almost stylized) methodology that originally was adapted from individual organism research. The evaluation system was essentially "built in" and was based on continuous measurement of the subject's behavior. That kind of scientific measurement is necessary to establish validity of a particular research or intervention strategy, but its relationship to the standardization and cost-effectiveness goals of some of the newer behavior modification programs has not been well worked out.

The final topic that emerged from the conference involved the question of accountability and ethics regarding the behaviorist in society. There was considerable attention and debate directed to the problem of ethical and social responsibility for those who can deliberately control the behavior of a client or subject, and are often paid to do so by someone other than the client himself.

Finally, it is appropriate to make some observations concerning the characteristics of the conference speakers, respondents and audience. First, the group was primarily of the applied behavior analysis orientation, as the obvious operant bias of the papers and comments undoubtedly reveals. Second, the speakers and respondents were primarily university-based researchers and teachers, not practitioners in applied settings. There were few, if any, philosophic opponents of the behavior modification approach at the conference. Most people who attended the conference accepted the importance of evaluating their own skills and programs from the perspective of improvement, and not abandonment.

ISSUES IN THE CERTIFICATION
OF BEHAVIOR MODIFIERS

W. Stewart Agras

It is particularly appropriate to begin this volume by discussing the certification of behavior therapists since professional certification is a possible solution to some of the problems which face behavior modification today. As criticism of these experimental, therapeutic approaches increases, particularly in the popular press, so the demand for self regulation in the form of certification can be expected to increase. This will be particularly true as the clamor becomes increasingly irrational by those equating, for example, behavior modification with the modification of behavior achieved by psychosurgery, or by the use of psychoactive drugs. It is muddle that is, I suspect, as embarrassing to the neurosurgeon or psychopharmacologist as it is to the behavior modifier.*

In what must now appear as a remarkably farsighted statement the Association for the Advancement of Behavior Therapy (AABT, 1969) noted in its By-laws six years ago that ". . . the growing interest in behavior therapy, alternatively known as behavior modification or conditioning therapy, poses new problems for the clinician. . . . There is a danger that clinicians, lacking an adequate background in learning principles and experimental methodology, and

---

* This chapter is based upon a paper: "Toward the certification of behavior therapists" which was published in the *Journal of Applied Behavior Analysis,* 1973, *6,* 167-172.

1

unaware of the complex theoretical and technical issues involved, may represent themselves as behavior therapists while employing techniques and procedures based neither on learning theory nor learning technology. On the other hand, persons trained in experimental methods may attempt the clinical application of laboratory research methods without sufficient regard for the need to acquire other skills essential to good clinical practice."

Reports in the news media of the use of apomorphine injections to punish infractions such as lying or swearing in prison populations, or the perhaps excessive use of isolation techniques under the guise of time-out procedures, seem to be, if they have been reported accurately, examples of the misuse of behavior therapy. These events give credence to the Behavior Therapy and Research Society's view (*Behavior Therapy and Experimental Psychiatry*, 1970), ". . . that it is urgently necessary to erect standards of training and competence in the field of behavior therapy and modification. . . ." A subcommittee of three members was chosen to ". . . formulate a list of charter clinical fellows on each of whom they would be unanimous" (Brady, Reyna, and Wolpe, 1971).

Such a move might well be protective of the solid, but still infant, body of research which is slowly increasing the competence of behavior modifiers to influence in a positive direction increasingly complex and difficult social problems. However, this step, which necessitates establishing criteria to define the kinds of knowledge and skills which a behavior therapist should demonstrate, deserves thoughtful discussion since it affects the future development of behavior therapy.

THE FIELD

What is meant by the terms behavior therapy, conditioning therapy, and behavior modification? One definition is that they encompass a set of clinical procedures based on established principles of learning. This list includes systematic desensitization; positive reinforcement procedures; aversive procedures, including punishment escape and avoidance procedures; classical conditioning and covert sensitization; implosion or flooding; modeling; paradoxical intent; negative practice; assertive training; and behavioral contracting. Lazarus (1971) extends this position by defining behavior therapy as ". . . a clinical undertaking which adds a series of specific techniques and operations (preferably derived from experimental psychology and certainly couched within a broad behavioral framework) to those few empirically validated procedures which have been part of traditional psychotherapeutic use. . . ." In this way behavior therapy is related to the general field of psychotherapeutic practice.

Although the above definition fits the interests of therapeutic practice by emphasizing the use of empirically validated treatment procedures, it poses some difficulties. While a procedure such as clinical application of selective positive reinforcement is closely tied to and clearly derived from basic research with a variety of organisms, others, such as implosive therapy or desensitization, have less clear ties. Even in the former case, the experimental analysis of the use of social attention or praise as contingent events poses new problems in definition, in quantification, and in the control of the complicated social interaction within which such events must be delivered. More difficult again is implosive therapy which claims to be based on the procedure of extinction (Stampfl and Levis, 1967). Full-strength fear arousing cues, presented verbally, are assumed to lead eventually to extinction of anxiety and avoidance behavior in the actual feared (or phobic) situation. In the identification of fear arousing cues, events based on assumed verbal symbolic relationships are often used. Here the relationship to the original experimentally defined procedure is nearer analogy than fact; replication of the treatment is difficult, as is analysis of effectiveness; and what is responsible for the effect is made difficult by the nature of the often dramatic interpersonal situation of therapy.

An alternative view of the field has been phrased in several different ways, depending on the background of the definer. Astrup (1965) defines behavior therapy as the application of conditional reflex theory and experiments (in particular) ". . . the detailed experimental study of the physiological basis of therapeutic mechanisms. . ."; Baer et al. (1968) define the field as ". . . the process of applying sometimes tentative principles of behavior to improve specific behaviors, and simultaneously evaluating. . . whether and which part of the application was successful." Yates (1970) most clearly represents this viewpoint when he notes that ". . .behavior therapy is fundamentally distinguishable from other therapeutic efforts by . . . the application of the experimental method to the understanding and modification of abnormalities of behavior." An applied behavior analysis which should, according to Baer et al. (1968), ". . . make obvious the importance of the behavior changed, its quantitative characteristics, the experimental manipulations which analyze with clarity what was responsible for the change, the technologically exact description of all procedures contributing to that change, the effectiveness of those procedures in making sufficient change for value, and the generality of that change." Like Yates, these authors emphasize the study of the single case; but no particular experimental method is advocated. This approach places behavior modification alongside experimental approaches to the modification of deviant behavior deriving from the biological sciences such as psychopharmacology; it also defines behavior therapy or modification as the application of the research methods and experimentally verified findings of the experimental behavioral sciences to the understanding and alteration of deviant behavior.

THE THERAPIST

The field may then be defined in two ways: clinical or procedure oriented on the one hand, and experimental-analytic on the other. What are the current definitions of the therapist? Wolpe (1968) suggests that the behavior therapist ". . . bases his strategy upon his knowledge of experimentally established principles of learning against a background of physiology." Ullman and Krasner (1965) list characteristics such as the ability to manage complex therapeutic relationships and concern for the patient's overall welfare, as well as more specific characteristics: knowledge of general and experimental psychology; ability to define problem behavior operationally; identification of reinforcers which maintain deviant behavior, and the ability to program schedules of reinforcement. Finally, Bijou (1970) characterizes the behavioral school psychologist as including the ". . . essential that the practitioner learn from first sources (1) the nature of the concepts and principles and supporting data, (2) the methodology of practical application and the basic literature on the behavioral technology of teaching, (3) the individual research methodology. . . ." In addition, ". . . practitioners should obtain experience in applying those principles."

The behavior therapist, then, must have knowledge of the principles underlying behavior modification, experience in the application

4

of such knowledge to human behavior problems, and experience in the experimental analysis of deviant human behavior, both for research purposes, and as an approach to the ongoing evaluation of clinical care. He must also, however, demonstrate certain less well defined characteristics, usually referred to as general clinical skills.

These skills consist of a cluster of behaviors which have not been rigorously examined, but which appear essential for good clinical care, and which are acquired to a greater or lesser degree during clinical graduate training in a more or less systematic way. They include the ability to form a working relationship with patients (clients, students), their families, the community, and other therapeutic staff. Such a working relationship embraces characteristics found in any helpful human encounter, including the ability to offer hope for a solution to problems, a rational context in which to understand problems, and a rationale for change. The clinician must also be aware of the total needs of the patient or client, and must be able to fit his endeavors into an overall program of care. This implies an awareness of the variety of problem behaviors encountered in any given population, and of the possible causes of such behavior, whether physiological or environmental, so that appropriate referral can be made and adequate consultation obtained.

Equally important is the willingness to follow through with a treatment program despite the uncertainties and vicissitudes which beset therapists. Indeed, the ability to deal with ambiguous and uncertain situations when operating within that vast, shadowy area of the partly known, and to carry through a therapeutic program despite these hazards, is an essential therapist characteristic.

Since many of these therapist characteristics, particularly those specific to the behavior therapist, are measurable, then the setting of performance standards, and also certification, is possible. The question is, should we move in this direction?

TOWARD CERTIFICATION?

The case for certification is straightforward and strong and, moreover, has historical precedent; the most recent is psychoanalysis. Following World War II, psychoanalysis faced the same issue that now concerns behavior therapy. It was felt that the profession had no protection against unqualified and self-styled psychoanalysts, and no way to protect the public from unscrupulous therapists. In response to those concerns, and after considerable controversy, psychoanalytic training and certification came under the supervision of a national body that established standards for training and membership in the American Psychoanalytic Association. There is no doubt that this technique worked very well. Psychoanalysis is a well-accepted therapeutic procedure even though its scientific basis is far weaker than the evolving experimental work of applied behavior analysis.

Just as the performance problems surrounding clinical work can be handled by certification, so the ethical problems concerning research activities could also be handled by an accrediting body. This, then, would provide an answer to some of the critics of behavior modification. Such criticism, for example, as expressed by an editor of the San Francisco *Chronicle* of March 12, 1974: "Behavior modification in the Iowa Prison System recently was declared to be cruel and unusual punishment by the U.S. Court of Appeals." After some four more paragraphs, which discuss apomorphine treatment, psychosurgery, medical research, and chemotherapy, all of which have apparently become significant tools of American law enforcement, the editorial continues: "If some of the more fervent believers in the theories of Dr. B. F. Skinner have their way, just about anybody who does not meet middle-class standards of behavior and thought would be put in the hands of the state. Already, there are dangerous tendencies in the treatment of so-called hyperkinetic children and the elderly." In the face of such outbursts it would be comforting to have a certification system. However, I have argued elsewhere (Agras, 1973) that the problems created by certification may outweigh the benefits.

PROBLEMS OF CERTIFICATION

The definitions of the field and of the therapist outlined earlier suggest that we are dealing with a continuum of partially overlapping interests, endeavors, and skills subsumed under the terms behavior therapy and behavior modification. To clarify this continuum, I studied the contents of three behaviorally-oriented journals: the *Journal of Applied Behavior Analysis (JABA)*, *Behavior Therapy (BT)*, and *Behavior Therapy and Experimental Psychiatry (BTEP)*. These journals have somewhat different editorial policies aimed at different audiences. The first is for "the publication of reports of experimental research involving . . . problems of social importance." *Behavior Therapy* is an interdisciplinary journal for the "publication of . . . research of an experimental or clinical nature which contributes to the theory or practice of behavior therapy or behavior modification in any setting"; while the last is designed to publish "research papers . . ." and ". . . to bring behavior therapy squarely into the domain of the psychiatrist." Thus all are interested in applied research; *JABA* is more experimentally oriented and less oriented toward therapeutics, and *BTEP* is more clearly aimed at the practitioner.

The papers in the latest complete volume of each of these journals were classified under a number of headings. The first classification was determined by whether the behavior studied was deviant or normal; behaviors classified as deviant were those defined as such by the author (e.g., delinquent, phobic, autistic, etc.). Second, each study was classified into experimental or non-experimental, depending upon the use of control procedures, and then according to the kind of experiment (i.e., an experimental behavior analysis or a group comparison). No attempt was made to assess the adequacy of the experiment. Other articles were classified into case reports as defined by the author or editor unless they in fact fell into the experimental category. Such reports were therefore primarily descriptive and not experimental-analytic. The final categories were discussion articles and technical notes.*

The results of the analysis are presented in Table 1, page 11. A significant gradient is apparent. *JABA* is the most experimentally oriented and deals less frequently with deviant behavior, more often outside a hospital or residential institutional setting; *BTEP* has fewer experimental articles, and deals mostly with deviant behavior, more often in a hospital setting than not. *BT* is midway between the other two journals on these indices. *JABA* most clearly exemplifies an experi-

---

* Dr. Larry Doke kindly helped me to estimate the reliability of the classification by independently classifying half the volumes of each journal (a total of 81 papers). Reliability was calculated as Agreements/Agreements + Disagreements x 100. The reliability of the definitions was as follows: Deviance 85%; Experimental 94%; Type of Experiment 97%; Case report 94%; Discussion Articles 98%; and Technical Notes 98%.

mental application of the behavioral sciences (e.g., 0% case reports), while *BTEP* exemplifies clinical application (e.g., 43% case reports).

These findings suggest, as do the editorial policies of the journals, that the continuum of interests under the term behavior therapy has two extremes—clinical and experimental—echoing the two definitions of the field: a treatment or procedure-oriented approach and an experimental approach. At present there is some overlap between the extremes, suggesting mutual interest. For instance, two authors published in both *JABA* and *BTEP*. More important, over one-third of the experiments reported in the latter journal are experimental analyses of behavior. But the overlap is small, suggesting that the inter-action between clinician and experimenter needs careful fostering lest it attenuate. Separation of the two tends to produce experimenters who investigate increasingly less important issues; convenience of population wins over social relevance. It is clear that a trend in this direction already exists since the more experimental *Journal of Applied Behavior Analysis* deals less frequently with deviant populations than the more clinical *Journal of Behavior Therapy and Experimental Psychiatry*. Many Ph.D. theses attest to the same failure, namely a tendency toward elegant triviality as indicated, for example, by the increasing preoccupation of experimenters with the mounting epidemic of snake fears among our undergraduate college students. Separation also produces clinicians who are uninterested in experimentally verifying whether or not their techniques work, or how they work; they concentrate on the details of technique rather than on experiments. This results in a dogmatic orientation not amenable to logical change, an attitude which has dominated the fields of counseling, psychotherapy, and education for many years.

Separation can also occur between the behavioral approach and closely related fields of inquiry. Many authors (see Krantz, 1971) have pointed to the separation of operant and non-operant psychology. While there are some good reasons for a separation between different kinds of scientific endeavor, much opportunity for fruitful interaction is lost. A potential exists for interaction between behavior therapy and other clinical approaches, and between the applied experimental behav-ioral sciences and other basic sciences concerned with behavior change. I am not advocating a wishy-washy eclecticism or a dilution of experi-mental rigor, but rather I am underlining the enormous relevance of the methods and technology of the behavioral sciences to the field of therapeutic behavior change, and the relevance of findings from other experimental fields to behavior modification and behavior therapy.

Separation or interaction is the crucial issue. It is my opinion that certification of behavior therapists may be just the kind of artificial distinction that will promote the separation of behavioral experimenter and clinician, and the separation of behavior therapy from other fields of inquiry. To return to our example of psychoanalysis, we find that the early psychoanalysts made observations about human behavior that provoked opposition from both the general public and professionals. In response to this opposition, and to early defections, Freud and his collaborators, known as the inner circle, strove for unity, often using rather authoritarian methods to gain their end. Following the institution of certification procedures, this authoritarian attitude was reinforced and finally led to psychoanalysis being taught and viewed as a static system with well substantiated therapeutic procedures (Alexander and Selesnick, 1966). Moreover, training requirements necessary for membership in the Psychoanalytic Society barred scientists of different persuasions from membership, and thus prevented other sciences from influencing the development of psychoanalysis.

Behavior therapy should take this unfortunate example seriously. If certification reduces scientific interchange, then the two ends of our postulated clinical-experimental continuum will separate, producing a technique-oriented school of psychotherapy (or method of remedial education) and a behavioral science of little relevance to the clinician. This is the very opposite of the field's present promise.

If certification of behavior modifiers is not the best solution to the present problems, we must ask ourselves whether reasonable alternatives exist. Other alternatives are proposed in this volume. Dr. Todd Risley, for example, suggests that programs should be certified rather than therapists. Moreover, unethical behavior and standards of training are also problems for the profession or discipline, and are not problems unique to behavior therapy. Since certification threatens bankruptcy for behavior therapy in the future, it seems preferable for behavior therapists to work within their existing professional organizations to strengthen current licensing and certification procedures.

That is, behavior modification is not a profession, but an experimental approach to the problems of human behavior (behavior analysis) and a technology based on that experimental approach (applied behavior analysis or behavior therapy). These terms, applied behavior analysis and behavior therapy, seem to be preferable to the term behavior modification which should be used to refer to all techniques which change or modify behavior, including such techniques as the psychotherapies, psychopharmacology and psychosurgery.

If applied behavior analysis develops as it should, with maximum interaction both within and outside the field, then there will be no such thing as a misrepresented behavior therapist. Our present clustering of interests should so influence others that all sciences interested in behavior change will borrow methods and procedures from this field and make them their own, and all therapists will use techniques which have been empirically validated. In this light the behavior therapist may be viewed as a transitional phenomenon, one who should not be ossified by certification.

Table 1. A Comparison of Three Journals showing Population Studied, Type of Article, and Type of Experiment Reported.

	Population	Type of Article			Type Experiment	
	Deviant	Controlled experiment	Case reports	Technical note	Experimental analysis of behavior	Group Comparison
Journal of Applied Behavior Analysis, Vol. 3	58%	82%	0%	14%	97%	3%
Behavior Therapy, Vol. 2	65%	48%	16%	4%	26%	74%
Behavior Therapy and Experimental Psychiatry, Vol. 1	70%	29%	43%	2%	36%	64%

REFERENCES

Agras, W. S. Toward the certification of behavior therapists? *Journal of Applied Behavior Analysis*, 1973, *6*, 167-172.

Alexander, F. G. and Selesnick, S. T. *The history of psychiatry: An evaluation of psychiatric thought and practice from prehistoric times to the present.* New York: Harper and Row, 1966.

Association for the Advancement of Behavior Therapy—By-Laws. New York: 1969.

Astrup, C. *Pavolvian psychiatry: A new synthesis.* Springfield, Illinois: Charles C. Thomas, 1965.

Baer, D. M., Wolf, M. M., and Risley, T. R. Some current dimensions of applied behavior analysis. *Journal of Applied Behavior Analysis*, 1968, *1*, 91-97.

Behavior Therapy and Research Society: By-Laws. *Journal of Behavior Therapy and Experimental Psychiatry*, 1970, *1*, 245-247.

Bijou, S. W. What psychology has to offer education now. *Journal of Applied Behavior Analysis*, 1970, *3*, 65-71.

Brady, J. P. Reyna, L. F., and Wolpe, J. Personal communication, 1971.

Krantz, D. L. The separate worlds of operant and non-operant psychology. *Journal of Applied Behavior Analysis*, 1971, *4*, 61-70.

Lazarus, A. A. Reflections on behavior therapy and its development: A point of view. *Behavior Therapy*, 1971, *2*, 369-374.

Stampfl, T. G. and Levis, D. J. Essentials of implosive therapy: A learning theory based psychodynamic behavioral therapy. *Journal of Abnormal Psychology*, 1967, *72*, 496-503.

Ullman, L. P. and Krasner, L. *Case studies in behavior modification.* New York: Holt, Rinehart, and Winston, 1965.

Wolpe, J. *Association for Advancement of the Behavioral Therapies 3.* 1968, pp. 1-2.

Yates, A. J. *Behavior therapy.* New York: Wiley, 1970.

RESPONSE

Jon S. Bailey

I cannot argue with Dr. Agras that abuses and misuses of the principles of behavior have taken place or that corrective steps need to be taken. It is clear from our newspapers and national magazines that clients have been shocked, restrained, and deprived of their rights, given drugs of questionable value and have had their brains operated on in the name of "behavior modification." In Florida two years ago we had a scandal of massive proportions at one of our Sunland Centers for the retarded. Children who swore had their mouths washed out with soap as a "punishment" procedure; others were forced to re-enact, in front of the staff, sexual behaviors they had been caught engaging in. Still others were locked in seclusion or deprived of their normal meals as punishment. These and other acts of inhumanity to the retarded were instigated or approved by a psychologist who claimed that he was a "behavior modifier."

These gross misapplications of principles, which have proven extremely helpful as well as humane in countless other instances, demand that we do something to prevent their reoccurrence. The principles do not apply themselves; they are interpreted and applied by people. Presumably, then, if we could be sure that these people had received the proper training and had been *certified*, our problems would disappear. I am not so sure. We do not have good imitative examples of the effects of certification in either law or medicine, disciplines that have practiced it for years. As I am inclined to do with other problems, I suggest that we do a quick behavior analysis of certification.

Certification is basically a procedure whereby a person is asked to emit a set of behaviors. He is then evaluated according to some standard, and if he exceeds the minimum requirement, he is then "certified" as competent to operate on his own, without supervision. A few features of the procedure need to be highlighted. First, the behaviors to be emitted usually occur in circumstances grossly different from where they are ultimately to occur (i.e., we would not expect 100% generalization). Second, because of practical constraints, the person will in all likelihood be tested on a small fraction of the behaviors he will be required to use in everyday practice. Finally, and possibly most importantly, the contingencies of the test are likely to be far different from the practical situation. For example, a law student may react in one way to a hypothetical question about bribery and in another way if he actually were bribed or asked by a high government official to bribe someone else.

I contend that these deficiencies in the certification model would be greatly multiplied if used in the field of applied behavior analysis. Allow me to briefly give a few examples of the nature of the problems that I see as a result.

Settings. A behavior modifier may find himself working in a variety of settings. Although he was trained to work with, say, the institutionalized retarded, he may find himself working in a mental institution, a public school, halfway house, prison, child clinic, rehabilitation institute, or government agency. Would he have to be examined in all of these settings to be certified to work in them?

Sources of authority. In each setting the sources of power and authority are different. Having learned to be successful in public schools does not guarantee that a person will not make mistakes in dealing with the often elaborate bureaucracy of an institution. Do we certify that a person can operate successfully given varying degrees of supervision or responsibility? If so, how can this be done? Surely a paper and pencil test over this repertoire would not be adequate.

Client population. The field of behavior analysis has caught on in so many fields that the range in subject population is vast. No training program I am acquainted with could possibly give training in all of them. Thus, a behavior modifier in training may spend some time working with an institutionalized retarded child or hyperactive child in a public school. But this does not assure us that he would be able to deal successfully with an adult mental patient, a delinquent, a drug abuser, a rapist, or even a child more or less retarded or hyperactive other than the ones he was trained with.

Problem behaviors. The range of behavior problems which can currently be affected positively by a behavior modifier grows daily. Teaching a normal child to tie his shoe, to discriminate red from green, or motivating him to complete his math assignments is far from working with a chronically unemployed adult who cannot hold a job because of his bad temper. The types of behavior problems that *can* be dealt with is enormous and most behavior modifiers are confronted with a large percentage of them in their training. In an age of specialization, would we need to certify some behavior modifiers to work with acquisition of behaviors in unmotivated subjects, and others to work with acquisition in motivated clients? What about maintenance behaviors? Would people be certified to work with them exclusively?

Procedures to be used. A few years ago the procedures a behavior modifier had at his disposal were relatively limited and unsophisticated. Extinction, reinforcement, shaping and fading could be taught in a few weeks of concentrated practice. Today, however, procedures are being developed which appear to be much more complicated. Overcorrection and restitution, social education, contingency contracting, home-based reinforcement systems and the procedure used by Azrin & Foxx for toilet training are but a few which come to mind. We can only expect that this trend toward the development of new procedures will continue into the future. Will behavior modifiers have to be recertified each time a new procedure comes out and before they can use it? At what point does a new procedure become acceptable so that it *can* be authorized for use? What happens when procedures become obsolete? How do we certify that people who learned to use them several years ago will not continue a procedure which has been replaced by a more effective one?

Who will certify? Certification, like abuse, is carried out by people. Who *will* be responsible for certifying our behavior modifiers? Will it be done by state or federal government agencies? Private consulting firms? Universities? Or will APA Division 25 or some similar group be chosen? And, who will do the choosing of those who will certify? Once it is decided who, then what will they certify? People? Procedures? Training programs? And what guidelines will they use? Finally, certification implies the authority to control the behavior of people or institutions. What will be the nature of the enforcement? Will it be benign or punitive? Will it involve incentives? And suppose someone is not certified by the group; will he have recourse to another group? The questions are almost endless and clearly suggest that certification is not to be entered into lightly.

Is certification the treatment of choice? The questions raised in this discussion should leave little doubt that I do not believe certification will solve the problems we are confronted with. As behavior modifiers we should actually be somewhat embarrassed to propose a solution that does not follow from the principles of behavior to which we subscribe so fervently, especially since there is a lack of any data to suggest that it is effective regardless of its origins.

Alternatives to certification. Perhaps we could consider some alternatives which may not be so involved or restrictive as certification. I would like briefly to suggest a few which come to mind.

1. *Educating the consumer.* Behavior modification, or behavior analysis, exists because there are consumers who will support experimentally developed therapeutic procedures which are more effective than anything else. One way of eliminating abuse might be to educate those consumers to know what to expect and what to watch for in their behavior modifier. A "Consumer Report" type of publication for behavior analysis might be useful in this regard.

2. *Regulate the use of certain procedures.* The most recent session of the Florida legislature considered a bill that would have disallowed the use of deprivation as an aversive control behavior modification procedure except under the most severe circumstances and then only under the scrutiny of authorized and approved personnel.

16

3. *Watchdog groups.* The same bill described above would have established, with legislative mandate, Human Rights Advocacy Committees for each region of the state. Any behavior modification program would have to be approved by this committee before it could be used in any institution for the retarded. Similar consumer committees made up of laymen from the community might represent the mentally ill, those in jail or prison, and so on.

4. *Online evaluation.* The Behavior Analysis Follow Through program at the University of Kansas and the Achievement Place program at the same institution have developed elaborate systems for monitoring the performance of their teachers and the teaching parent respectively. Both of these methods are described in detail later in this symposium. I would suggest that this method might be adaptable to behavior modifiers in general.

Final thoughts. Ideally, it seems that the problem of abuses in our field ought to be submitted to experimental analysis by our best and most productive researchers. Studies should be run to discover which method is the most effective in reducing abuse in its many forms, from simple passive neglect to actual physical harm. I urge that we avoid the temptation to rush to certification for a quick solution to our problems and instead follow the tradition of carefully analyzing and researching the problem of abuse directly.

RESPONSE

Margaret E. Lloyd

In order to discuss the issues involved in the certification of behavior modifiers Dr. Agras, both in his 1973 article and at this conference, has attempted to define the field of behavior modification. He has done so in terms of the skills and knowledge that behavior modifiers should possess; i.e., an understanding of the principles underlying behavior modification and, more uniquely, in terms of the characteristics of the articles published in three major journals. He suggests that the field is a continuum of overlapping interests ranging from experimental-analytic interests represented roughly by the publications of the *Journal of Applied Behavior Analysis* to clinical or procedure-oriented interests represented by the publications in *Behavior Therapy and Experimental Psychiatry*. This continuum appears to be largely one of scientific rigor; from the experiment at one pole to the case study at the other; from research to clinical practice. Dr. Agras argues against certification by saying that it would damage the field by splitting the two poles of the continuum, research and practice, still farther apart.

While this argument may turn out to be a compelling one, it seems to me that, as it stands, it is based on an oversimplified definition of the field. We actually are dealing not with one continuum but two.* Some time ago Keehn and Webster (1969) made an analysis of the field of learning theory-based therapies. They separated those therapeutic practices which were largely based, at least by convention, on respondent psychology and labelled behavior therapy, from those practices

---

* Keehn, J. D. and Webster, C. D. Behavior therapy and behavior modification. *The Canadian Psychologist*, 1969, *10*, 68-73.

based on operant psychology, labelled behavior modification. The separation was probably a useful one since the two areas have certainly not developed synchronously.

The work being done in *each* of these two areas, behavior modification and behavior therapy, could be spread along a continuum of rigor such as the one suggested by Dr. Agras. Such a continuum might include basic animal research at one pole, applied research somewhere in the middle, and treatment (e.g., therapeutic intervention in which the controlling effect of the independent variable is not verified) at the other pole.

Behavior modification spreads across its entire continuum. If one wished to continue the journal analogy, then it spreads from *JEAB* to *JABA* to various descriptions of behavioral treatments such as those reported in the newsletter, the "Boulder Behaviorist," and other local newsletters. Behavior therapy, however, does *not* spread entirely across its continuum. There clearly is treatment in behavior therapy. Behavior therapy also occupies the applied research area of its continuum as demonstrated by the work of Dr. Agras, Peter Lang and many others. There is very little activity in behavior therapy at the basic research pole of the continuum. Behavior therapy (even in the absence of a certification procedure) has already become separated from basic research. Possibly because of this behavior therapists do not appear to apply the laws of behavior variously to complex human situations. Rather, standardized procedures have been developed which seem to be evolving more or less autonomously. One example of such a procedure is implosive therapy which Dr. Agras has described as more an analogy to an extinction procedure than the fact of an extinction procedure. Desensitization, assertive training and the like are also tied only loosely to the respondent conditioning literature. Behavior therapy and behavior modification also differ in the focus of their therapeutic efforts. The behavior therapist alters a client's internal responses so that externally he responds differently to an unchanged environment. In this sense, behavior therapy is not that different from more traditional psychotherapies. The behavior modifier, on the other hand, alters the relationship between a client's responses and his environment by changing the environment.

The areas of behavior modification and behavior therapy differ along at least three dimensions: (1) the literature from which they were originally derived; (2) their current degree of separation from that literature; (3) the focus of their therapeutic efforts.

If the two areas do differ, then it is important to decide if the problems which are the occasion of the push for certification exist to the same degree in both areas; and if problems do exist in both areas, would certification affect both areas in the same way or might its effects be different? The last question needs to be considered both in terms of the efficacy of certification in alleviating the problem, and in terms of the reaction that certification might have on either area.

Any method of treatment which is effective is likely to be misused, either for some antisocial goal, or seized upon by people who do not have the background or skill to use it correctly. Consequently, both behavior modification and behavior therapy are likely candidates for misuse. It seems strange, then, that the preponderance of the more sensational reports of misuse, for example those reported in *Time* magazine (March 11, 1974) and the preponderance of legal suits filed by ACLU and others, appear to involve behavior modification. A possible explanation is that much of behavior therapy falls within the traditional private-practice framework of altering internal responses in one-to-one or small-group settings. Consequently, misuse in this area may be handled through the traditional channels: threats of malpractice suits and revocation of state licensing. Although these channels may not be completely adequate, especially when aversive techniques are at issue, they at least appear to be available.

On the other hand, society seems temporarily at a loss about how to handle misuse which occurs in conjunction with changing or restructuring environments. This is especially true when the individuals involved in the restructuring are not participating voluntarily, such as behavior modification programs in prisons, mental hospitals and hospitals for the retarded. The lack of machinery for handling misuse in these situations is, I think, very real. Authority, and therefore responsibility, is often quite diffuse and, perhaps more importantly, personnel in such institutions are usually excluded from state licensing requirements. The fact is that most state licensing procedures affect only those therapists in private practice and therefore exclude from control those very people working in the areas where the problems are most acute. It seems likely then that the publicity and law suits relative to the misuse of behavior modification are being generated, at least in part, because there are no other easy channels available for dealing with misuse. This would certainly argue for serious consideration of other control channels, including certification of behavior modifiers by the profession itself.

It is interesting to speculate about the possible reactive effects of certification on the field of behavior modification. The question raised by Dr. Agras is whether certification would result in a disruption of communication between those persons who weren't certified and those who were. If the traditional certification distinctions were made (though there is no need to assume they would be), it would be between those people involved in research and those not so involved. I certainly agree with Dr. Agras that such a disruption of communication would not be at all desirable. But it doesn't seem that the *fact* of certification alone could do this. However, if other conditions varied with certification; if, for example, certification entailed drastic changes in training programs or drastic changes in professional organizational membership, then communications could become a problem. This variance would depend on details of the certification procedure worked out by the profession. Basically, I feel that as long as we all belong to Division 25 we are relatively safe (it sometimes occurs to me that the greater threat to maintaining communication between research and technology may lie in the current trend toward the professional degree).

In brief summary, it seems to me that the problem in behavior therapy is different from the problem in behavior modification technology and that we therefore might well look for different solutions for each area.

WHAT IS "APPLIED"
IN THE APPLIED ANALYSIS OF BEHAVIOR?

W. Scott Wood

THE NATURE OF THE APPLIED ANALYSIS OF BEHAVIOR

Scientific perspectives. There have been many attempts recently to describe operant behavior modification, or the applied analysis of behavior, in order to characterize clearly its approach in dealing with human behavior. I would like to discuss some of these today and try to point out a few of the implications that follow from accepting one or the other of these different perspectives.

One frequently stated viewpoint emphasizes the importance of using behavioral laws to change human behavior in desirable ways. In general, this position holds that behavior modification is best described as the systematic application of certain fundamental principles of environmental-behavioral control to human behavior. These principles, such as reinforcement, extinction, stimulus control and punishment, are said to be firmly established by basic research with many different species, and in applied research as well, and as such they best represent what is scientifically known today about the nature of behavior as influenced by environmental events.

Texts that emphasize this perspective, whether intended for laymen, students, or professionals, characteristically devote considerable space to the research origin of these relationships and then usually present a matrix of problem-solving strategies for their use in dealing with certain classes of human behavioral problems.

A second popular way of presenting behavior modification is to stress its methodological features. In this approach the procedures, in some sense, take precedence over the principles. Here we find first the injunction to define the target response objectively, or in such a way that two or more human observers can agree that a behavior is or isn't occurring. Continued measurement, coupled with systematic environmental manipulations, becomes the essential procedure; the behavioral laws are relegated to a "try-it-and-see" status while the fundamentals of the observation system are elaborated in detail.

These two perspectives are neither mutually exclusive nor, in fact, even found separated from one another in most efforts to describe applied behavior analysis. They usually represent different emphases on what is most important in dealing with human behavior in a scientific manner. These differences in emphasis, however, can lead to real differences in interpreting psychological events. For example, some authors of the first school are willing to consider the extension, at least for explanatory purposes, of certain behavioral relationships to a realm of undisclosed activities; private events, if you will. A classic version of this theoretical extension can be found in Skinner's chapter "Private Events in a Natural Science" in *Science and Human Behavior*(1953). Michael, in his analysis of the depressed behavior of the typical rehabilitation client, gives another good example of utilizing behavioral laws to analyze private activities (Michael, 1968). And, of course, Lloyd Homme has his "coverants." And the logic of certain behavioral intervention programs may be based upon such extensions. For example, behavior therapists frequently try to alter overt behavior through the use of imagined events and activities.

More methodologically oriented behaviorists tend to oppose such accounts, referring to these kinds of efforts as speculative. The usual basis for such opposition is the publicly unverifiable nature of the events or activities in question. For some, this may be seen only as a contemporary problem of instrumentation, while others may question the very reality status of some of the referrants.

The behavioral view. Even though the area of private events remains troublesome, both perspectives describe the applied analysis of behavior as an extension of a scientific philosophy and methodology to human behavior. However, a somewhat different view of the field can be obtained by turning from an account that is "scientific" to one that is "behavioral." In this latter approach, an attempt is made to categorize behavior analysis by the different classes of behaviors that behavior analysts engage in, the situations in which they occur, and their consequences. It is an attempt to discover what the behavior analyst does that is different from the activities of other persons with similar interests in manipulating (controlling, influencing) the behavior of others, under what circumstances he does them, and what results are produced; a contingency analysis, so to speak. It may then be possible to eliminate further references to other conceptual systems, including whether it is or isn't more "scientific." It at least has simplicity to recommend it as a strategy. In fact, it may seem almost too simple to take seriously. However, it is not without precedence. Behavior analysts themselves frequently recommend just this approach when they are confronted by a client with a clinical diagnostic label, and Day (1968) provided a similar but considerably more sophisticated logic to identify the radical behaviorist.

Differences between the two perspectives. However, there are other differences besides simplicity that result from contrasting a behavioral interpretation of the nature of applied behavior analysis with those which emphasize scientific content or methodology. First, the scientific analyses, by and large, are interpretations primarily based upon the form, or topography, of what it is that the behavior analyst says or does, since science for many means either an abstract set of procedures, or rules, which are sequentially followed in a given investigation; or else it refers to a set of statements which are said to represent the subject knowledge of a given area. The behavioral interpretation must specify both the situation and the consequences; the form of the response becomes relevant only insofar as the appropriate outcome of behavioral control is reliably produced within a given setting.

That is not to say that either knowledge of scientific methods or that understanding of the laws of nature are without consequence, or that they are a hollow set of rules and descriptions without purpose. However, specific goals do tend to become vague. I don't want to belabor this point with a lengthy digression into the philosophy of science, but the concrete objective of predicting and controlling a given person's behavior is considerably more specific than the abstract "empirical knowledge" which is often mentioned as the goal of a science.

Another distinction can be made between the scientific and the behavioral perspectives on an objectivity versus subjectivity continuum. It could be claimed that one of the advantages of emphasizing scientific methodology and content is its objectivity. Although the methods must be followed by someone in order to have any meaning, it is possible to talk about the scientific methodology of behavior analysis, or any other discipline, as an abstract set of procedures. Presumably, the consequences of following those procedures would be the same regardless of who followed them. Similarly, "knowledge" as a set of descriptions of lawful relationships is ordinarily thought to be independent of the "knower." The laws of nature are assumed to remain constant regardless of who understands them.

The behavioral approach, however, must focus more attention on the individual person because the distinguishing elements of the behavior modifier's repertoire are themselves subject to behavioral control. Many factors can affect them, including changes in consequences, whether or not there are strong alternative response classes, and the presence or absence of ancillary verbal repertoires, such as problem-solving skills, self-descriptive behaviors and, possibly, the extent to which the behavior analyst is able to see contingency relationships in the behavior of others (Skinner, 1972).

The importance of these factors is not unknown in science, of course. They often are represented as the "trait" or "personality" variables that lead one to describe different scientists as dedicated, insightful, creative, scholarly, and so on. These differences are obvious even though all scientists may have been exposed to the same facts and research methods in their training. One possible advantage of the behavioral view is that such "personalities" can begin to be specified more precisely, and possibly even deliberately trained.

Finally, we come to the issue of values. Here, perhaps, the contrast between the traditional scientific interpretation of applied behavior analysis and the behavioral one is most clear. Science, typically, is considered to be value free; it is a case of knowledge for its own sake. Questions involving the social applicability of scientific knowledge in a given area are said to be "value" questions, ones which are commonly regarded as beyond the realm of the subject area itself.

Even when a scientist becomes involved in decisions to use or not to use the knowledge of his discipline for certain purposes, these acts are commonly attributed to the scientist's philosophic, political, or religious beliefs and not the result of his scientific training. More often than not the responsibility for seeing that the scientist's skills and knowledge are put to "good" use is left in the hands of his employers: the government, state, corporation, university, school or hospital. In the past, this has been an arrangement which has worked quite well. Unfortunately, some people today have begun to view science more as a threat than as a benefit to "the good life."

Psychology has always been very sensitive to the obvious social implication of its science. The American Psychological Association has its handbook of ethics to guide psychologists along the path of higher values, and blatant violations of normal social mores are, naturally, illegal. I fear, however, that because psychology has rarely been "misapplied," at least to the extent of evoking great public concern, it is more a testimony to the weakness of its methods than to the efficacy of APA handbooks, the precision with which legal sanctions determine psychologists' behavior, or the moral character of the average psychologist.

Those days have probably passed, and primarily due to the demonstrable power of contemporary behavior theory. We now are confronted by a public, by governing agencies, and by other colleagues whose concern is not whether our methods and principles are scientifically valid, but rather what we intend to do with them. Today it is our values, not our science, that are being questioned.

But values, from a behavioral view, are simply part of the contingencies that identify a scientist or applied behavior analyst, or at least they should be. A "value" can be viewed as nothing more than a reinforcer (Skinner, 1972). The values that someone holds are the events and activities that shape and maintain his behavior. There is no necessity to evoke a mysterious realm of understanding beyond the ken of science to deal with such issues; we have the knowledge here and now to talk effectively about questions of value for psychology. It is not a matter of not understanding values, or of values not being part of our discipline; it is simply a matter of determining what values we wish to incorporate as part of the contingencies that define the field of applied behavior analysis.

27

Let me now summarize briefly what I believe to be the critical distinctions between a behavioral perspective on the nature of applied behavior analysis and a traditional scientific view of the field. The scientific view emphasizes only certain behavioral categories, specifically those of research skills and subject area knowledge. The behavioral analysis, which must also specify that conditions and consequences be complete, forces one to identify the behavior modifier not only in terms of specific response categories, but also when and for what purposes those skills and knowledge are put to use.

IMPLICATIONS OF A BEHAVIORAL PERSPECTIVE

Discriminative stimulus control. The best way to compare some of the implications of the behavioral perspective with those of the scientific interpretation of the nature of applied behavior analysis is to move precisely through the three basic elements that make up a behavioral contingency. First, let us consider the nature of the discriminative stimuli which are important in distinguishing the applied behavior analyst. Obviously, he should be controlled by changes in the behavior of others. We are behavior controllers; we must react appropriately to changes in the behavior of those we seek to control. Of course, this is true of the relationship between almost any scientist and the events he seeks to study. Presumably this is what scientific methodology is all about, arranging circumstances so that the scientist is best able to see the effects of his experimental efforts and to recognize which are the important independent variables that enter into functional relationships in a given area of research.

But scientific methodology can be the source of a problem in the area of discriminative stimulus control. The rules of science are usually taught as a set of standardized procedures that eventually may come to govern the behavior of the researcher more strongly than his own reactions to the subject. Sidman (1961) has indicated the importance of behavioral research that follows the data and not the experimental design. We should guard against allowing our research design strategies to overwhelm our interest in gaining effective control of the behavior of our subjects—even if it costs us that particular publication.

In a similar vein some research procedures are clearly superior to others for arranging good discriminative control over the researcher by the behavior of his subjects. The advantages of recording and attempting to alter an individual organism's *rate* of responding through experimental manipulations of environmental consequences lie in this area. This approach, which has been called the experimental analysis of behavior, is a particular contingency arrangement between experimenter and subject that produced large and rapid advances in behavior control techniques, and not accidentally. Psychologists were studying the behavior of rats long before Skinner designed the first operant conditioning chamber and cumulative recorder. The key to the greater success of the experimental analysis lies in the special arrangement of contingencies between important aspects of the behaviors of both the subject and the experimenter (Skinner, 1968).

Those who seek to redesign or to develop new methodological procedures for applied behavior analysis should consider carefully the implications of their resultant discriminative stimulus control over the researcher. Of course some techniques, such as group comparisons, are often justified for reasons other than their contribution to basic or applied research; e.g., to convince a public that has difficulty reading cumulative records. In these cases, the goal is not new or improved behavioral control methods but rather a public relations task. Nonetheless, many readers, including new students, may miss that point and come to understand that all "scientific" methods are equal in behavior analysis. And that is an error; some are simply better than others and for very good behavioral reasons.

Another issue involving stimulus control is the question of how behavior analysts identify the social problems they attempt to solve. What is it about a person's behavior that distinguishes him as a target for behavioral engineering? Very broadly speaking, it seems to be nonproductive deviance. In other words, behavior that is conspicuously different from that of most other members of the individual's peer group and not especially beneficial. This could include behavioral deficits such as those of the retarded; antisocial acts such as those of the delinquent or criminal; and extremely unusual behavior generally characterized as mentally ill. Behaviorists attempt to normalize such behavior patterns either as a result of somebody else's concern, such as a parent, teacher, or social agency, or simply as a result of their own cultural conditioning, or both. Fortunately or unfortunately, we just happen to be better at it than most. Because of this, we tend to be singled out for special criticism from those who are generally or specifically opposed to some aspect of cultural conformity.

I don't believe we have any apologies to make for our efforts along these lines. We have been able to establish programs that provide more humane environments for those institutionalized and we have also initiated training programs which increase the likelihood of their successful return to noninstitutional settings. We have developed programs to eliminate or prevent behavioral conflicts between children and their parents or teachers, and we have taught parents and teachers how to do the same. We have devised training programs for people without important behavioral repertoires, such as self-care and language, thus opening the door for them to a more socially independent future. We have established programs which have had the effect of counteracting early childhood isolation from traditional educational stimuli, helping to equalize the opportunities for success for many youngsters in traditional educational programs. Many other examples can be given. However, we should keep in mind what features of behavior evoke concerns for intervention. All social problems and goals may not fall within the areas of remediation and prevention of social differences.

Behavioral training. The behavior of our discipline is just that—behavior. We know a great deal about behavior and how to analyze and control it. There seem to be several implications from this perspective. Verbal knowledge about behavioral control and being able to control behavior are not the same thing nor are they necessarily taught in the same fashion. This does not deny that verbal behavior concerning behavioral research strategies and principles of behavioral control is not facilitative of actual behavior control skills, but indicates that they are very different repertoires. And as such, they contribute quite different things to our discipline.

To have behavior control skills without derivative verbal description of procedures and principles is unscientific—or more precisely, prescientific. It represents an era of guilds and apprenticeship training programs. On the other hand, the mere presence of an elaborate verbal superstructure without the associative demonstrable control over behavior is at best presumptuous, and more often merely hypocritical.

Now these are things we all know, but I believe that emphasizing the scientific features of the field rather than its contingency aspects may obscure a clear separation between these behavioral repertoires. Knowledge of behavioral principles, or knowledge of research design, can mean both verbal and nonverbal skills, but often it means just the first, something that is obtainable from our students in quite traditional ways. We should not forget, however, the other repertoire in our training programs, whether for the layman or the beginning behavioral psychologist.

And it has only been quite recently that our training efforts have taken on the appearance of "practicing what they preach" in the sense of trying to develop behavioral skills through behavioral methods. All who have had the experience of trying to develop a behavioral program which requires new skills from the staff know that academic-type classes in behavior principles are inadequate. Unfortunately, knowledge from these experiences hasn't always been consistently applied in our college programs where verbal skills are often the primary focus. We usually manage to assure that our preprofessional students acquire the necessary behavioral skills through practicum or thesis requirements, but I suspect that many service courses and workshops aimed at the nonprofessional neglect all but the verbal repertoire.

If we are going to be successful in disseminating behaviorism broadly in this society, then we must improve our instructional technology. And our interests in improved teaching must also include the area of behavioral as well as verbal skills. Most of us are well aware of what needs to be done, and many are working on just these kinds of programs. There are, however, a couple of possible areas that deserve more attention. For example, many educational programs in applied behavior analysis have discontinued or de-emphasized basic operant research with animals, and for a variety of reasons. Lack of support, lack of student interest, and lack of dramatic scientific advances are often given as reasons and many of them are possibly valid. I would like to suggest, however, that animal operant laboratories behaviorally represent an excellent starting point for acquiring behavior control skills.

Certainly the behaviors we use to control a rat's or a pigeon's behavior are topographically quite different from those that we use when dealing with human behavior in a classroom or hospital; but they are still a class of behaviors, an operant, maintained by their effectiveness in controlling the ongoing behavior of another organism. This may be important since function, not form, determines the definition of an operant. We want to teach behavior control skills, and strengthening one class of responses, controlling animals, should strengthen others. Certainly many of the components of a successful behavior controller's repertoire have little to do with the particular species whose behavior he is working on.

There seem to be three obvious benefits that can result from using the basic operant laboratory for this purpose. First, and possibly most important, the mistakes that beginning behaviorists may make are considerably less costly. Second, the educational objectives can be optimally arranged to insure the students' success, since there need be no further consideration made in the laboratory beyond the educational effects of this experience on the student. Third, the student can see clearly how subtle and complex contingencies control behavior in a very orderly fashion. Such observations in the natural environment are often· the result of interpreting environmental control rather than demonstrating it.

There is no guarantee, of course, that animal laboratory experiences will produce an effective behavior modifier any more than a textbook course will. We all know instances where they decidedly have not. I suspect, however, that a greater potential may exist for establishing a generality from an animal training environment than from a strictly academic one. In the first case, one is relying upon the generalization of certain response classes involving actual behavioral control; in the latter, it is an effort to produce new behavior through a type of verbal stimulus control.

Before I mention another kind of behavioral repertoire entirely, let me summarize this point quickly. It is not a plea for more basic research per se, although I think there are good reasons why we should continue a strong experimental operant program. It is rather a suggestion for applied training programs to use the animal research paradigm to shape and strengthen behavior control skills in our students. And obviously I don't mean just reading about animal behavior; I mean actually learning to control the behavior of animals in a laboratory setting.

My other point is considerably more speculative; it has to do with how and why we teach verbal skills about behavior control procedures. Most people believe that we teach an extensive verbal repertoire to communicate effectively, both within our discipline and to others, how behavioral control is accomplished. I would like to suggest that there is a somewhat neglected area, within-the-individual communication, which serves primarily to facilitate a person's own efforts to control behavior as a particular class of problem-solving skills (Skinner, 1968).

I suspect, for example, that most good behavior modifiers have many behavioral skills which are "unconscious." We learn to function as a behavior analyst by being shaped in many ways; learning to react to subtle cues, looking for small differences, selecting an effective consequence, and so on, and these can occur without the person necessarily being aware of the stimuli that become relevant in determining such behaviors. The reason for this, of course, is simply that being aware of what you are doing is a more complex behavioral repertoire than being unaware (Skinner, 1957). In fact, there are physical activities where active "awareness" can even be deterimental, as in a golf swing, for example. However, for most activities, being able to verbally abstract the relevant controlling variables and then to react to the abstraction as a separate set of discriminative stimuli has decided advantages. This is particularly true where the goal is to train someone else to the same level of performance. The presence of verbal cues in some ways obviates lengthy exposure to the actual contingencies which themselves were originally necessary to arrive at those rules. Behavior under the stimulus control of rules, of course, is by no means the same operant class of behaviors as those under contingency control, even when the responses are topographically similar. However, behavior can begin as rule-governed responding and end by being contingency-managed (Skinner, 1968).

I believe that we are still faced with the somewhat incomplete set of "rules" in our own area of applied behavior analysis. But I don't believe that those particular abstractions I am referring to here will come from the kind of research that most members of the field now engage in, which is aimed primarily toward technological expansion rather than the terminological refinement which some still see as necessary (Day, 1971). I believe that better self-descriptive skills will help us improve this situation. I doubt that many of us deliberately observe our own ongoing behavior as data to be analyzed, nor do we have training programs to instruct students in these behaviors. I believe such an effort both on our own parts and as an adjunct to our training programs would produce some clear benefits for the discipline in the area of refined terminology.

I realize that such efforts will inevitably raise the question of "reliability" for many behavior analysts. But the problem of reliable observations is basically a behavioral one; it unfortunately hasn't received the attention it deserves because the "scientific" question has tended to obscure the underlying behavioral one. The behavioral problem of how one learns to make accurate, or even *if* one can learn to make accurate, observations where there is no opportunity for appropriate audience control is an area where both analysis and research is needed. All scientists frequently have the opportunity to make observations in the absence of the public. The question of private events, where one is observing one's own behavior in a fashion that is not available for the public to observe, is only part of the picture involved in the reliability issue.

Briefly, if we think of our own "principles" essentially as verbal abstractions of our methods of behavioral control, then they are probably still too broad to account for the real differences observable in the success of their application to human behavior. One possible avenue toward helping to improve this situation is through more deliberate training in self observation. We may be able to react to subtler differences in our own behavior than our observational techniques currently permit us to see in the behavior of others. The question of the reliability of such observations is a real one, but it too is primarily a behavioral question.

Consequences as values. Finally, we come to the last element of a contingency analysis, the consequences which maintain responding and stimulus control. The immediate consequence for the behavior analyst that has been implicit throughout the discussion is the ability to control behavior. It is our first "value." This consequence has its analogs in most branches of science, and is only replaced in some areas where control is physically impossible by prediction, as in astronomy. This particular value of control, however, is not the one I wish to address today. Admittedly there are those critics who speak out against learning how to control another person's behavior as a proper scientific goal on the grounds that it is either impossible or immoral to do so. But the free will versus determinism argument has been addressed so often, and by such better proponents, that I will forego that debate and discuss instead some other questions of value. Specifically what are, or should be, the values we display when we do in fact control someone else's behavior as behavior anlysts?

The controversies about values or goals tend to begin only at certain levels of scientific development and tend not to occur at others. For example, basic researchers rarely have their laboratory goals called into question except occasionally by Hollywood screenwriters. Most of society's members accept the purposes of basic research and object only to expense, trivial topics, and unnecessary harm to living subjects. Generally speaking, applied research has been granted similar grace. For instance, the kind of research that often takes place on university campuses, where large groups of sophomores are pitted against one another in some monumental card sorting task, rarely attracts much criticism. However, there are efforts to constrain the researcher in these and similar settings, and the American Psychological Association's ethical guidelines are one example in this area, providing sanctions against unnecessary deception, producing "psychological" harm without subsequent counseling, and other instances of unacceptable behavior by the researcher. Thus what emerges in applied research as value questions primarily concerns the indirect manner in which the research may harm its subjects while attempting to accomplish some other purpose. This situation has been considered at length, by several groups, and their deliberations provide insight into society's level of acceptance for certain kinds of research strategies utilizing human subjects.

But it is really social implementation, not basic or applied research, that focuses the attention of the public on a given discipline. Any science that contributes a technology to society must face the issue of the purposes for which that technology is used. Some do, of course, by flatly denying that their responsibility extends to public utilization. Unfortunately, applied behavior analysis is at a double disadvantage in this regard. First, it has a history of blending applied research with social implementation and obscuring any meaningful distinction between behavior analysis and engineering. Second, we can and should talk behaviorally about social issues, which includes placing our own social efforts under the scope of our analysis. Questions involving purposes weren't always raised because applied behavior analysis began in settings where benefits were clear. In fact, being able to do anything with some of the early subjects was generally seen as progress. Those days are gone. Schools, prisons, and housing projects are not environments where behavior can be intentionally controlled by psychologists without their answering legitimate questions about the purpose of such control.

I believe that there are certain implications for this field that come from confronting the issue of values directly. First, we should teach more about ethics and values. Students should be at least prepared to talk intelligently about ethical concerns when they are raised. The "I'm just a scientist" model may do the field a disservice in the sense that we implicitly leave the questions of direction in the hands of others who, in fact, may be less qualified to make such decisions. Even without a clear behavioral ethic, the applied behavior analyst who is able to talk about values in a traditional manner may at least become involved in decisions regarding the direction of implementation, and not regarded merely as a hired gun, an engineer to complete someone else's blueprint for society.

Beyond traditional ethical considerations, we should look carefully at Skinner's interpretation of social development in terms of immediate and distant consequences. Skinner suggests that social technologies should be judged by their contribution to the survivability of the culture and not necessarily by their immediate consequences. The social implementation problem becomes one of developing better cultural self-control, foregoing immediate benefits in the interest of long-range objectives. As teachers we should consider this perspective when we begin to establish reinforcers for our own students as behavior controllers. Most new behaviors learned in school are acquired with immediate and often quite artificial reinforcers. Grades, teacher and parental praise, and peer-group pressure are often used to shape behaviors which presumably will be maintained later by social benefits. We might consider how to move more deliberately from the immediate and the artificial to more natural social consequences in our own training programs, and to reinforce students for valuing the social implications of their developing skills as well as the immediate benefits of grades, professional status, and publications. This possibly could be accomplished by directing some of these immediate reinforcers toward the actual solution of behavioral problems rather than exclusively toward more demonstrations of reversible behavioral control strategies.

Second, we will profit by increasing our efforts to enhance the public's awareness of the social risks and gains of deliberate behavioral control. There would seem to be two immediate benefits for these efforts. We will increase the number of those who can, in fact, apply behavioral principles effectively, and also provide a more knowledgeable audience to shape our own behaviors. I don't think we teach enough behaviorism today in public schools. We use behavioral techniques to develop traditional school repertoires, such as reading, math, social behavior, and so on; but very few behaviorists have addressed the problem of teaching elementary behavioral concepts as a separate subject area. There is no special reason to make an effort to develop a behavioral rationale for this point since the traditional justification involving twigs and trees does it quite well.

Finally, I would like to return to a point I raised earlier about the behaviors that we in society tend to regard as problems. As I suggested then, our interest in the remediation and prevention of culturally deviant or deficit behaviors may be a somewhat restricted view of where we have valuable social contributions to make. Unfortunately, society's reinforcers are primarily directed toward those programs which have the immediate effect of eliminating behavioral differences, not generating them. To the extent that we depend upon these social benefits for our own research and program development, we too are relatively restricted to these objectives. For example, it would be much more difficult to raise funds to work as extensively with those youngsters called "gifted" than it is to obtain funds for programs for the retarded. However, the accelerated development of a few individuals also may have considerable benefits for our society. Some behavioral differences are beneficial; some may even be highly productive.

In light of these considerations I would like to suggest that we consider establishing a private behavioral foundation whose primary purpose would be to generate support for programs that do not readily qualify for available public funds, but that do meet rigorous standards as behavioral programs (assuming that we can reach some general agreement on those standards, and I believe that we can). The secondary purpose of such a foundation would be to advocate the implementation of broader behavioral programing within society. For example, simply publishing descriptions of successful programs and also establishing its

37

own criteria for acceptable behavioral designs available to the public would help counteract some of the recent press criticism that has been lodged against behavior modification.

As professionals, most of us contribute to various agencies that allegedly provide beneficial social programs, or at least we are regularly pressured to do so. Most of these programs are completely ineffective and we all know it. We may as well contribute to a project whose responsibility to its members and to society at large is directly and intentionally in accordance with our own knowledge about the nature of behavior control.

REFERENCES

Day, W. F. Radical behaviorism in reconciliation with phenomenology. *Journal of the Experimental Analysis of Behavior*, 1969, *12*, 315-328.

Day, W. F. A comment on current objections to behaviorism. A paper presented at Drake University, 1971.

Michael, J. L. Rehabilitation in *Behavior modification in clinical psychology*. Neuringer and Michael (eds.), New York: Appleton-Century-Crofts, 1970.

Sidman, M. *Tactics of scientific research*. New York: Basic Books, Incorporated, 1960.

Skinner, B. F. *Science and human behavior*. New York: The Macmillan Company, 1953.

Skinner, B. F. *Verbal behavior*. New York: Appleton-Century-Crofts, 1957.

Skinner, B. F. *Technology of teaching*. New York: Appleton-Century-Crofts, 1968.

Skinner, B. F. *Beyond freedom and dignity*. New York: Alfred A. Knopf, 1971.

RESPONSE

Richard W. Malott

Scott did a conceptual behavioral analysis of behavior analysis. I would like to comment on one category of the three-term contingency (S^D–R–S^R); namely, the reinforcer component. What are the reinforcers for behavior analysis?

By your reinforcers ye shall be known.

First. One doth not live by prediction and control alone. There is also understanding. Holland and Skinner (1961) and Staats and Staats (1963) called it interpretation. It's relatively easy to evaluate the extent to which a conceptual framework correctly predicts and controls. Understanding is not so amenable to a straightforward empirical analysis. Perhaps it is as much a problem of logic as it is of empirics.

Can we say that our conceptual framework helps us to understand a phenomenon under specific conditions? Does it allow us to interpret the phenomenon in terms of the principles, the laws, the causal relationships contained within our conceptual framework? Can we also make this interpretation with logical consistency?

Beware, all ye who openly admit to conceptual, analysis-generated understanding as a source of reinforcement, lest ye be accused of conceptual imperialism.

Second. There does indeed exist a profession called behavior analysis and it is distinct from the public school teacher, speech therapist, correctional officer, etc. This is just as true as the fact that there is a mathematics profession independent of any specific set of applications. A professional behavior analyst finds it reinforcing to apply behavior analysis successfully to the understanding of phenomena and the solutions of problems. He may not find it reinforcing to be intimately involved in acquiring the details of other professions that receive the benefit of such analysis.

Beware, lest ye be called arrogant.

Third. Professional behavior analysts find creative analyses reinforcing be they novel analyses of old problems or standard analyses of new problems.

Beware: lest ye become a behavior-analysis butterfly flitting from one superficially analyzed area to the next once the bloom of novelty has worn off. Understand that the analysis can be superficial whether it is conceptual or experimental. Our behavior is more immediately reinforced by clever innovations than by stable, long-range solutions.

Following loosely from this conceptual analysis of existing reinforcers and Scott's paper, let me make a few brief recommendations for the improvement of the efficacy of the profession of applied behavior analysis.

First. What ever happened to the world's first token economy? How's it doing? Does it still exist? I think not. There are no professional reinforcers for the maintenance of existing behavioral systems. We can't write an article for *JABA*, or go to a meeting and report that we have been running this behavior modification program now for the last 15 years and it is still running just as well as when it was first described as a novel project one year after its inception. We need to consider as failures those projects that do not maintain. We need to train our students to be as concerned with systems maintenance as with implementation. And we need to provide professional recognition for cleverly managing to arrange for systems' survival.

Second. We want our profession to be more involved with solving problems of long-range social consequences. This goal will not be accomplished by attempting to increase the reinforcing value of the solution of long-range social issues while our professionals are still graduate students. I believe our behavior is controlled more by the immediate than our historical (e.g., graduate school) environment. We should develop post-graduate consequences (e.g., professional recognition) contingent upon behaviors that have long-range social consequences. Of course, we should teach our students skills which will facilitate problem solving.

Third. While the generalist behavioral engineer may not be interested in the details of the disciplines he is helping, he must recognize that he is an engineer and acquire the orientation and skills of a general systems engineer or systems analyst.

Finally. I would like to support Scott's recommendation for the establishment of a behavioral foundation to accomplish the goals he has outlined.

RESPONSE

Julian D. Ford
William R. Hutchison

We agree with the overall position of Dr. Wood's paper that a behavioral viewpoint has several distinct advantages in looking at our own professional behavior. The useful implications which follow from this have been pointed out throughout this conference, and even more thoroughly in his paper. The most important implications for this conference on professional issues are in the areas of ethics and controlling the behavior of behavior modifiers, which in the behavioral view are the same. Along with Dr. Wood we wish to avoid less productive discussions using the philosophical language associated with values and teleology. The power of this behavioral approach applied to other "high-order" behavior can be seen, for example, in the demonstrations of "self-control" behavior in Mahoney's dogs and Rachlin's pigeons that make no reference to internal constructs such as "will power."

Dr. Wood reminded us that a value is nothing more than a reinforcer. This simple consideration explodes the myth that scientific behavior is value free. The problem for us is that we do not control most of the reinforcers that determine our behavior. However, many of the problems that *seem* to confront us result from a too restricted analysis of contingencies. A case in point is Dr. Wood's statement: "Unfortunately, society's reinforcers are primarily directed toward those programs which have the immediate effect of eliminating behavioral differences, not generating them. To the extent that we depend upon these social benefits for our own research and program development, we too are relatively restricted to these objectives." Further, he does not believe we have any apologies to make for our efforts along these lines.

Society has developed the practice of reinforcing scientific behavior because of the benefits which accrue. This would recommend to us maximum sensitivity to long-term rather than short-term contingencies of our behavior. Then, following a behavioral self-control model, we arrange the immediate contingencies over which we have control, and which control us, in order to maximize long-term consequences. Outside our immediate control, society may be reinforcing practices which do not contribute to cultural survival. In such cases, if we can sustain efforts to develop alternative practices and demonstrate their superiority, we can anticipate more desirable outcomes for ourselves.

During this conference a number of very useful proposals for rearranging contingencies have been made; e.g., public education in behavior modification, community forums, providing guidelines for practice of behavior modification, improved training and mid-career education for behavior modifiers, accountability, efforts at lobbying, and others. It has been a useful advance in thinking to apply our behavioral approach at this level. But the steps suggested are not going to be taken by themselves, or automatically, or through some mysterious progression. Let us suggest that we raise our analysis one level higher to determine how to generate and maintain these efforts effectively. Although there have been many statements saying "we *should* do this, we *ought* to do that," our feeling is that we have not thought about this in behavioral terms; and where we have, we are depending on the public and government to provide aversive control and negative reinforcement to prompt action. We would hope that behavior modifiers could do better. We should not go home feeling *too* satisfied about having come up with a good analysis and possible solutions to our problems unless we have also begun to think about how to generate and maintain the behaviors required to carry them out.

As Dr. Wood has noted, a behavioral analysis of the many levels of professional practice must deal with the discriminative stimuli, topography, and consequences that both characterize and control those behavior modification practices. We would emphasize, even more so than does Dr. Wood, that the behavioral-analysis perspective includes the wider view that behavior modifiers, and all scientists, are subject to many strong social influences *as well as* the scientific emphases on objectivity and precision.

43

We have two comments regarding discriminative stimuli that set the occasion for behavior modifiers' professional practices. First, we would go one step beyond Dr. Wood's astute suggestion that behavior modifiers must deal not only with "nonproductive deviant behavior" but also with already adaptive behavior. It is desirable not only to enhance gifted persons' repertoires, but also to facilitate the "normal" behavior of the "average" person; e.g., self-paced, individualized instruction in education, or programs training parents simply to be more effective parents.

Second, as behavior modifiers move out to many new applied settings, beyond mental health, education, and correctional systems into business, economics, and environmental design, it is extremely important that they carefully observe the complex social and physical milieu before planning any interventions. A one-week frequency count of one or two target behaviors is clearly insufficient baseline data to fully sensitize the behavior modifier to the many discriminative stimuli that are in effect. This also argues for developing behavior modification *within* current professions rather than as a separate profession through certification, or at least working very closely with the established professions.

Concerning the topographies that characterize behavior modifiers' practices, we strongly agree with Dr. Wood's conclusion that both nonverbal and verbal communication skills are essential in assessment, program design, and intervention; and that training programs for behavior modifiers must emphasize these competencies. We would add, however, that communication skills, as opposed to direct behavior-change skills, are often underrated by action-oriented behavior analysts. Behavior modifiers often underemphasize the development of rapport with individual clients, and (until this conference) the necessity of convincing influential social groups and the general public of the desirability and efficacy of behavior modification.

We also stress that behavior modifiers must be more creative in finding alternative routes to their goals. Aversive control techniques, for instance, often produce swift short-term improvements, but are socially and ethically objectionable in many instances. The behavior analyst who is truly sensitive to the consequences of his behavior should be able to operationalize this "sensitivity" in the form of alternate strategies.

In regard to the consequences that influence behavior modifiers, we have stressed the need to design the short-term contingencies that directly influence our professional practices, and over which we have direct control, so that they produce behavior that is congruent with the crucial long-term reinforcers (i.e., values) and contingencies that are in effect. We agree with Dr. Wood that public education, which makes the public better able to appraise and appreciate the value of behavior modification and to make behavior analysts accountable for their practices, is one promising way. Training programs must also be structured to fade out immediate and artificial consequences in favor of natural, long-range social consequences. And contingencies that influence mid-career professionals must also be structured to maintain socially and ethically responsible practices.

Finally, behavior analysts must begin to formulate programs for evaluating the potential self-management strategies suggested by Dr. Wood. The target behaviors and environmental stimuli to be measured and evaluated objectively must first be determined. Unobtrusive measures, such as the frequencies of hiring behavior analysts, are good candidates. Second, we must formulate feasible research designs. Multiple baseline and randomized control-group designs would be appropriate, the latter particularly to answer questions of relative *utility* of the different strategies.

We conclude by strongly endorsing Dr. Wood's behavioral analysis of behavior modifiers' professional practices, and his suggestions for self-control strategies that could enhance their social and professional standing. We look forward to the implementation and controlled evaluation of these programs in the near future.

BEHAVIORAL COMPETENCIES
FOR THE EVALUATION OF BEHAVIOR MODIFIERS

Beth Sulzer-Azaroff, Jack Thaw, and Carol Thomas

New England is awakening to the value of behavior modification. Despite the dire warnings by self-described "humanists" that behavior modification is leading the march into the big brotherhood of 1984, more and more practitioners are beginning to accept the proposition that their most humane function is effectively and efficiently assisting clients to achieve the goals they set for themselves or their dependents. Community clinics are beginning to treat their client's troubling behaviors with behavioral procedures. Schools are training their staffs to use behavioral contingencies to help students increase their learning. Attempts are even being made to establish behavioral programs in group homes for persons en route from institution to community. Institutions for those labeled retarded, emotionally disturbed, and delinquent are beginning to incorporate token economies and other behavior modification procedures into their treatment programs. So successful have many of these programs been that behavior modification has been publicly endorsed by various agencies. For example, the Connecticut Office of Mental Retardation has adopted a set of guidelines for the treatment of behaviorally disordered retarded persons. The guidelines call for supervision of certain treatment programs by "a trained behavior modifier" (Thorne, 1973).*

---

*Thorne, G. D. Standards for the care of mentally retarded clients with behavioral disabilities, O.M.R. Policy No. 9, Office of Mental Retardation, State of Connecticut.

Those of us who label ourselves "behavior modifiers" draw a breath of satisfaction—but only for a moment, because then the question arises: "Just who is this 'trained behavior modifier'?" Is he the person who uses shock to decrease dangerously self-abusive behavior and decides to try the same technique with people who use vulgar language? Is he the person who knows that when a usually hyperactive person is slowed down his behavior is modified, and then calls his prescription of tranquilizers, heavy enough to make that person a zombie, behavior modification? Is he the person who has heard about M&M's and gives them out indiscriminately, non-contingently? Everybody knows that behavior modifiers are dispensers of M&M's! Does he use isolation for prolonged periods and call it "time out," a well-known behavior modification procedure? Or does he modify behavior by performing surgery on the brain? Is he (heaven forbid, yet not beyond the realm of conjecture) a person who acquaints himself with all of the known principles of behavior modification and uses them to his own personal advantage and to the detriment of others? Fortunately, in a retardation facility in the State of Connecticut such abuses are unlikely because the same set of guidelines also spells out carefully all the necessary procedures for safeguarding the rights of the behaviorally disordered retarded person. It also provides for a board to act as that person's advocate in the selection of goals and any aversive procedures.

So in the present instance we may be accused of creating a straw man. Yet the straw man, like Ray Bolger in the *Wizard of Oz*, may actually contain a vital core simply camouflaged by exterior wisps of straw. Malpractice under the name of behavior modification does exist (witness the Sunland, Florida episode). Popular fear of the application of the method, largely based on folklore and misunderstandings, is sparked by demonstrable instances of actual abuse. And that popular fear has begun to have a repressive effect on one of the most positive, therapeutic teaching methods yet developed. According to Lesley Oelsner in the *New York Times* (February 19, 1974), ". . . the Law Enforcement Assistance Administration said it would no longer use funds appropriated under the Nixon Administration's anti-crime legislation for behavior modification. . . ." Also mentioned in the same column was the fact that Sam Ervin, Chairman of the Senate Subcommittee on Constitutional Rights, wrote a letter asking the Chairman of the Law Enforcement Assistance Agency to "consider a moritorium" on funding behavioral research.

The freedom to practice behavior modification methods is clearly being threatened. Attribute this threatened repression to folklore, mass hysteria, misunderstanding, conflicting philosophies, and actual abuse. To the list, however, add several more. One, quoted in the same *Times* article, should cause those of us who describe ourselves as behavior modifiers to do some soul searching. I quote: "To some extent the present impasse is the fault of the proponents of behavior modification themselves, for often they have given little thought to the sociological or legal ramifications of the methods they have been developing." The second relates to the competence of the individual labeling himself a behavior modifier. It is too much of a temptation to dismiss behavior modification abuses with a wave of the hand and to call the abuser incompetent. We would surely not engage in such abuse; it's only those incompetents out there. Or we can dissociate ourselves from the whole thing by calling ourselves "behavior analysts," etc. But how long will it take that label to become besmirched? And who will protect the public that consumes the services of the behavior modifier? How can it tell who is competent and who is not? It is the thesis of this paper that some tool must be developed for sorting out the competent from the incompetent, or we all shall be thrown out with the bath water sullied by the malpractitioners.

There is a real dilemma, however, about how to perform such a sorting process. Certification by examination through state agencies or through one of the American Psychological Association's divisions is anathema to many practitioners. Most of the reservations concern certification, particularly that behavior modification practice may become too rigid; e.g., if examination is by paper and pencil test, only verbal behavior is measured, and a practical test may be difficult to administer. Many fear that this type of certification will cause us to weigh ourselves down with millstones of outmoded tools and techniques, much in the same manner as more traditional behavioral treatment methods. Additionally, not all behavior modifiers are psychologists. Some are in speech, criminology, psychiatry, education, and other human service areas. Clearly those people would not qualify for certification through a division of the American Psychological Association.

Another viable alternative is to certify training programs; however, there are still many difficulties in their accreditation. Does the presence of a course title and credit on a college transcript guarantee that the person who has earned the course credit is capable of putting into practice the content that was taught? Is there a necessary relationship between a course title or description and the behavior that the student actually acquires? Another solution proposes the philosophy of the market place: let the consumer decide whether the behavior modification product is worth buying. In other words, have the clients and agencies who utilize the services of the behavior modifier give testimony to the efficacy of those services. Because behavior modification utilizes constant objective measurement, perhaps such consumer evaluation makes sense after all.

Given all of the problems about the sorting process one is initially tempted to say "forget it" and rationalize that ultimately the competents will surface and the incompetents will disappear. The very fact that we are attending a conference on professional issues in behavior analysis attests to an unwillingness to engage in such avoidance behavior. Alternatives must be explored, so we plunge in.

Our approach was to employ the methods we have used in the past to go about analyzing any other behavioral problem situation; e.g., specify the problem, operationalize the term "behavior modification competency," target the behaviors to be achieved, and specify under what conditions the responses should occur and the criteria by which attainment of those target behaviors should be evaluated. Feeling, however, that unilateral identification of the component responses would be far too presumptuous, we decided to survey the respected leaders and productive members of the field to identify competent responses at several practitioner levels and to ask how the identified competencies should be utilized. The material we are presenting today is, therefore, only a first step in the arduous process of identifying the requisite limits of competency in behavior modifiers. Decisions about how to begin to implement the results of the survey still remain, along with the equally weighty decisions about certification, training programs, and evaluation of component responses. (Our survey attempted to tap some of those issues as well, but as you will see from the results, there is quite a diversity of thought on those particular issues.) Following are the steps we followed.

METHOD

Designing the questionnaire. Jack Thaw, Anthony Cuvo, and I sat down and generated a list of responses that we thought were either necessary or desirable for behavior modifiers to be able to perform, the conditions under which the responses should be performed, and criteria for assessing the attainment of each of those responses. Eleven response categories were identified:

1. Behavior modification model

2. Assessment, goal formulation and targeting

3. Ethics, law and philosophy

4. Behavioral observation: recording and contingency specification

5. Measurement

6. Design

7. Behavioral procedures

8. Communication

9. Training and consulting

10. Administration

11. Research

As many of the component responses that we could think of were listed under each category. Then, at APA in Montreal, I asked several respected behavior modifiers and other involved persons if they would be willing to look over the material we had assembled. The material was sent to them and comments were sent to Stewart Agras, Scott Wood and his students, Patricia Strang, Bill Hopkins, Howard

Sloane.* Where possible, we attempted to incorporate the suggestions into the competency list and questionnaire. One major suggestion was that several levels of behavior modifier responses be identified and so, accordingly, four levels were listed:

1. The Behavior Analyst (conceptualizer, supervisor, evaluator)

2. The Behavior Technology Coordinator (supervisor, trainer)

3. The Behavior Technologist Engineer (designer and implementer)

4. The Behavior Co-Technician (carries out day-to-day operation of projects, programs)

No further definitions of those titles were given since it was assumed that respondents finding such designations appropriate would have no difficulty assigning functions for each level. This apparently was not such a good idea because many people expressed difficulty in responding to the four different levels. We should have given a few illustrations of the types of functions that people at those levels would tend to perform. A full list of competencies is provided (see appendix, page 80).

A questionnaire was designed, and respondents were asked to rate each of 70 items by checking those they felt were necessary or desirable for a person functioning on the designated level and omitting checks when they felt that the response was unnecessary for someone at that level.

In addition, a second questionnaire was included so that characteristics of the respondents could be identified: their background, training, and behavior modification activities. Respondents were also asked about the utilization of the survey; i.e., who should

* The authors wish to express their thanks to Mr. Francis Kelley, Superintendent of Mansfield State Training School and Hospital, to the staff of the institution, to our colleagues working in mental retardation facilities in the state of Connecticut and elsewhere for their suggestions and encouragement. Anthony Cuvo helped conceptualize the project and to him we wish to express our appreciation. A special thanks to Irene La Bonte and Laurette Metelsky who shared in the typing as well as to Barbara Tomasi for her role as project assistant.

function as a supervisor attesting to the person's achievement of competencies, as well as if and how often such surveys should be conducted.

Subjects and survey procedure. Two hundred and fifty-two questionnaires were sent out, primarily to editors and contributors to the *Journal of Applied Behavior Analysis* (*JABA*). All editors and editorial board members for *JABA* from 1969 to the present were surveyed. Ten senior authors of recent *JABA* articles were selected by taking a single issue (Fall 1973) and selecting every third senior author. In addition, 6 editors of *Behavior Research and Therapy* (*BRAT*) and 3 authors from the August 1973 edition were surveyed. (There is a great deal of overlap of editors and authors between *JABA* and *BRAT*.) Twenty-two editors of *Behavior Therapy and Experimental Psychiatry* (*BTEP*) and 6 authors from a current issue (June, 1973) and 29 editors and 8 current authors (May, 1973) from *Behavior Therapy* were surveyed, as well as 3 persons who have expressed interest in this issue. It was anticipated that results would be analyzed to determine if there were differences in responses between *JABA* affiliates and those primarily affiliated with the behavior therapy journals. Questionnaires were sent out in early December 1973 and subjects were asked to respond by January 15, 1974. Stamped, addressed envelopes were enclosed to facilitate the response. Respondents were also asked to indicate their desire to receive a copy of the completed paper.

RESULTS

Responses. There were a total of 92 responses to the survey. There were 13 refusal letters; Table 1 lists the reasons given for refusal (see page 63).

Eleven persons sent only the biographical sheet and two people sent only the competency check list. There were 66 complete returns. Responses from people affiliated with *JABA* accounted for 54 of the complete returns, *BRAT* for one, *BTEP* for 5, and 3 interested people and 3 anonymous respondents accounted for the other completed returns. (Since there were only a total of six returns from people affiliated primarily with the behavior therapy journals, no comparison between *JABA* and *BRAT*, *BTEP* and *BT* has been made.)

Biographical data of respondents. Table 2 (page 64) lists the backgrounds of the respondents: the degrees they attained, their major and minor fields, and their academic or nonacademic backgrounds. Of the 75 persons who returned this sheet, different numbers responded to each of the questions. Therefore the number of respondents to a particular item is listed under its heading.

Almost all of the respondents, 68, hold doctoral degrees, and 70 either majored or minored in psychology. Thirty-two report a nonacademic affiliation, primarily working as institutional or community clinicians. Fifty-seven report having academic affiliations, most reported that they are affiliated with psychology department faculties. Table 3 (page 65) indicates the behavior modification activities of the persons responding to those items. Of the 72 persons responding to that item, 98% report engaging in behavior modification research, 93% in college or university training, 65.2% in on-the-job training, and 72.5% in inservice training. Of the 66 persons reporting that they perform some sort of behavior modification clinical treatment, 12 work with children, 15 with mentally retarded persons and the remainder with a variety of subjects.

Survey utilization. Seventy-three people responded to the items related to survey utilization. Table 4 (page 66) presents those results. There is apparently no clear concensus about whether or not the individual should keep a copy of his own check list, although 60% of the respondents endorsed the item that suggests the supervisor should keep the list. Using the check list as a basis for state certification was either rejected or not answered by most respondents; only about one-third endorsed that item. Respondents were stronger in their endorsement of the list as a guide for graduate training, and for in-service training. Approximately half of the group felt that the list could be used as a self-training guide.

Who attests to competency achievement? There was a strong endorsement for someone who has already achieved the competency himself to attest to its achievement; 55 of the 73 respondents selected that item. (See Table 4.) This particular question generated quite a few open-ended comments which are presented in Table 5, page 67. There were two comments in particular that were written in by several persons. Five suggested that a state board or committee of various professionals attest to competencies and nine persons indicated that people with more than one of the competencies should function in that role.

Continuation of survey. There was a strong voice of support for repeated surveys of this type. Fifty-two respondents endorsed a regular repetition of similar surveys while four rejected the idea and three felt that one was sufficient. Several open-ended comments were added to this question. (See Table 6, page 68.) A few of those responses refer to the technical aspects of the questionnaire, some to provisions for flexibility, and some to simplification of data collection.

General comments. Many of the respondents (42) wrote general comments of their own when responding to specific items. Additionally, 10 people took the time to write letters in response to the questionnaire. Four letters rejected the idea of conducting surveys of this type and spelled out their reasons. One letter expressed the view that limiting the practice of behavior modification to the operant approach ". . . is dangerously parochial." The writer expressed the view that where and by whom a person was trained ". . . will continue to be a first indicator of what an individual should be expected to do . . ." and also finds it curious that ". . . we should be trying to imitate the medical model that we have rejected so strenuously at the level of professional practice." Another letter voiced the feeling that certification should be avoided since it ". . . will act to perpetuate established practices and retard experimentation with new ideas"; the writer doubts that suitable criteria can be formulated. Another writer endorsed establishing ethical guidelines and rejected specifying procedural guidelines and explicit divisions of labor; he questioned the efficacy of the behavior therapies, especially operant techniques, implying that the survey is premature. He also expressed the fear that "such an effort will merely cause us to repeat the 'sins' of schools of therapy." Another letter expressed the fear that state certification would place the state in the position of supporting, training and treating certain segments of the population and implied that state involvement would serve to increase and perpetuate ". . . the bureaucracy of the welfare state." A fifth letter writer, while not actively rejecting the project, did express his anxiety that it would intensify rivalries among the various therapies. He also questioned the supervisory function and suggested the possibility of certifying training programs, along the lines that the Association for the Advancement of Behavior Therapy (AABT) is currently following, rather than certifying people.

The remaining general comments are presented in Table 7, page 69. In a few cases comments were rephrased and grouped with those that were essentially synonymous. Of those comments, 14 could be construed as supporting the project; 5 do not. Some respondents suggest alternative approaches; i.e., the empirical approach: locate a group of "super-competents" and identify the competencies they possess; describe position competencies rather than "level of functioning" competencies. In addition to those contained on Table 6, page 68, seventeen respondents reported problems with filling out the check list. Eight respondents suggested various uses for the results of the survey; e.g., training, placement, etc.

Responses to behavior modification check list. Sixty-eight people responded to the behavior modification check list. Table 8, page 70, presents the frequency of endorsements of each item, as necessary or desirable, and the percentage of those endorsements for each of the 4 categories: Behavior Analyst, Behavior Technology Coordinator, Behavior Technologist Engineer and Behavior Co-Technician. The number and percentage of those not endorsing an item, which is the equivalent of saying that the response is unnecessary, are not included in the table (the figures may be easily calculated by adding the frequency for the necessary and desirable items and subtracting them from 68). No item was endorsed as desirable by over 50% of the respondents but, aside from the latter category, many items were scored by a majority of respondents as either necessary or desirable. Sixty-four of the 69 items were considered necessary for the Behavior Analyst by the majority of respondents while the other 5 were considered either desirable or unnecessary. Only 43 of the items were considered necessary for the Behavior Technologist, while 22 were considered as either necessary or desirable by a majority. One item (develops model or theory) was considered unnecessary for the Behavior Technologist. For the Behavior Technologist Engineer only 22 items were considered necessary, 25 either necessary or desirable, and 20 items were considered unnecessary. The respondents endorsed most items as being unnecessary for the Behavior Co-Technician; 13 items as either necessary or desirable; and only 3 as necessary: behavioral observation for the contingencies, for goals, and conduct measures. A similar distribution is reflected by the mean percentages for each role category at the end of Table 8.

The next set of tables lists the response items that were selected most and least often for each of the practitioner levels. Items selected are listed in descending order.

Behavior Analyst. The competency responses endorsed most frequently for the Behavior Analyst related to familiarity with and incorporation of the essentials of the behavior modification model; individual and program goal assessment; familiarity with ethical standards and philosophical issues. They offered a rationale for and appropriate use of experimental designs, written and oral communication, and those responses that indicate a critical consumption of current research. (See Table 9, page 74.) The Behavior Analyst was seen more as an individual who can define, illustrate and offer alternative behavioral procedures, but not necessarily someone who applies the procedures. He was less often seen as a behavioral observer, one who does direct measurement, a trainer, consultant, administrator, researcher, or someone who should be able to prepare Audio-Visual media.

The Behavior Technology Coordinator. The Behavior Technology Coordinator is also apparently supposed to be familiar with the behavior modification model, individual and program goal assessment, and ethical and philosophical issues; to be able to give the rationale for and select appropriate experimental designs, and to communicate orally and in writing. (See Table 10, page 75.) The desirability of the Behavior Technology Coordinator's ability to conduct behavioral observations, measurement, to define and effectively apply procedures and to conduct in-service training was strongly endorsed. Most consulting, administrative, and research skills were not considered crucial for the person functioning in this role.

The Behavior Technologist Engineer. Table 11 (page 76) indicates that there were no very strong necessary endorsements for responses in this category. However, there did seem to be some strong trends in the selection of functioning in this role. Responses selected as necessary or desirable by over 70% of the respondents are included in the table. Observation measurement, design, and the application of behavioral procedures were among those categories that received endorsement at that level. Less complex oral and written communication skills were among those listed as well as ethical items, familiarity with the behavior modification model and specification of program goals. Excluded as being unnecessary for persons functioning as Behavior Technologist Engineers were items in research, administration, training and consulting.

The Behavior Co-Technician. Only three items were endorsed as necessary by the majority of the respondents for this category. Table 12, page 78, indicates that aside from behavioral observation and measurement, no response items were heavily endorsed. Specifically rejected for practitioners at this level were administrative, research, design, training, consulting, and communication skills.

DISCUSSION

Any conclusions based on this report must be considered to represent the viewpoints primarily of productive researchers and editors at the post-doctoral level who have published in the *Journal of Applied Behavior Analysis.* Most of the respondents hold academic affiliations and half have non-academic, probably clinical, affiliations; they conduct behavior modification with varied populations. Since there were so few responses from people representing the "behavior therapies," it would not be appropriate to generalize about that group.

There is no clear support for a system to determine the competency of an individual to perform behavior modification activities. State certification is apparently a controversial issue; the responses are almost evenly divided among those who are for it, those against it, and those having no opinion. The comments of respondents also give evidence of the controversy. Perhaps the suggestion of one letter writer, that we stick to judging according to *where* and *by whom* a person was trained, can serve as the prime guide for competence. Since most respondents endorsed using a list of competencies, such as those presented as a guide to graduate training, training departments might publicly indicate the competencies that their programs are designed to achieve. Trainers (or trainees) who have already achieved the competency could attest to its achievement; it is a notion supported by the majority of respondents.

Since most of the respondents endorsed conducting surveys of this type (hopefully with technical improvements), perhaps a more definitive system for identifying competent behavior modifiers will evolve. In the meantime something must be done immediately. There is no longer any doubt that people in need of the unique services that behavior modification can provide are being threatened with denial of those services. We feel that one effective way to combat that threat is to maximize the competencies of people functioning as behavior modifiers and to have a system for identifying those with the competencies.

The competencies themselves. Almost all of the responses listed were considered necessary for the Behavior Analyst by the majority of the respondents; only the items related to media and manual preparation, designing apparatus, model or theory development were rejected. Interestingly enough, perhaps because respondents were not asked specifically to do so, no additional competency responses were suggested. Possibly we did a superb job of isolating relevant competency responses or perhaps our respondents were simply exhausted by the time they completed the check list and weren't giving thought to additional items. At any rate, there seems to be a consensus now that describes what a competent Behavior Analyst should be able to do, from the most necessary, and necessary or desirable, to the least necessary or undesirable. Because flexibility of competency requirements seems to be so important to so many of the respondents, and since support for similar surveys in the future was heavy, we hope to repeat a modified form of the survey in a couple of years.

For the other three role categories, competency requirements were not as strongly supported. Yet the responses to the Behavior Technology Coordinator do meet with our concept of what a behavior modifier at the pre-doctoral level should be able to do. The person described by the respondents resembles many of the highly skilled behavior modifiers we have seen conducting projects and programs in institutions, schools, clinics and other service facilities. It is likely that people who obtain these competencies, but who are not researchers or administrators, are often graduates of master's level programs. The Behavior Technologist Engineer's profile resembles those who tend to function as research assistants in behavior modification projects or programs. We have seen graduate research assistants as well as undergraduate students and talented persons without college educations performing the functions described. Since a majority of the competencies were not deemed necessary for persons functioning at this level, perhaps they should not be called behavior modifiers. Either research assistant, project or program assistant, or Behavior Technology Coordinator would be more appropriate.

The Behavior Co-Technician cannot be called a behavior modifier since he is expected to do observation and measurement functions only. The person described here, while frequently crucial to a behavior modification program, is usually given a different title: research, project or program assistant, observer, behavior co-technician recorder, etc. He is not called a behavior modifier. We have seen many people with varied backgrounds function in this role: parents, students at all levels, volunteers, etc. Usually they have received on-the-job training; occasionally they have been trained in an in-service or college course.

It seems, therefore, that at least two and perhaps three specific behavior modifier roles have been identified: the Behavior Analyst and Behavior Technology Coordinator. The Behavior Technologist Engineer might be called a behavior modifier since he does apply behavioral procedures systematically and with the requisite experimental controls.

Several aspects of the responses were quite gratifying. People who applied behavioral procedures are expected to include experimental controls, thereby providing for accountability. If behavior modifiers do regularly incorporate such controls into their projects and programs, they will continue to operate from an empirical base rather than from faith. Fortunately the inclusion of experimental controls in projects is a characteristic which should be apparent to those attempting to locate competent people. The public, as well as the profession, should realize, however, that the sort of controlled data collection that behavior modifiers conduct makes their results more public, open to closer scrutiny, and possibly to more criticism by the consumer and the general public. For the behavior change agent who keeps his records privately in his safe, public scrutiny and consequent evaluation is almost impossible.

A second gratifying aspect of the survey was the large number of respondents. Sixty-eight persons filled out the check list, 73 the biographical data sheet and 10 respondents wrote separate letters. Responding to the questionnaire was time consuming and difficult for many of the respondents, yet they did take the time to reply. (We shall take the advice of several respondents the next time and seek the services of a professional questionnaire developer, in the hope that the task will be somewhat simplified.) Such commitments of time and effort attest to the interest in and concern for this topic.

The fact that strong endorsements were given to the items on ethics, such as ethical guidelines, community standards and laws was also pleasing, especially in light of Oelsner's comments about the failure of behavior modifiers themselves to give little thought to the sociological and legal ramifications of the methods being developed. One ethical consideration, however, was disappointing to us: only 75% of the respondents thought it necessary for behavior analysts to include in proposals a section addressing itself to the major ethical issues relevant to the particular case. We feel that every behavior modification proposal should incorporate such a section as testimony to the fact that ethics have been considered in the design of the method. The section on ethics should address itself to community standards, laws, prevailing philosophies, the individual freedom and responsibility of the clients through informed consent as well as the client's attitudes and feelings. In the event that clients are not competent to communicate that information, their caretakers and advocates should participate instead. Many universities and institutions have human research subject committees. Our behavior modification proposals should meet the ethical requirements for our subjects as well. Some behavior modifiers, especially those who work in schools and institutions, may protest the absurdity of this argument. "What ethical concerns should we have about teaching arithmetic effectively, toilet training someone or teaching him how to tie his shoe?" Our rejoinder is that it is important to include the section and to mention that teaching arithmetic is part of the curriculum endorsed by the school board; that being toilet trained and being able to tie one's shoes are goals for all institutional residents and that parents and other advocates have agreed to these goals. It is better to do all that than not mention the topic at all. Rather the occasionally superfluous statement than the error of neglecting ethical issues in more ambiguous areas such as social behaviors and sex roles. In addition there is the more powerful, pragmatic argument, that if we are not overly cautious about our own ethics, society may take over the role and sharply curtail our activities and the services we can perform.

We thus offer, as our first formal recommendation, that behavior modifiers be ethically overscrupulous; that they apply the principle of informed consent, as well as publicly announced ethical concerns and solutions, prior to instituting their procedures.

A second recommendation derives from the apparent interest by behavior analysts in coping with the problem of competency. Concern has been expressed by behavior analysts; competencies have been identified; alternatives for attesting to competency achievement are under consideration. Yet publicity occasionally places us in a bad light, for reasons described earlier in this paper. We recommend that a strong effort be made to inform the public of the accomplishments that behavior modification has been able to achieve. As a corollary, we should publicly admit our limitations. We should caution against overzealous regard for techniques that are relatively new and in some cases in need of more extensive study. Basically we have available a self-correcting method, effective in many but hardly in all areas of behavioral problems. An accurate and responsible view of our method should be communicated to the general public.

The third recommendation is that some method or set of alternatives be selected soon for identifying the competencies that individual behavior modifiers have achieved. In Connecticut, when psychologists participating in an in-service workshop had met criteria for achievement of specific competencies, records of their accomplishments were placed with their consent in their personnel folders in the central office. Other methods might include placing evidence of competency achievements in placement folders, student records, or elsewhere, or one of the alternatives suggested by the respondents to our survey.

Finally, this is probably the time to constitute a committee charged with the responsibility of recommending regular procedures for establishing competency criteria, their evaluation, and a means for attesting to their achievement. The committee subsequently should consider providing national guidelines and, in close collaboration with national and local agencies, seek their adoption in each of the 50 states.

Table 1. Reasons for Refusal

Letters

13 Refusals to respond

  1 no time

  1 no problem identifying those competent

  2 sabbatical

  7 weren't qualified in behavior modification or mental retardation

  1 medical excuse

  1 sought justification for responding to this one (survey) out of 50 surveys per week

Table 2. Respondents' Background and Occupational Activities (n=75)

Degree (n=72)	F	%	Major Studied (n=69)	F	%	Minor Studied (n=31)	F	%
Masters	4	5.6	Psychology	62	89.9	Science	2	6.4
Ph.D.	65	90.3	Education	4	5.8	Liberal Arts	1	3.2
M.D.	2	2.8	Technology	1	1.8	Psychology	8	25.8
Ed.D.	1	1.4	Medicine	1	1.4	Other	20	64.5
			Speech	1	1.4			

Occupation (n=32)

Non-Academic	F	%	Academic	F	%
Community Clinician	5	16.6	Student	1	1.8
Institutional Clinician	15	46.9	Psychology faculty	36	63.2
Medical School	2	6.2	Psychiatry faculty	4	7.0
Community Administrator	2	6.2	Medical School other faculty	3	5.3
Staff Trainer	1	3.13	Education, Special Education faculty	5	8.8
Researcher	7	21.9	Audiology, Speech faculty	1	1.8
			Human Development	3	5.3
			Other	4	7.0

Table 3.   Respondents' Behavior Modification Activities

Activity (n=72)	Yes F	Yes %	No F	No %
Behavior Modification Research	71	98.6	1	1.4
Training				
College, university	66	93	5	
On-the-job	45	65.2	24	34.8
In-service	50	72.5	19	27.5
Clinical Treatment	66			
Population:				
School children	12	18.2		
Mentally retarded	15	22.7		
Emotionally disturbed	1	1.5		
Physically handicapped	1	1.5		
Sex problems	1	1.5		
Alcoholics	1	1.5		
Unspecified others	35	53.0		

Table 4. Survey Utilization (n=73)

Checklist	Yes F	No F	NR
Who keeps checklist?			
Individual keeps in own personal file	32	40	1
Supervisor keeps it	28	44	1
Use for state certification	23	18	32
Guideline for graduate training	62	1	10
Guideline for in-service training	55	2	16
Self training	39	5	29

Who Attests to Competency Achievement?

	Yes F	No F	NR
Person who has already achieved competency himself	55	2	16
Member of AABT	11	9	53
Member of APA Division 25	10	9	54
Direct line supervisor	16	8	49
College or university professor	17	9	47
Anyone to whom evidence is shown	6	11	56

Surveys Like This Should Be Conducted

Regularly: 52   Only once: 3   Not at all: 4

Table 5.   Open-Ended Comments on Attesting to Competency

Who or what should function as supervisor attesting to individual's achievement of given competencies?

State committee or board of various professionals	5
Follow AMA	1
Faculty of the training institute or college	2
Licensing agency	1
Certifying board—national structure	1
Conventional methods suffice—degree, institution	1
Licensed individual	1
Maybe just you and me???	1
Consensus of people, selected by applicant	1
Whoever is qualified—1 person for each competency	2
Clients	3
Professor teaching a relevant course	2
Anyone who can interpret data	1
Person with more than 1 of the competencies	9

Methods of qualifying

State records and evaluates responses to standardized filmed stimuli	1
Published research productivity	1

Table 6.   Open-Ended Comments on Survey Usage

Surveys like this should:

Develop a coding system for objectives on checklist	1
Use APA meetings for data gathering	1
Be scheduled to review objectives, build checks, revisions	1
Checked for validity and reliability of items	1
Have a multiple alternative model	1
Be psychometrically refined	1
Be conducted every 2 or 4 years	1
Call in survey testing expert to construct questionnaire	1
Help define issues	1
Have check-list criteria more performance-related	1

Table 7. General, Open-Ended Comments from Questionnaires and Letters

Necessary for practitioners	1
Needed for clinical or applied practitioners only	1
Positive reinforcement—"a good first step," etc.	9
Difficult problem	2
Need—because of changing values, accountability	1
Specialization in operant techniques required in children's services	1
Questions own validity	1
Certification to be avoided—too inflexible	1
Limit to operant approach to behavior modification too narrow	1
Rejects imitation of medical model	1
Against power grabs	1
AAMD and APA ethics suffice	1
Difficult to train	1
Competency criteria based on criterion group (empirically derived)	3
Describe specific position competencies	1
Need to know more about modifying environments than modifying behavior	1
Problems with filling out checklist:	
Difficulty with role specification at each level	12
Difficulty with filling out	3
Vague	1
Too long	1
Use survey for:	
Better training programs	2
State wide directory	1
Developing certification titles within teaching profession	1
Self modification	1
Job placement	1
State certification	1
Proposals to agencies for review (APA, institutions, state, etc.)	1

Table 8. Responses to Behavior Modification Check List

CATEGORY		PRACTITIONER RESPONSE	Behavior Analyst (Conceptualizer, Supervisor, Evaluator)				Behavior Technology Coordinator (Supervisor, Trainer)				Behavior Technologist Engineer (Designer and Implementer)				Behavior co-Technician (Carries out day-to-day operation of Projects, Programs)			
			Nec. No.	%	Des. No.	%	Nec. No.	%	Des. No.	%	Nec. No.	%	Des. No.	%	Nec. No.	%	Des. No.	%
I. Behavior Modification Model	a.	Lists steps	61	89.7	2	2.9	55	80.9	4	5.9	45	66.2	9	13.2	14	20.6	26	38.2
	b.	Writes proposal	61	89.7	2	2.9	49	72.1	9	13.2	35	51.5	15	22.1	4	5.9	25	36.8
	c.	Writes report	60	88.2	2	2.9	46	67.6	11	16.2	26	38.2	20	29.4	4	5.9	25	36.8
II. Assessment, Goal Formulation and Targeting	a.	Assesses and refers	55	80.9	5	7.4	48	70.6	8	11.8	29	42.6	11	16.2	11	16.2	19	27.9
	b.	Specifies program goals	59	86.8	2	2.9	50	73.5	8	11.8	36	52.9	13	19.1	10	14.7	17	25.0
	c.	Specifies system goals	57	83.8	3	4.4	40	58.8	13	19.1	27	39.7	14	20.6	5	7.4	15	22.1
III. Ethics	a.	APA guidelines	58	85.3	2	2.9	48	70.6	7	10.3	41	60.3	8	11.8	25	36.8	16	23.5
	b.	Community standards	59	86.8	2	2.9	51	75.0	7	10.3	43	63.2	9	13.2	32	47.1	14	20.6
	c.	Knows federal, state laws	56	82.4	5	7.4	47	69.1	10	14.7	35	51.5	17	25.0	22	32.4	20	29.4
	d.	Identifies issues	56	82.4	3	4.4	46	67.6	10	14.7	28	41.2	26	38.2	10	14.7	26	38.2
	e.	Describes ethical system	50	73.5	6	8.8	37	54.4	17	25.0	21	30.9	25	36.8	9	13.2	20	29.4
	f.	Includes in programs	51	75.0	7	10.3	42	61.8	11	16.8	21	39.7	16	23.5	12	17.6	18	26.5
	g.	Responds to criticisms	55	80.9	7	10.3	44	64.7	14	20.6	30	44.1	17	25.0	18	26.5	18	26.5
IV. Behavioral Observation	a.	Contingencies	52	76.5	3	4.4	52	76.5	3	4.4	49	72.1	6	8.8	39	57.4	14	20.6
	b.	Goals	51	75.0	5	7.4	50	73.5	5	7.4	46	67.6	7	10.3	35	51.5	14	20.6
	c.	Trains others	50	73.5	8	11.8	51	75.0	3	4.4	36	52.9	12	17.6	14	20.6	18	26.5

TRAINED BEHAVIOR MODIFIERS

			n	%	n	%	n	%	n	%	n	%	n	%	n	%	n	%
V.	*Measurement*																	
	a.	Defines systems	60	88.2	4	5.9	51	75.0	5	7.4	39	57.4	10	14.7	11	16.2	23	33.8
	b.	Selects systems	58	85.3	3	4.4	52	76.5	5	7.4	38	55.9	14	20.6	11	16.2	24	35.3
	c.	Conducts measures	47	69.1	10	14.7	51	75.0	7	10.3	44	64.7	9	13.2	39	57.4	11	16.2
	d.	Designs measures	52	76.5	8	11.8	47	69.1	9	13.2	44	64.7	12	17.6	8	11.8	24	35.3
	e.	Uses apparatus	39	57.4	13	19.1	40	58.8	11	16.2	42	61.8	12	17.6	31	45.6	16	23.5
	f.	Designs apparatus	34	50.0	18	26.5	26	38.2	21	30.2	27	39.7	19	27.9	6	8.8	18	26.5
	g.	Trains others	51	75.0	8	11.8	55	80.9	4	5.9	32	47.1	14	20.6	7	10.3	17	25.0
VI.	*Design*																	
	a.	Lists variables	61	89.7	4	5.9	43	63.2	14	20.6	35	51.5	18	26.5	9	13.2	21	30.9
	b.	Gives rationale	63	92.6	1	1.5	43	63.2	13	19.1	33	48.5	18	26.5	4	5.9	28	41.2
	c.	Traditional designs	51	75.0	3	4.4	44	64.7	14	20.6	33	48.5	16	23.5	5	7.4	19	27.9
	d.	Irreversible behavior	55	80.9	5	7.4	34	50.0	20	29.4	27	39.7	19	27.9	1	1.5	18	26.5
	e.	Selects appropriately	60	88.2	2	2.9	41	60.3	16	23.5	30	44.1	19	27.9	2	2.9	19	27.9
	f.	Conducts research	45	66.2	14	20.6	24	35.3	28	41.2	18	26.5	17	25.0	0	0.0	19	27.9
VII.	*Behavioral Procedures*																	
	a.	Operational definitions	64	94.1	2	2.9	50	73.5	10	14.7	42	61.8	12	17.6	17	25.0	21	30.9
	b.	Illustrates with examples	58	85.3	4	5.9	48	70.6	13	19.1	39	57.4	12	17.6	14	20.6	23	33.8
	c.	Lists rules for applications	53	77.9	7	10.3	44	64.7	16	23.5	34	50.0	13	19.1	13	19.1	19	27.9
	d.	Applies procedures	49	72.1	11	16.2	43	63.2	17	25.0	39	57.4	15	22.1	19	27.9	23	33.8
	e.	Demonstrates effectiveness	52	76.5	8	11.8	42	61.8	16	23.5	39	57.4	13	19.1	15	22.1	18	26.5
	f.	Offers alternatives	58	85.3	3	4.4	45	66.2	15	22.1	38	55.9	13	19.1	6	8.8	25	36.8
	g.	Discovers new procedures	46	67.6	12	17.6	24	35.3	23	33.8	21	36.9	14	20.6	2	2.9	19	27.9
VIII. **(1)**	*Communication: Oral*																	
	a.	Describes procedures	59	86.8	8	11.8	51	75.0	11	16.2	36	52.9	18	26.5	17	25.0	28	41.2
	b.	Presents project or program	60	88.2	8	11.8	43	63.2	17	25.0	28	41.2	21	30.9	5	7.4	23	33.8
VIII. **(2)**	*Communication: Written*																	
	a.	Writes steps	61	89.7	4	5.9	43	63.2	16	23.5	38	52.9	12	17.6	11	16.2	14	20.6
	b.	Writes project proposal	61	89.7	6	8.8	39	57.4	19	27.9	32	47.1	17	25.0	3	4.4	17	25.0

PRACTITIONER RESPONSE

TRAINED BEHAVIOR MODIFIERS

	Behavior Analyst (Conceptualizer, Supervisor, Evaluator)				Behavior Technology Coordinator (Supervisor, Trainer)				Behavior Technologist Engineer (Designer and Implementer)				Behavior co-Technician (Carries out day-to-day operation of Projects, Programs)			
	Nec. No.	%	Des. No.	%	Nec. No.	%	Des. No.	%	Nec. No.	%	Des. No.	%	Nec. No.	%	Des. No.	%
c. Writes program proposal	58	85.3	6	8.8	37	54.4	19	27.9	24	35.3	19	27.9	3	4.4	12	17.7
d. Writes project report	57	83.8	6	8.8	36	52.9	19	27.9	22	32.4	19	27.9	2	2.9	13	19.1
e. Writes program report	52	76.5	8	11.8	29	42.6	21	30.9	17	25.0	17	25.0	0	0.0	11	16.2
f. Publishes project or program report	42	61.8	21	30.9	20	29.4	25	36.8	12	17.6	19	27.9	1	1.5	12	17.6
g. Writes progress report	55	80.9	9	13.2	35	51.5	20	29.4	22	32.4	19	27.9	4	5.9	14	20.6
VIII. Communication: **(3) A.V.**																
a. Draws	25	36.8	21	30.8	21	30.9	22	32.4	27	39.7	16	23.5	8	11.8	25	36.8
b. Prepares media	19	27.9	29	42.6	17	25.0	28	41.2	19	27.9	22	32.4	7	10.3	13	19.1
IV. Training and Consulting																
a. Conducts single session workshop	43	63.2	17	25.0	33	48.5	21	30.9	14	20.6	22	32.4	3	4.4	9	13.2
b. Conducts workshop series	38	55.9	23	33.8	32	47.1	21	30.9	9	13.2	19	27.9	1	1.5	9	13.2
c. Consults on training	40	58.8	23	33.8	31	45.6	22	32.4	12	17.6	18	26.5	1	1.5	9	13.2
d. Teaches course	37	54.4	27	39.7	29	42.6	25	36.8	9	13.2	20	29.4	1	1.5	8	11.8
e. Conducts in-service training	39	57.4	22	32.4	37	54.4	20	29.4	13	19.1	20	29.4	3	4.4	9	13.2
f. Prepares training manual	32	47.1	24	35.3	25	36.8	27	39.7	14	20.6	15	22.1	2	2.9	8	11.8
g. Consults on methodology	41	60.3	21	30.9	26	38.2	25	36.8	13	19.1	17	25.0	3	4.4	9	13.2
X. Administration																
a. Agency policies	50	73.5	10	14.7	27	39.7	16	23.5	10	14.7	13	19.1	4	5.9	11	16.2
b. Staff organization	50	73.5	9	13.2	27	39.7	18	26.5	5	7.4	18	26.5	0	0.0	7	10.3

	Behavior Analyst				Behavior Technologist				Behavior Technologist Engineer				Behavior Co-Technician			
c. Uses natural contingencies	46	67.6	14	20.6	36	52.9	17	25.0	17	25.0	18	26.5	13	19.1	19	27.9
d. Obtains administrative approval	50	73.5	8	11.8	33	48.5	15	22.1	11	16.2	13	19.1	4	5.9	7	10.3
e. Staff contingencies	48	70.6	12	17.6	34	50.0	15	22.1	10	14.7	19	27.9	4	5.9	7	10.3
f. Coordinates, supervises	46	67.6	11	16.2	40	58.8	12	17.6	7	10.3	18	26.5	0	0.0	6	8.8
g. Directs agency project or program	44	64.7	12	17.6	21	30.9	19	27.9	3	4.4	11	16.2	0	0.0	5	7.4
XI. Research																
a. Reads research	59	86.8	6	8.8	42	61.8	12	17.6	28	41.2	13	19.1	6	8.8	21	30.9
b. Identifies trends	53	77.9	12	17.6	29	42.6	19	27.9	16	23.5	19	27.9	3	4.4	14	20.6
c. Formulates research questions	48	70.6	14	20.6	19	27.9	22	32.4	14	20.6	15	22.1	0	0.0	12	17.6
d. Integrates findings	50	73.5	13	19.1	22	32.4	20	29.4	13	19.1	12	17.6	0	0.0	8	11.8
e. Writes research proposal	40	58.8	19	27.9	14	20.6	26	38.2	11	16.2	11	16.2	2	2.9	7	10.3
f. Conducts experimental research	40	58.8	23	33.8	19	27.9	24	35.3	17	25.0	10	14.7	2	2.9	8	11.8
g. Applies research tools*	38	55.9	20	29.4	16	23.5	24	35.3	13	19.1	11	16.2	2	2.9	6	8.8
h. Evaluates research	51	75.0	10	14.7	20	29.4	17	25.0	13	19.1	9	13.2	1	1.5	8	11.8
i. Develops model or theory	28	41.2	24	35.3	21	30.9	21	30.9	6	8.8	10	14.7	1	1.5	5	7.4

*Written as "Applies all" on check list by mistake.

Mean Percentages for Each Behavior Modification Role Category

Role	Behavior Analyst	Behavior Technologist	Behavior Technologist Engineer	Behavior Co-Technician
Necessary	72.1	53.4	36.9	12.3
Desirable	14.5	22.4	21.8	22.7
Unnecessary	13.4	24.2	41.3	65.

Table 9. Behavior Analyst
(Conceptualizer, Supervisor, Evaluator)

More than 90% necessary:
Operationally defines behavioral procedures
Gives rationale for experimental design
More than 90% necessary or desirable:
Communication (oral)
    *Presents project or program
    *Describes procedures
*Reads research
*Writes project proposal
*Writes steps
*Lists variables (confounding)
*Writes progress report
*Measurement; defines systems
*Writes program proposal
Behavior modification model:
    *Lists steps
    *Writes proposal
*Writes project report
Publishes project or program report
Integrates research findings
Formulates research questions
Consults on methodology
*Illustrates behavioral procedures with examples
*Selects appropriate design
*Responds to criticisms (of behavior modification)
*Writes report
More than 80% necessary:
Items with * above as well as the following competencies
Offers alternative behavioral procedures
Knows community standards
Specifies program goals
Assesses and refers
Selects design for irreversible behavior
APA ethical guidelines
Selects systems of measurement
Knows federal, state laws
Identifies ethical issues
Less than 50% necessary (=50% or more desirable or unnecessary):
Develops theory or model
Communication: A.V. Draws
Prepares media
Prepares training manual
Less than 50% necessary or desirable
None
*See first item under *More than 80% necessary*

Table 10. Behavior Technology Coordinator
(Supervisor, Trainer)

Over 90% necessary:
None

Over 80-90% (necessary):
Behavior modification model; lists steps
Measurement; trains others

Over 90% necessary or desirable:
Communication (oral); describes procedures

Over 80% necessary or desirable:
Measurement; defines systems
Measurement; selects systems
Behavioral observation contingencies
Ethics, community standards
Measurement; conducts measures
Assessment, goal formulation and forgetting
Specifies program goals
Behavioral observation goals
Behavioral procedures; operational definitions
Behavior modification model; writes proposal
Assessment, goal formulation and targeting; assesses and refers
Ethics, APA guidelines
Behavioral procedures; illustrates with examples
Ethics; knows federal, state laws
Designs measures
Writes report
Behavior modification model
Ethics; identifies issues
Behavioral procedures; offers alternatives
Design, traditional
Behavioral procedures; lists rules for applications
Design; lists variables
Design; gives rationale
Behavioral procedures; applies procedures
Communication (oral); presents project or program
Communication (written); writes steps
Behavioral procedures, demonstrates effectiveness
Design; selects appropriately
Communication (written); writes project proposal
Communication (written); writes program
Training and consulting; conducts in-service training
Communication (written); writes project report
Communication (written); writes progress report

Less than 50% necessary or desirable (=50% or more unnecessary):
Research; develops model or theory

Table 11. Behavior Technologist Engineer
(Designer and Implementer)

Over 90% necessary:
None
Over 90% necessary or desirable:
None
Over 80% necessary:
None
Over 80% necessary or desirable:
Behavioral observation, contingencies
Measurement, designs measures
Over 70% necessary or desirable:
Behavior modification model; lists steps
Ethics; identifies issues
Behavioral procedures; operationally defines, applies, illustrates with
   examples
Measurement; conducts measures
Design; lists confounding variables
Behavioral procedures; demonstrates effectiveness
Measurement; uses apparatus
Design; gives rationale
Behavioral observations; goals
Behavioral procedures; offers alternatives
Ethics; knows federal, state laws
Ethics; knows community standards
Measurement; selects systems
Behavior modification model; writes proposal
Communication written; writes project proposal
Ethics; APA Guidelines
Assessment; specifies program goals
Design; selects appropriate traditional designs
Communication (oral); presents project or program
Communication (written); writes steps
Behavioral observations; trains others
Less than 50% (>30%) necessary or desirable: (=50 to 70% unnecessary)
Administration, staff organization
Research; evaluates research
Administration; coordinates and supervises
Training and consulting; conducts workshop series
Training consulting; teaches course
Administration; agency policies
Administration; staff contingencies
Administration; obtains administrative approval

Table 11 (Continued)

Research; writes research proposal
Communication (written); publishes project or program report
Communication (written); consults on training
Training consulting; conducts in-service training
Training consulting; consults on methodology
Research; integrates findings
Research; applies research tool
Research; formulates research questions
Research; conducts experimental research
Training and consulting; prepares training manual

Less than 30% necessary or desirable (=70% or more unnecessary)
Administration; directs agency project or program
Research; develops model or theory

Table 12. Behavior Co-Technician
(Carries out Day-to-Day Operation of Projects, Programs)

More than 90% necessary:
None

More than 90% necessary or desirable:
None

More than 80% necessary:
None

More than 80% necessary or desirable:
None
(Highest % necessary = 57.4)

More than 50% necessary:
Behavioral observation; contingencies
Measurement; conducts measures
Behavioral observation, goals

Less than 30%–11% necessary or desirable
(More than 70-89% unnecessary)
*Design; conducts research
*Communication (written); writes program report
*Administration; staff organization
*Research; formulates research questions
*Research; integrates findings
 Design; irreversible behavior
 Communication (written); publishes project or program report
 Training and consulting; conducts workshop series
 Training and consulting; consults on training
 Training and consulting; teaches course
 Research; evaluates research
 Communication (written); writes project report
 Training and consulting; prepares training manual
 Research; writes research proposal
 Research; conducts experimental research
 Research; applies research tools
 Communication (written); writes project proposal
 Communication (written); writes program proposal
 Training and consulting; conducts single session workshop
 Training and consulting; conducts in-service training
 Training and consulting; consults on methodology
 Research; identifies trends
 Communication (written); writes progress report
 Administration; agency policies
 Administration; obtains administrative approval

Table 12 (Continued)

Administration; staff contingencies
Assessment, goal formulation, and targeting; specifies system goals
Communication (A.V.); prepares media
Assessment, goal formulation, and targeting; specifies program goals
Less than 10% necessary or desirable:
(More than 90% unnecessary)
*Administration; directs agency project or program
*Administration; coordinates, supervises
Research; develops model or theory

*Zero % necessary

Appendix. Competencies for Behavior Modification Practitioners

Category	Conditions and Practitioner Response	Criteria for Assessing Achievement
I. Behavior Modification Model[1]	a. Lists the essential steps in designing and conducting a behavior modification program.	a. Orally or in writing. The model should include targeting (or goal refinement); a selection of a behavioral procedure; contingency specifications; the provision of a favorable environment; procedural applications; operant level assessment; evaluation or control techniques; maintenance and generality programming; results analysis and communication. At least these essential elements must be included, although terminology and order of presentation may vary.
	b. Writes a proposal for a behavior modification project.[2]	b. Submits to supervisor; *all* essential elements shall be adequately covered (see directly above).
	c. Writes a written report of a behavior modification project.	c. All essential elements adequately covered.
II. Assessment, Goal Formulation and Targeting	a. Assess individual's problem and refers to people who have demonstrated competencies.	a. Agency to which individual referred concurs orally or in writing that referral was appropriate.

80

b. Given a behavioral problem situation, specifies appropriate and realistic project or program goal.[3]

b. The program goal shall be of value to the clients themselves (according to those individuals or their advocates); shall have a reasonable likelihood of being achieved (contingency control adequate, response close to current repertoire); and shall be practical (adequate time, funds, personnel facilities available).

The goal shall be stated in behavioral language. Conditions under which responses should and should not be emitted shall be specified along with a criterion for the achievement of the goal.

c. Given an expressed need to alter or improve system strategies, specifies system goals.[4]

c. Same as b. Should be acceptable to the practitioners within the system.

III. Ethics, Law and Philosophy

a. Is familiar with APA Ethical Guidelines.

a. Objective short answers quiz (10 items or more based on information contained in current APA Ethics Code, answered at 90% accuracy level).

b. Is familiar with the ethical standards and practices of the agency, community, state, as well as other legal precedents.

b. (1) When written ethical standards available, answers objective quiz at 90% level.

Category	Conditions and Practitioner Response	Criteria for Assessing Achievement
		(2) When standards not explicitly written but implied, writes a summary of those standards. Approved by appropriate agency head.
	c. Is familiar with federal and state laws as they affect practice of behavior modification.	c. Passes short answers test (90%) over relevant laws. Does not violate laws in proposal or practice.
	d. Identifies major ethical issues: Whose agent is the behavior modifier? Who has the responsibility for the client? Who decides what is best for the client; On what grounds? How does one decide who receives treatment and who doesn't? How much information is given to the client? What type? What are the pros and cons for: changing behavior? using aversive consequences?	d. In writing or orally at least five major ethical issues related to the practice of behavior modification should be listed and illustrated. For an illustrative problem situation, conflicts should be enumerated and a resolution reached for each. The adequacy of the responses should be assessed on a pass-fail basis by a panel of at least two judges.

reporting procedures and results? How are the human rights of the individual and his family best safe-guarded? Others?

e. Discusses a behaviorally rational ethical system with which the given behavioral practices are consonant (the system may place constraints upon those specific practices as well).

f. Provides for ethical concerns in behavior modification projects, programs and systems.

g. Is familiar with major criticism regarding behavioral control and responds to those criticisms in a logical, rational manner (i.e., issues of freedom and dignity; identifies current uses of behavioral control procedures outside of the behavior modification area: the media, schools, accidental contingencies, social, religious, legal sanctions).

e. For three sample situations (i.e., ward, school, community agency) a paragraph is written that justifies the behavioral approach selected in terms of a system of ethics. The source for the system should be presented to and accepted by the policy-making board of the organization.

f. Each behavior modification proposal shall have a section addressing itself to the major ethical issues relevant to the particular case. Judgment by immediate supervisor as to adequacy of handling.

g. From a pool of current criticisms, supervisor selects a sample of approximately five. Response to the criticism should be judged adequate by supervisor and by one person who is outside of the field of behavior modification and has expressed concern over at least one of those issues in the past.

Category	Conditions and Practitioner Response	Criteria for Assessing Achievement
IV. Behavioral Observation: Recording and Contingency Specification	a. Observes in the natural setting; identifies individual responses and the stimuli that appear to be contingent upon those responses.	a. In sample situations (observation room, videotape, film or in real-life setting school, institution, etc.) at least five observable, measurable behaviors are listed along with a precise description of the antecedent and consequent events. Judged by supervisor as being objectively measurable.
	b. Observes in setting where actual problems exist (clinic, school, home, institution, etc.) for purposes of goal formulation and targeting.	b. At least 3 behaviors in need of modification are targeted and measured for at least 15 minutes each for at least 2 sessions. Criteria for acceptability are the presentation of observational logs.
	c. Trains others to observe in the natural setting.	c. Under supervision, trains at least three persons to observe according to Criteria a and b above.
V. Measurement	a. Operationally defines observational recording systems.	a. Orally or in writing, according to standard text in behavior modification.
	b. Given a list of target behaviors, appropriate observational systems are selected.	b. 90% accuracy as judged by supervisor.

c. Conducts measurement.	c. Measures via procedure designed by others; 80% reliability for 3 sessions using independent, trained observers as reliability standard.
d. Given sample behavioral targets, selects appropriate measure, develops scoring method (data sheet design, instrument selection, etc.), and conducts measurements of target reliably.	d. Data collection method and set-up approved by supervisor. For each response measure, a reliability coefficient of over 80% shall be demonstrated by comparing the observation recorded by 2 independent observers; such a demonstration should be obtained for 3 sample target behaviors.
e. Uses measurement apparatus.	e. Records data for two sessions using apparatus (i.e., stop watch, timer, camera, etc.).
f. Designs measurement apparatus.	f. Measurement apparatus should be reliable and safe; instrument works without technical disruption or deviation at least 10 times in a row; safety judged by professional technician (electrician, etc.).
g. Trains others to measure behavior in the natural setting (a through d above).	g. Under supervision, trains at least 3 persons to measure reliably according to Criteria under a through d above.

VI. Design

a. Lists variables that frequently confound results of behavior modification projects and programs.

a. At least five, such as maturation, extra attention, etc.

Category	Conditions and Practitioner Response	Criteria for Assessing Achievement
	b. Gives rationale; specifies the necessity for the inclusion of experimental controls in all behavior modification projects and programs.	b. Necessity for demonstrating effectiveness of procedures and that the procedure itself and not some artifact was responsible for the change.
	c. Defines and illustrates traditional behavior modification designs: reversal multiple baseline.	c. Baseline, treatment, baseline plus illustrative study cited from current literature. Baseline, treatment; repeated at different time, plus illustration cited from current literature.
	d. Describe designs for nonreversible responses, transition states: direct and systematic replication schedule control multiple schedule designs others.	d. Specifies operation, cites source and illustrate from current literature.
	e. Selects appropriate design for proposed projects and programs.	e. Proposes programs to increase, decrease, maintain and teach behavior. Supervisor judges that major confounding variables are controlled.

f. Conducts research on experimental designs.

f. Publishes or presents paper on experimental findings related to refinements, elaboration, or innovation in experimental design.

VII. Behavioral Procedures

a. For the behavioral procedures which follow writes operational definitions, including specification of the behavior; contingent consequential and prior stimuli; and the operation performed.

a. The operational definitions should conform to those offered in standard texts for behavior analysis, behavior modification or behavior therapy.

At least 90% of the definitions must be correct.

Behavior Procedures:

   operant conditioning
   positive reinforcement
   negative reinforcement
   differential reinforcement
   stimulus change
   shaping
   chaining
   fading
   schedules of reinforcement
      ratio
      interval
      multiple
      differential rate
   extinction (operant)
   avoidance

Category	Conditions and Practitioner Response	Criteria for Assessing Achievement
	timeout response cost punishment satiation reinforcement of incompatible behaviors respondent conditioning respondent extinction desensitization flooding (implosion) aversion therapy sensitization others. Example: Differential reinforcement. In the presence of stimulus A (S_A^D) Response R_X is followed by the presentation of a stimulus (S^+). In the presence of stimulus B (S_B^D) response R_X is not followed by the stimulus S^+ (S^+ is withheld).	

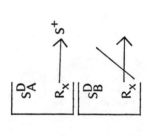

$$S_A^D$$
$$R_x \longrightarrow s^+$$

$$S_B^D$$
$$R_x \longrightarrow$$

As a result of these operations the rate of R_x is predicted to increase in the presence of S_B^D.

b. Illustrates each procedure listed under VIIa with an example from an applied setting.

c. For each procedure listed under VIIa above, specifies rules for effective application of the procedure, the rules based upon the following variables:

    temporal
    schedule
    quantitative

b. Each illustration must include essential stimulus and response elements.

c. 90% correction quiz, criteria for correctness based upon current knowledge in behavioral psychology.

Category   *Conditions and Practitioner Response*

qualitative
social
collatoral events:
    facilitating, suppressing
subject variables:
    history
    deprivation
    physiological
    others.

Example: Small quantities of the
reinforcer should be delivered every
time, and immediately following the
emission of the response. The individual should be deprived of the
reinforcer. (Skinner, 1938)

The example specifies a quantitative
variable (small quantities), a tem-
poral variable (immediately after),
a schedule variable (every time), and
a variable (deprivation condition)
related to the condition of the subject.

d. Applies the above procedures in a laboratory or natural setting.

e. Applies at least one procedure from each of the following categories, with a concommitant demonstration of procedural effectiveness:

   increase in behavioral rate
   decrease in behavioral rate
   maintenance of behavioral rate
   teaching new behavior.

f. Given a behavioral problem from each of the 4 categories listed directly above, offers alternative procedures to *remedy the problem.*

d. For each procedure, a response should be selected, a baseline recorded and a behavioral change generated that tends to move in the predicted direction. Adequate demonstration of the application shall be based on a graph showing the rates under the two conditions. Approximately 1/3 of the procedures listed above shall be applied and documented in this manner.

e. Same as above but in addition, a demonstration of control via some experimental control technique (i.e., reversal, multiple baseline, others).

f. Procedures are applied. Supervisor judges that procedures selected are defensible on basis of knowledge in field.

   Each of four categories of problems is effectively remedied as a consequence of the application of one of the procedures. Effective remedy is defined as achieving the preset terminal objective.

Category	Conditions and Practitioner Response	Criteria for Assessing Achievement

	g. Discovers new information:
	
	    by demonstrating the superiority of one procedure over another, under specific conditions
	
	    or by demonstrating the effectiveness of a refinement of a procedure
	
	    or by replicating a procedure with a new population
	
	    or by isolating a variable that affects a given behavior modification procedure
	
	    others.
		g. Criteria shall rest solely on the acceptance of a paper written on the study and accepted for publication by a journal or for delivery at a major convention (national or regional professional organization) or accepted as a thesis or dissertation in a graduate program.

VIII. 1. Communica- tion: Oral	a. Describes rationale and procedure to parents, paraprofessionals, persons who manage contingencies; answers questions in a clear, comprehensible, non-threatening manner.	a. Under observation of supervisor, a specific procedure is described and a rationale for the selection of the procedure is offered. Supervisor should judge the comprehensibility of the presentation based on language selected listener response and questions. Subjective judgment that audience not threatened (anger, hostility not apparent,

gestures and statements of approval apparent).

b. Presents completed project or program orally.

b. All essentials included; replicable; questions answered adequately; judgment based upon pooled opinion of audience or supervisor, or accepted by convention review board for presentation.

2. Communication: Written

a. Writes procedural steps to be followed.

a. All essential steps included; check list provided as supportive data.

b. Writes project proposal.

b. All essential elements of a behavior modification project included; methodology judged by supervisor to be sufficiently clearly written that an independent person would be able to carry out the project in the same manner (supervisor's check list for supportive data).

c. Writes program proposal.

c. Same as b but for group treatment program.

d. Writes project report.

d. All essential elements included, both those essential to a behavior modification model plus those required by the *Publication Manual of the American Psychological Association*; supervisor's check list as supportive data.

e. Writes program report.

e. Same as d but for program.

Category	Conditions and Practitioner Response	Criteria for Assessing Achievement
	f. Publishes project or program report.	f. Paper accepted for publication by journal.
	g. Prepares periodic progress reports for all relevant persons.	g. Progress report judged acceptable by supervisor.
3. Communication: Audio-Visual	a. Draws figures, graphs and diagrams.	a. At least three figures and diagrams according to APA specification; check list as supportive data.
	b. Prepares slides, videotapes, films. Objectives of presentation stated.	b. 80% of objectives achieved or endorsed by supervisor.
IX. Training and Consulting in Behavior Modification	a. Conducts a single session workshop.	a. Written objectives pre-specified and evidence offered that objectives were met (i.e., questionnaires, quizzes, oral audience responses, etc.).
	b. Conducts a workshop series.	b. Written objectives, procedures and evidence of achievement of objectives.
	c. Acts in a consultation training capacity.	c. Brief report of consultation activities with notation of problems and suggestd solutions.
	d. Teaches course in behavior modification.	d. Course objectives, curriculum, methods, data on student performance.

94

e. In the natural setting (i.e., classroom, ward, factory, etc.) conducts in-service training program.

f. Prepares written training manual; trainee population specified, objectives listed.

g. Having demonstrated competence in the practitioner response in the area of proposed consultation according to the above criteria, consults with others about:

    alternative modification procedures

    control methods

    graphing procedures

    reference sources

    administrative or practical problems others.

X. Administration

a. States agency administrative policies that relate to a given behavior modification project or program.

b. Describes staff organization and roles and how those resources could be best organized to carry out a behavior

e. 80% of objectives achieved; or endorsed by a recognized expert in behavior modification field.

f. Same as e.

g. Letter of endorsement from agency or individual served.

a. Agency head certifies.

b. Same as a.

95

Category	Conditions and Practitioner Response	Criteria for Assessing Achievement
	modification project or program most effectively.	
	c. Utilizes natural contingencies in the natural environment.	c. Appropriate staff supervisor certifies.
	d. Obtains appropriate approval from administrative and supervisory authorities.	d. Written approval for proposed program.
	e. Applies appropriate contingencies to staff.	e. Same as a.
	f. Coordinates a project or program in behavior modification; acts as supervisor for the line personnel.	f. Same as a.
	g. Serves as director of agency project or program in behavior modification.	g. Same as a.
XI. Research	(See Discovery of new information, under Procedures and Section VI above). In addition:	

a. Reads current research.

b. Identifies current research trends.

c. Formulates new research questions.

d. Integrates findings from published research into paper.

e. Writes research proposal; integrates issues in field to provide rationale for study.

f. Conducts experimental research.

g. Applies research skills or tools (i.e., statistical analyses, computer programming).

h. Research evaluation; reads research report and writes critical evaluation.

i. Develops a model or theory of behavior.

a. Written summaries of at least ten current research articles in the field; all essential elements included.

b. Written list of three major trends in field, with cited studies as supportive data.

c. At least five written research questions, independent and dependent variables clearly identified.

d. Integrative paper written.

e. Supervisor judges that rationale for conducting the study is adequately supported by evidence from the research literature.

f. Research report in publishable form.

g. Utilizes research skills or tools such as statistical analyses or computer programming in analyzing results of at least one project or program.

h. Written critique or evaluation of research for granting agencies, journals or other agencies.

i. Publication in a professionally recognized source.

Footnotes to Appendix

[1]Model: Refers to a specific procedural approach; e.g., a behavioral model, a client-centered model.

[2]Project: Refers to the design of a treatment approach for an individual. An individual organism ABAB design is an example of such a project structure.

[3]Program: Refers to a group treatment unit (such as a token economy for a cottage or ward of mildly retarded adolescents), and considers its goals, structure (including projects and model) and staffing.

[4]System: Refers to overall strategy within an area of behavior intervention. Such an area might include a hospital, a community, or a school district.

Someone yesterday mentioned the lack of women speakers for the conference. We have now had two women speakers and they are among the few to present data to support what they are saying. Beth Sulzer-Azaroff's paper nicely emphasizes many of the recurrent themes of this conference. For instance, our field has arrived in the sense that there are many demands for behavioral services and behaviorally trained employees; there have been abuses of people's rights and expectations of good and humane treatment by other people who rightly or wrongly have called their work behavioral programs; there are threats to the field as a result of these abuses; certification will be forced upon us, by our own subgroups or by state agencies, whether we like it or not; we may as well try to sort the good certification issues from the bad. However, behavioral principles are ubiquitous. They are at work in every home, factory, institution and school. There is no way we can reasonably restrict usage of our technology to ourselves, even if we wanted to. In a real sense that technology will eventually become part of the repertoire of virtually every professional, and a part of the natural repertoire of every person.

However, Beth has gone beyond what most of us have been doing. Most of us have been throwing out our individual opinions (sometimes I think we have strained to make sure that our opinions are at least a little different from those of other speakers and discussants). Beth, instead of giving us her opinion, has given us the opinions of 92 people.

Beth acknowledges, correctly I think, that the opinions are probably from the wrong people. Certification, when it comes, will not most directly effect *JABA* authors and academicians, but the practitioners out in the field. I am not sure that the first two groups should tell the third what to do.

Responses to the questionnaires were interesting and sometimes predictable; the members of the sampled groups do not at all agree on the general issues of certification; super-level behavioral practitioners should have more skills than subordinate technicians; super-level behavioral practitioners should have just about all listed skills.

Scott Wood will note that there is some skepticism about training people to be theoreticians and Dick Malott may not be relieved to see that he doesn't have to train his people to be audio-visual experts. I hope, I am sure, that Scott and Dick will continue teaching these skills to their students even though we have told them that they need not.

The arguments have said that we must be ethical; we must offset the bad publicity we are getting; we should begin to catalog competencies; we should form a committee to begin to specify criteria for competencies. I would like to argue, at least with the simplicity of these last two recommendations, even though I suspect the argument will be in vain. Our field is young. Sixteen years ago Jack Michael must have been writing to Ted Ayllon in Canada to tell him to quit baiting the psychiatrists and get on with his dissertation. Just 11 years ago Montrose Wolf, Todd Risley and Hayden Mees were nervously sitting out Dick's temper tantrums. Only 9 years ago Ullman and Krasner gave the field a name—a name we are coming to regret because it is so nonspecific that it can be applied to practically every damned-fool idea that comes along.

The field grew out of some wild extrapolations from basic research and deductions from theory which must have required almost unbelievable faith. It borrowed an empirical approach from the *Journal of the Experimental Analysis of Behavior* and set out to make the world a better place to live in. It has generated a great deal of technology both for remediating many kinds of problems and testing new ways to handle problems.

Now we are beset by professional problems and public pressures; the uninitiated have hopped on our bandwagon and sullied our good name; we are finding that our name wasn't too good to begin with. Some people don't like our methods, some don't like our results;

some bureaucrats want to quickly define us to avoid more thorough and arduous looks at our work; politicians and reporters want to do away with us because they are reinforced by making news about protecting humanity from real or imagined evils; competing professions would like to restrict us; we fight among ourselves about whether it is more important to help a group of retarded children, publish a paper in the *Journal of Applied Behavior Analysis (JABA)*, develop a jazzy slide show, or teach a good college-level course.

We will probably have certification on at least some levels and in some areas before long. The pressures will make that happen. We won't agree too well on many aspects of how to certify; we won't like certification once we have it; and certification probably will not make our practice any more beneficial to our clientele. But, let's certify and be done with it.

There is another approach which I think has a greater chance of long-range payoff for everyone. I believe this alternative will be pursued by at least some of us and will eventually prove superior to the path we are about to take towards certification. Certainly the alternative bears closer resemblance to the developmental model we say we apply to other people's problems. I believe the alternative incorporates many of the ideas various members of the conference have been pushing. Let me briefly outline the model.

1. When we commit ourselves to work in an area, let's make sure that we are working for, and working closely with, our clients—kids, parents—whoever the potential beneficiaries of our work may be. Let's try to set up these relationships so that these beneficiaries have real, immediate control of our behaviors. In this way we can get real approval or rejections of our results and our methods. I believe this is what we have been calling accountability. There are several implications of such a move. It would insure at least the local public acceptance of our work. It might provide us, if we do good jobs, lay allies in fighting off attacks from jealous professions. It might mean that we should avoid, as much as possible, working for bureaucracies or else we should advocate the elimination of bureaucracies. Whenever we go to work for bureaucracies, we are at once insulated from feedback from a large part of our

constituency. This condition leaves us free to do poor work or to work for our own interests at the expense of our clients. It keeps our constituency from knowing about the good work we do. It bothers me that so much of our field is oriented to providing services for governmental units.

2. Once committed to an area and with the heat of accountability on us, perhaps we will develop or copy the best possible service programs our skills and technology allow.

3. Let us analyze these programs to determine what kinds of competencies are sufficient to make them run. I believe this might be certification of procedures.

4. Let us, then, develop methods to train people to man these service programs. I expect we will be surprised by the successes of our training programs once we are clearly committed to producing certain competencies—competencies that are not arrived at by rational argument and compromise votes, but that have been empirically derived.

5. If our students have the specified competencies at the end of training, both the student and the training program are temporarily certified for the specified service programs.

6. Let us teach and help our clients to continue the on-line monitoring and certification of the service programs, the people who man them, and the procedures they use. If we did the above, I suspect that we would end up with different kinds of competencies for different kinds of settings and problems. Therefore, I suspect that the immediate development of a general list of competencies as Beth suggests will prove inadequate and perhaps even an eventual impediment. I also suspect that the specialists will do better jobs as defined by our clients than will generalists.

7. However, let's keep some generalists around to carry information about new ideas and procedures from one kind of

program to another and perhaps to be the pioneers when we go into a new area and do not yet know which competencies are important. Let's use an empirical approach for deciding the specialist versus generalist issue.

8. Let us tie our research, training and practice closer together so that research is at least sometimes dictated by the real problems of the practitioner and his clients rather than by cute ideas we have about independent variables. Similarly let's make sure that our practice is dictated by the results of our research and the interests of our clients rather than our advisor's opinions or sume fuzzy, yet untested, notion. I believe our research can only be supported on a large scale as long as it pays off for the beneficiaries of our practice. Our practice should only be bought as long as it constantly improves from research. Our teaching is probably worthless unless it supports one or both. If we don't all need each other, there is something wrong with our system and model. I do not believe that surveying professionals' opinions about competencies and criteria fits this model.

9. If it gets in our way, let's change our name. If we engineer our field at the same time, perhaps we can avoid besmirching whatever new name we adopt.

10. Finally, the one non-behavior modifier in the crowd yesterday, Dr. Hussein, said something that was awfully appealing. We are problem oriented. To at least some extent let's quit devoting all of our time to putting Band-Aids on huge open sores that result from society's malpractices. Let's begin to find ways to teach normal people to raise normal children, and to be productively nice to each other. Maybe then there will not be so many problems. Maybe that is a way to begin to build our public image.

The greatest abuses involving behavioral principles are not our using our technology when we should not, or other professionals' using inhumane and unwise forms of it. The greatest abuse is all of the instances when nonprofessionals or untrained professionals misuse, un-knowingly and in good faith, the many everyday extensions of the principles. The second greatest abuse probably results from our failure to carry out procedures as well as the state of our technology allows. Let's begin to teach the world, including ourselves, the generality of the principles.

You see I think we are all correct. I believe I agree with just about everything that has been said at the conference. I do not agree with the occasional implication that the suggestions and ideas are mutually exclusive. I think the world demands just about all of them. If we have been wrong up to this point, it is because we have allowed the field to evolve, and we have not applied to it the developmental model we try to apply to everything else.

Let me conclude by telling you about an analogy that I attri-bute to Barney Salzberg. Maybe you have to know Barney to completely appreciate it. Barney Salzberg is one of the world's genuine good guys. He worries about things. He takes obligations, responsibilities and the state of the world seriously. One day he came by my office worrying about something he had just heard a presumed authority tell a group of students. Barney said something like this: "The world we call the behavioral and social sciences is like a huge mountain of shit. It's made up of all the garbage put out by the Freudians, the pretenses at rele-vance of a lot of worthless basic researchers trying to make cases for unbelievably weak variables, the politicians and astrologists trying to make a fast buck, and the education authorities' current, unvalidated bunk. Somewhere on the side of this enormous mountain of shit is this little bunch of behaviorists. They are scratching away and there *is* a dent where they're shoveling away the shit. And, they are all running around slapping each other on the back and saying, 'Man, look at the dent we're making in this mountain of shit.' And, what they never know is that there are a thousand times as many of those other guys on the top, piling it on much faster than the behaviorists will ever be able to scratch it away."

I am willing to live with the uncertainty of eventual success implied by the analogy. I just don't want us to start contributing to the mountain ourselves.

SECTION II:
Evaluating Programs and Procedures

QUALITY CONTROL
IN THE BEHAVIOR ANALYSIS APPROACH
TO PROJECT FOLLOW THROUGH

Don Bushell, Jr., Donald A. Jackson, and Lynn C. Weis

The words "quality control" immediately suggest assembly-line manufacturing or the inspection procedures of service stations like Mobil and Exxon, and franchise restaurants like Sambo's and the ubiquitous McDonald's. Whether attention is focused on precise adherence to parts specifications, clean restrooms or uniform menus, the process of quality control is the process of insuring procedural replication. The outcome of this process is intended to assure both the satisfaction of the consumer, and the reputation of the service provider. And it is in this sense that quality control procedures are as important in applied behavior analysis as they are in the production of pharmaceuticals.

Because of ambiguities in usage, it is more difficult to distinguish between the procedures and functions of quality control and the procedures and functions of certification. This is especially true because a certificate is often used to document a quality control procedure (the restroom is certified clean and the beef is certified choice). Nevertheless, it is the thesis of this paper that there are (or should be) some important differences between the functions of quality control and those of certification. The distinction is between preparation and performance.

In the context of this conference it seems that the certification of behavior analysts is a general notion that is straining to cover two different sets of issues. One concern is that those who advertise themselves as behavior analysts have their claim legitimized by a background of experience and preparation which promises competent performance according to the current standards of the discipline. This is the union-card type of certification which attests that the bearer has paid his dues in time and study and has mastered the fundamental techniques of his trade. The utility of such a practice is evident. The certificate provides a formal badge of identity for the members of a profession; it enables standard setting by the group; it screens out those who have not met the requirements; and it indicates to the general public that superior performance is to be expected from certificate holders. For those who seek to hire qualified behavior analysts (e.g., hospitals, clinics, school districts), a certification procedure may have important benefits.

The disadvantage of certification is that it can only require and recognize what is conventional. As a statement of appropriate standards, the certificate tends to be static and intolerant of innovation. Further, the certificate does not traditionally provide any measure of actual on-the-job performance. Just as school teachers are certified by the state as qualified teachers *before* they are allowed full teaching responsibility, most certificates are prerequisites to practice rather than statements about quality performance. Measures of the job performance, together with procedures for supporting high quality performance and clearly identifying performance inadequacies, is quality control. That is the second concern that seems to be at issue in the conference, and it may be a concern that is entirely independent of certification. Moreover, it is in the area of quality control that the technology of applied behavior analysis can make particular contributions.

Our perspective on this thesis is the direct result of experience over the past six years in the federally funded elementary school program called Project Follow Through. It has been our responsibility in Follow Through to replicate a classroom instructional model in several hundred classrooms that are scattered from Massachusetts to Montana in a variety of community and school settings. The experience has developed a chronic preoccupation with quality control and, through an often painful sequence of trial and error, has led us to the development of some standard and economical procedures for monitoring performance in these far-off places. Consequently, the following discussion is presented in the hope that our experiences may have some relevance to the broader professional issues that are the subject of this conference. Before that is possible, however, we need to describe the general nature of Follow Through and something of the procedures and history of our particular model which is called Behavior Analysis.

THE BEHAVIOR ANALYSIS APPROACH
TO PROJECT FOLLOW THROUGH

In the fall of 1968, five school districts that had been awarded Federal Follow Through Grants elected to begin implementing the Behavior Analysis approach to Follow Through sponsored by the Department of Human Development at the University of Kansas. Behavior Analysis is one of 20 different intervention strategies that are in Follow Through. The several approaches differ in theoretical orientation and procedure, but all are attempting to improve the school experience of poor children as they enter school from Head Start and progress through the third grade.

During that first program year, our work was with 29 classrooms that served 740 children who were starting their elementary school careers. That original group of children has now "graduated" from Follow Through, but as they advanced through the primary grades others entered and additional communities elected the Behavior Analysis approach for their Follow Through projects. As shown in Table 1, page 122, we are now working to meet the needs of over 7,000 children in 300 classrooms of 15 projects in 12 communities. These communities are, on the average, 700 air miles from the University of Kansas.

The children are black, white, Puerto Rican, and Indian. Their teachers range from first-year people with provisional certificates to those with more than 20 years of classroom experience. They live in urban and rural settings. Their school buildings range from very new to very old, and are operated by local school boards, Catholic Missions, and The Bureau of Indian Affairs. About the only thing that is general across all the sites is that the children are poor and, on an actuarial basis, are expected to do poorly in school. It is our job to defeat those actuarial predictions and to break the prevailing relationship between a low income and a low probability of success in school.

To accomplish this task, we have translated some key principles of reinforcement into an educational program for the primary grades that fits within the financial and political characteristics of Follow

Through. Because others might translate the same principles into a different program, a brief description of our procedures is in order. (Also see Bushell, 1973; Bushell and Ramp, 1974.)

The elements of a Behavior Analysis classroom. Most of the elements of the Behavior Analysis classroom are familiar to elementary education. Our objective has been to assemble these elements in a way that would substantially improve children's early mastery of basic academic skills.

Expanded classroom staffing. Whether it is called "teaching" or "shaping," it is generally agreed that the process is most effective when the learner engages in many behaviors that are followed by differential consequences. One teacher cannot meet this requirement for 25 to 35 children simultaneously. Title I(ESEA) money provides a permanent aide to most Follow Through classes. In addition, Behavior Analysis has employed two parents to complete a team of four adults for each class of children. This staffing pattern allows an extraordinary degree of small-group instruction, and correspondingly increases the amount of attention that can be given to each child's behavior.

If you were to visit a Behavior Analysis classroom, you would see each of the four adults teaching a group of six or seven children. Typically, the lead teacher would be teaching reading to one group while the permanent aide would be teaching arithmetic to another and the parents would be teaching spelling and handwriting to the remaining groups.

Curriculum selection. To complement the advantages of small-group instruction, Behavior Analysis has selected curriculum materials according to criteria that derive from our understanding of the shaping process. Whenever possible we opted for commercially available series, and thereby managed to avoid getting to the business of curriculum development in all but two specific cases (beginning reading and beginning handwriting). In making our selection we have given priority to materials that clearly describe the behavior they will develop; allow the individual initial placement; require frequent observable student responses; contain regular imbedded criterion-referenced tests; and permit different rates of individual progress.

Systematic motivation. To maximize the effectiveness of small-group instruction with carefully selected materials, Behavior Analysis classes support motivation with a token reinforcement system. As the children work in small groups, the teacher is able to provide frequent praise and encouragement for their progress and improvement. Praise is often accompanied by the presentation of a token. In each group, the adult moves quickly from child to child in a random sequence providing correction and help where needed, and tokens and praise where appropriate.

The tokens accumulated during an instructional period can later be exchanged for a variety of privileges and activities that the children select according to their preference and the number of tokens they have acquired. Throughout the day instructional periods alternate with exchange periods that allow the children to choose from the changing lists, or menus, of games and activities such as art projects, stories, dancing, playground activities, singing, and even the opportunity to do extra reading or arithmetic.

The delivery system. It would undoubtedly be possible to marshal substantial experimental support for each of the preceding practices, but it is likely that those experimental data would arise from rather well-controlled settings that were convenient to the experimenter. The real challenge of Follow Through is that it requires the replication of the basic program model in remote sites that are remarkably inconvenient and regularly beset by teachers' strikes and acts of God.

The basic elements of a Behavior Analysis classroom have been the same since 1968, but our training and support procedures have changed and developed continuously. Without recounting all of the things we have done wrong, it may not be possible to appreciate our current practices. Nevertheless, it seems charitable to avoid long descriptions of past sins. At this point there are four parts to our delivery system.

First, each Behavior Analysis project is the direct and personal responsibility of a professional behavior analyst who is designated as the District Advisor. The District Advisor uses the telephone, the mails, and monthly visits to see to it that the local project staff receives appropriate in-service support and technical training. Initially, when a project is small, the Advisor may provide classroom training personally, but as the project grows these functions are assumed by local training specialists, called Staff Trainers, who are themselves trained by the District Advisor.

Second, our current design calls for two training positions for every 10 classes. These two trainers, one who concentrates on the needs of lead teachers and permanent aides, and the other who concentrates on supporting the teaching parents, continually work in the classroom to improve the performance and refine the teaching techniques of the entire project staff. With practice and continued support from the District Advisor, these trainers have, in many cases, become extremely skilled behavior modifiers.

Third, each project operates its own demonstration and training classes that provide intensive individualized practicum experience for other teachers, aides, and parents in the program. These settings provide the opportunity to rehearse observation and recording techniques, specific curriculum strategies, planning, and management techniques with the help of the demonstration teacher and the Staff Trainer.

Fourth, the basics of the Behavior Analysis approach to classroom behavior management and the teaching of each curriculum subject are specified in a series of training manuals (Bushell, 1973; Bushell and Ramp, 1974; Bushell, 1974; Jackson, 1974; Becker and Jackson, 1974). These materials clearly describe the procedures that are to be used in teaching, scheduling, and evaluation.

Measures of effect. While skillfully avoiding detail, we have, nevertheless, reached the point where you should have a general picture of what a Behavior Analysis classroom looks like and how it gets into operation with the help of curriculum manuals, training classrooms, Staff Trainers and District Advisors. Perhaps the most fundamental feature of all, however, is the system we use to measure the effects of the program as they are revealed in the children's academic progress.

Since 1969, our teachers have been providing us with reports called *Weekly Individual Progress Records (WIPRs)*. At the end of each week a class roster is sent to us reporting the book and page number each child was working on that Friday in reading, arithmetic, handwriting and spelling. For each curriculum series in use we have constructed a simple chart. Along the vertical axis of this chart is a series of steps, each step consisting of a number of pages. The steps have been constructed so that each requires about the same amount of time to complete. The horizontal axis of the chart indicates 26 of the 40 weeks of the school year. By entering the number of children who are working on each step every week an informative record of class progress is created.

Figure 1, page 123, provides the example of 25 weeks of progress in reading by 22 kindergarten children. The heavy line has been added to locate the median child each week. Simple inspection of these records provides information on the rate of general progress, the degree of individualization, the placement range, and where there seems to be difficulty with the materials (e.g., indicated by the slow rate of progress through Step 4). As a monitoring device, these charts have been invaluable.

For the past two years we have been building the next logical extension of this system, the rapid feedback of prescriptive recommendations based on *WIPR* data. The new system, called BANCS (Behavior Analysis National Communication System), uses the technology of high speed data communications to put us in closer, more supportive touch with each Behavior Analysis classroom (Weis, 1974). The teacher initiates the system by completing a weekly roster containing each child's curriculum placements and absences. These rosters are then collected by an aide who translates each placement into a series of marks that can be "read" by an optical mark reader manufactured by OpScan Corporation. The OpScan machine reads the placement information on each child and transmits it by telephone to the University of Kansas Computation Center. The computer analysis evaluates current placement against previous placements and then determines how much progress should be made by each child during the coming week in order to reach individual, pre-set, year-end targets. This new target information is then automatically transmitted back to a teletype in the local district. The aide returns the report to the classroom teacher and gives a copy to the local Staff Trainer. It is a process that takes less than 18 hours to complete. The form of the feedback report is illustrated in Figure 2, page 124.

This fictitious report indicates that T. Bailey was reading on page 126 of *Programmed Reading Book 14* (Buchannan and Sullivan Associates, 1973) on September 24. This placement corresponds to Step 44 in the reading curriculum. Under the heading "Success Ratio," the entry "—14/39—" indicates that Bailey advanced only 14 pages during the previous week which was less than the 39 pages targeted. Hence the minus next to the 14. Further, the "—" following "39" indicates that if he continues to progress at the rate of only 14 pages per week, he will end the year below his pre-set, individual, year-end target. In order to prevent this, his target for October 1 is set at page 23 of *Book 15*—a 40-page target.

With this information, Bailey's teacher is able to adjust his instructional schedule appropriately in order to get him back on target toward his pre-set, year-end objective. In this case, the adjustment might consist of increasing Bailey's reading instruction by shortening his math period since the report indicates that he is progressing well above the expected rate in math.

As the local Staff Trainer monitors these reports, he can move to assist in specific and timely ways rather than simply dropping into a classroom to ask "How's it going?" Further, when a class report begins to show an increasing proportion of minus signs in the "Success Ratio" columns, indicating that too many children are falling behind targets, intensive training and support can be mobilized to correct the problem. When the proportion of pluses indicates increasing numbers of children are exceeding targets, the Trainer can tell the Principal that he has an outstanding teaching team on his staff.

The performance certificate for Behavior Analysis teachers. Whatever our training and support procedures have been, they have always been more effective with some teachers than others. Early in our history we began searching for relevant reinforcers that we could use to recognize and support our more cooperative and effective teachers. A variety of school district regulations prevents the differential treatment of teachers on any grounds except seniority. Consequently, we have focused on public approval and social attention as recognition for achievement. One rather concrete type of recognition is provided by the award of a certificate which indicates that a teacher has successfully met a series of performance criteria. (See Nelson, Saudargas and Jackson, 1974a.)

In contrast to several earlier versions which proved cumbersome to manage, our current set of performance criteria seems both parsimonious and relevant. This procedure has not been in use long enough to permit its complete evaluation, but reactions from teachers and Staff Trainers thus far have been uniformly positive. The procedure can be entirely managed by the local Staff Trainer (see Nelson, Saudargas and Jackson, 1974b), and it allows teachers and aides to earn their certificates in as little as four weeks if all goes well. Three sets of criteria are considered in the procedure.

Instructional teaching criteria. When he wishes to earn a certificate, the teacher invites the Staff Trainer to conduct a formal observation during a small-group instruction period. The 10-minute observation yields data on the nature of the teaching interactions (contacts). If these data support a "yes" answer to each of the following items, the first set of performance criteria have been met.

1. 80% of the children are on-task.

2. 100% of the teacher's contacts are to on-task children.

3. 100% of the teacher's contacts contain praise.

4. 100% of tokens are delivered with praise.

5. 90% of the teacher's contacts that include prompts also contain descriptive praise and a token.

6. 0% of the teacher's contacts contain disapproval.

7. 80% accuracy demonstrated by 4 children (picked at random and checked by the trainer).

8. Time-out, if needed, is applied appropriately (as specified in training materials).

Exchange teaching criteria. A second evaluation, also conducted at the invitation of the teacher, follows the same general routine, but the behaviors of interest are different. These criteria specify the operation of the classroom motivational system, and the Staff Trainer's observation will determine whether the system is functioning properly. The criteria include: the back-up (exchange) activities are planned and

115

prepared beforehand; the content and prices of the back-ups vary at the two exchanges observed on the same day; prices are set independently by each instructional group but are the same for all children within a single group; each child is allowed to choose any activity for which he has enough tokens; children who elect not to exchange or do not have enough tokens sit quietly during the exchange period; the first child ready to exchange is allowed to do so without having to wait for the others; at least one back-up contributes to academic skill; the adults participate in the back-up activities; adults praise appropriate interaction during the exchange; and at the end of the exchange period, instruction begins with the first child who comes to the table.

Student progress criteria. The final performance criterion requires that, for a period of 4 weeks, 80% of the children in the teacher's own instructional groups be reported "on target" by the computer feedback. This can be 4 weeks, each of which are at 80% or better, or an average of 80% for 4 weeks combined.

The total procedure requires a criterion teaching performance and a criterion exchange performance on each of two occasions at least four weeks apart. These observations, coupled with four weeks of criterion progress by the children, complete the procedure. If any performance drops below criterion, trainer's handbooks (Nelson, Saudargas and Jackson, 1974b; Jackson and Minnis-Hazel, 1974) provide specific training recommendations that can be used to correct problems.

Functions of the certificate. It has already been observed that the purpose of the certificate is to recognize the excellent performance of our teachers. That is still true. The procedure, however, may be the most important aspect because the three sets of criteria serve as excellent training objectives. In their present form these objectives are clearly understood by the teachers, and they precisely define the training tasks that must be met by the local Staff Trainer.

The Behavior Analysis Specialist Certificate must be earned annually. It is not a license for anything. Instead, it is recognition of skill mastery. In a few cases we have seen preferred positions go to those who have earned certificates, but such events are too rare to function as effective reinforcers. The certificate is documentary recognition of specific excellent performance that enables the District

Advisor to send the teacher a complimentary letter with a copy for the personnel file in the Superintendent's office and a copy to the building Principal.

DISCUSSION

The preceding description of the Behavior Analysis approach to Follow Through should provide the basis for a discussion of the implications which our experience may have for the broader field of applied behavior analysis. The central theme of this conference reflects our growing concern over the appropriate use of behavior modification procedures. That concern is expressed in two different ways. First, how can we protect the consumer of our services from abuse; and, second, how can we protect the reputation of behavior analysis from the abuses of incompetent or unethical practitioners. Both of these concerns have influenced our work with Follow Through schools.

Consumer protection. Three closely interrelated factors seem necessary for the protection of clients and consumers: choice, information, and consent. In varying degrees, Follow Through's unique program design has approached each of these requirements. At the outset, when a community was given the opportunity to participate in Follow Through, it was also given the opportunity to choose which of the several sponsored approaches it would implement. In order to help them make that decision, Follow Through provided program descriptions from several sponsors of different orientations. Planning groups of parents, teachers, and administrators then studied these descriptions in an effort to determine which would best meet the needs of their particular community. Neutral consultants provided additional help, and communities often asked several sponsor representatives to make personal presentations and respond to questions. When a decision was made, the mutual consent of all parties was embodied in a three-party agreement between the community, the sponsor, and the U.S. Office of Education.

Obviously, Follow Through has been a developmental program. Many of its requirements and problems could not be anticipated fully at the time of the initial agreement. Consequently, the enabling agreement has been renewed annually. In some cases, local communities have decided not to renew the agreement with their original sponsor. In other cases, sponsors have found they could no longer work with a particularly uncooperative community. The periodic renewal of the sponsor-community relationship in the light of increased experience and information has served to preserve the community's right to choose and reaffirm their original consent.

The fact that the community has the right to choose, and the right to change its choice, also influenced *our* behavior. If our client communities were going to make annual decisions about the continued implementation of our program, they needed a great deal of information—information that described program effects in clear and relevant terms. Of all the sponsors in Follow Through we were best equipped to meet this need. The standard data-oriented conventions of applied behavior analysis provided the appropriate guidelines.

Awkwardly at first, but progressively with greater refinement, we have been able to specify our objectives in ways that are easily measured and clear to our clients. Our curriculum materials permit statements of objectives that are operational rather than conceptual, and they allow descriptions of children's progress to be continuous rather than occasional. The certificate that specifies the desired teaching behavior also provides clear measures of training effects and continuous descriptions of improved approximations. When these two types of information are combined, they also describe the performance of the local Trainers and our District Advisors.

Because behavior analysis teaches us to state our objectives in measurable terms and to monitor our progress toward those objectives, we have been able to respond effectively to the clients' legitimate need for information. The data on student and classroom progress carried by the BANCS system provides for public monitoring of performance on a weekly basis. Each classroom observation made by a Staff Trainer results in a clear description of how closely the teacher's performance meets each of the teaching criteria.

Each site visit by a District Advisor results in a formal report to the parents, teachers and administrators connected with the program. These reports describe progress where it occurs and offer specific recommendations for change where progress is lagging. Every six months comprehensive reports are distributed that describe the effectiveness of every Behavior Analysis classroom in the country. In these reports the descriptors are the same for the Hopi program as for the Bronx, and all may assess the progress of each classroom in its relationship to all the others.

It would be tempting to assert that we do all of these things because we are "good guys" and responsible professionals, but there lingers the strong suspicion that we might be less assiduous in our reports of progress (or the lack of it) if our client communities did not have the annual option of continuing or terminating our services. It may be a point that has general relevance. Our experience in Follow Through has indicated that the conventional procedures of applied behavior analysis offer exactly the kind of information that is fundamental to the protection of its clients.

Protecting our honor. In addition to the issue of consumer protection, there remains the issue of protecting the reputation of the field from the abuses of a few who claim the name, but are not competent, in the practice of applied behavior analysis. More specifically, it is a question about how we are protecting you, our colleagues, from our incompetence as a Follow Through sponsor. Or, to put the matter less delicately, how have our procedures protected us from the unthinkable possibility that one of you may have goofed.

Because we work in several of the major urban areas of the country we have frequently been compared with others who were identified as "behaviorists" of one sort or another. In some cases the comparison allowed us to benefit from a temporary halo effect; in others, we found it helpful to shape clearer discriminations between us and them. Either way, the methods and procedures of applied behavior analysis have protected us and you. From the description of our program, you have seen that our procedures have been drawn from your research. When your procedures were clear, we have been able to replicate your effects. When we are unable to replicate your procedures, our data systems showed no effects and the practice died of extinction. At a more general level it seems fair to observe that as long as we hold to our professional tenets that emphasize the production of data that will control our behavior, we guarantee ourselves the ultimate protection of "natural selection." Put simply, regardless of what they call themselves, those who cannot replicate our procedures stand little chance of replicating our effects and little chance of being reinforced by clients. Those who can replicate our procedures *and* our effects *are* our colleagues—regardless of what they call themselves.

A concluding recommendation for contracts rather than certificates. As we indicated at the beginning of this paper, we consider the need to maintain quality performance by behavior analysts to be separate from and perhaps unrelated to certification. Our experience in Follow Through has strengthened the conviction that it is the results of our performance that have been judged, not our credentials. Six years ago we understood only our objectives. In the years since we have learned how to reach those objectives, but we could not have certified our expertise or our procedures before the fact. Instead, we learned to depend on and respond to the public data from repeated measures of children's progress—we learned how to use a quality control system.

At a very general level the process of quality control merges with the law in the area of contracts. Contract law is a quality control system of huge proportions that focuses on procedures which are very similar to the conventions of applied behavior analysis. For example, a behavior analyst usually begins working with a client or agency by reaching some agreement on what the outcome of the service should be. In the law, this kind of agreement affirms "mutuality of contract" that protects the rights of each party. After the initial agreement, the behavior analyst and the client agree on how they will decide when the objective has been reached (i.e., measures are established), and they agree on the procedures to be followed. In the law, these are called the "terms of the contract." In applied behavior analysis, when we observe shoddy performance, we contemplate certifying only those who are competent. In the law, however, breach of contract leads to a court which can command performance or award damages to the aggrieved party.

The point is a simple one. Recent discussions with our colleague (and law graduate), Neil Minkin, are leading to the conclusion that applied behavior analysis already speaks the language of contract law, but most of us have not mastered its technology. Our usual conventions of specifying terminals, devising clear and public measures of effect, stipulating precise contingencies, and altering our tactics according to our data are the ingredients of an excellent contract. Moreover, the law constitutes an entire social technology that is already capable of protecting clients and practitioners alike; and it comes with a

120

built-in enforcement system: the courts.

It seems likely that the issues which have stimulated this conference and made it so timely would not have become a cause for concern if behavior analysts already followed the convention of drawing contractual agreements with their clients, whether the clients were individuals or agencies. Where certification tends to require uniform qualifications and does not safeguard performance, legal contracts might even stimulate innovative and cost-effective problem solutions. Given the behavior analysis tradition of accountability, the step to formal contracts deserves consideration as the next approximation toward fully responsible professional conduct.

Table 1.   Behavior Analysis Follow Through Projects in Operation
            1973-74

Location	Grades	Schools	Classes	Children
(U) Bronx, New York	K-3	2	20	539
(R) Hopi Reservation, Arizona	K-3	5	25	317
(U) Indianapolis, Indiana	K-3	4	17	401
(U) Kansas City, Missouri	K-3	3	24	618
(U) Louisville, Kentucky	K-3	4	47	1003
(R) Meridan, Illinois	K-3	2	20	421
(R) Northern Cheyenne, Montana	K-3	3	16	405
(U) Pittsfield, Massachusetts	K-3	3	8	169
(U) Philadelphia, Pennsylvania	K-3	3	53	1427
(R) Portageville, Missouri	K-3	1	15	383
(U) Trenton, New Jersey	K-3	8	36	898
(U) Waukegan, Illinois	K-3	1	24	550
Totals		39	305	7131

(U) Urban
(R) Rural

This table shows the 12 cities in which Behavior Analysis operates
Follow Through programs. Two of the sites, Northern Cheyenne and
Hopi, are Indian reservations. Two of the sites, Bronx and Philadelphia,
have multiple projects making a total of 15.

Figure 1. Class Progress Record

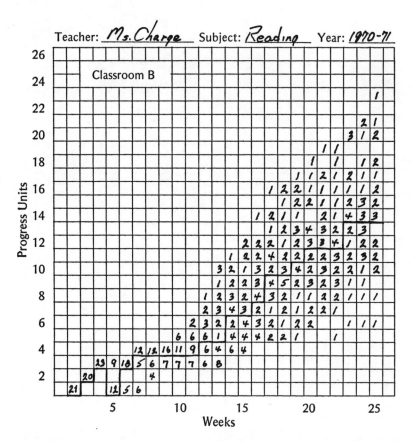

This is a Class Progress Record showing the weekly distribution of reading book and page placements for all children. These placements have been converted to a Progress Unit, thus providing a more uniform metric. The solid line denotes placement of the median child.

Figure 2. Standard Feedback Report

BEHAVIOR ANALYSIS REPORT TO: REPORT NO.2, VERSION - H   CASEBIER CODE - 050413160   WOODLAWN   TRENTON 3RD

| | | READING | | | | | MATH | | | |
STUDENT ID NAME	ABS	09/24 BK-PG	STEP	SUCCESS W*RATIO*Y	10/01 TARGET	TRG OPT	09/24 BK-PG	STEP	SUCCESS W*RATIO*Y	10/01 TARGET
01 BAILEY, T	1	14,127'	44	− 14/ 39−	15, 23	C:A	3,162	43	+ 10/ 7+	3,170
02 BREECH, C		21, 25	57	+ 24/ 23+	21, 48	A:A	3,160	42	+ 10/ 10+	3,170
03 BINION, T	1	18, 73	52	− 5/ 21−	18, 95	A:A	3,163	43	+ 8/ 7+	3,171
04 BRITTAIN,	4	19, 1	53	+ 5/ 5−	19, 26	A:A	3,163	43	+ 2/ 3−	4,171
05 DAVIS, RO		18, 62	51	+ 24/ 24+	18, 86	A:A	3,150	42	+ 12/ 11+	3,161
06 GLADNEY,		20,142	56	+ 12/ 10+	21, 7	A:B	3,180	43	+ 16/ 13+	3,192
07 JOHNSON,	1	19, 56	53	− 19/ 20+	19, 80	A:B	3,200	44	+ 12/ 11+	3,211
08 KENNY, JU		23,144	62	NO TARGET SPECS		A:A	4, 1	51	− 4/ 5+	4,106
09 PORTER, R		17,132	50	+ 25/ 65+	18, 53	B:A	3,141	42	+ 11/ 11+	3,152
10 POWERS, T	1	121		MISSING BOOK NO.		A:A	3,150	42	+ 12/ 9+	3,159
11 RUSSELL,		21, 21	57	− 18/ 23+	21, 44	A:A	3,	CONFLICTING PAGE NO'S		
12 WALKER, R		18,130	52	+ 21/ 21+	19, 7	A:A	3,151	42	+ 9/ 9+	3,160
13 CROSS, MA		17,130	52	+ 26/ 25+	18, 11	A:A	3,180	43	+ 10/ 8+	3,188
14 FOWLKES,		20, 21	55	− 5/ 11--	20, 33	A:A	4, 5	51	+ 5/ 4+	4,110
15 GAILLIARD	1	6,100	27	+ 8/ 8−	6, 109	F:C	3, 20	35	+ 10/ 10−	3, 30
16 MORRIS, L		20, 18	55	+ 12/ 11+	20, 29	A:A	4, 12	51	− 1/ 5+	4, 13
17 HARRIS, O		19, 44	53	+ 24/ 20−	19, 60	A:A	3,131	41	+ 13/ 12+	3,143
18 JONES, AN		21,130	57	− 21/ 10−	21, 144	A:A	3,167	43	+ 13/ 8+	3,174
19 LEACHMAN,	1	18, 1	51	UPDATED PLACEMENT		A:A	3,182	44	UPDATED PLACEMENT	
20 REVENGE,	2	20, 31	55	UPDATED PLACEMENT		A:A	3,190	44	UPDATED PLACEMENT	
21 WRIGHT,	1	19,122	54	UPDATED PLACEMENT		A:A	3,180	43	UPDATED PLACEMENT	

This is a standard feedback report used to describe each child's weekly absences, book and page placement, progress since the last report, and target for the next week. The left portion concerns reading and the right portion, math. The numbers in the STEP column refer to the progress unit corresponding to each book and page placement.

REFERENCES

Becker, J. and Jackson, D. A. *The Behavior Analysis phonics primer.* University of Kansas Support and Development Center for Follow Through, Department of Human Development, University of Kansas, Lawrence, Kansas, 1974.

Bushell, D., Jr. *Classroom behavior: A little book for teachers.* Englewood Cliffs, New Jersey: Prentice-Hall, Inc., 1973.

Bushell, D., Jr. *Tokens for the Behavior Analysis classroom: A teaching guide.* University of Kansas Support and Development Center for Follow Through, Department of Human Development, University of Kansas, Lawrence, Kansas, 1974.

Bushell, D., Jr. and Ramp, E. A. *The Behavior Analysis classroom.* University of Kansas Support and Development Center for Follow Through, Department of Human Development, University of Kansas, Lawrence, Kansas, 1974.

Jackson, D. A. (ed.), *Curriculum procedures for the Behavior Analysis classroom: A teaching guide.* University of Kansas Support and Development Center for Follow Through, Department of Human Development, University of Kansas, Lawrence, Kansas, 1974.

Jackson, D. A. and Minnis-Hazel, M. *A guide to staff training: The ultimate wrap-up.* University of Kansas Support and Development Center for Follow Through, Department of Human Development, University of Kansas, Lawrence, Kansas, 1974.

Nelson, A., Saudargas, R. A. and Jackson, D. A. *Behavior Analysis certification: How to become certified as a Behavior Analysis specialist.* University of Kansas Support and Development Center for Follow Through, Department of Human Development, University of Kansas, Lawrence, Kansas, 1974a.

Nelson, A., Saudargas, R. A. and Jackson, D. A. *Behavior Analysis certification: Observation and training procedures for the Staff Trainer.* University of Kansas Support and Development Center for Follow Through, Department of Human Development, University of Kansas, Lawrence, Kansas, 1974b.

Weis, L. C. The dilemma of education-intervention research. Unpublished manuscript. University of Kansas, Lawrence, Kansas, 1974.

RESPONSE

J. Grayson Osborne

If the papers presented at this conference have demonstrated one major oversight, it has been the failure to define what is meant by phrases like "Quality Control." It is the meaning of these phrases that is at the heart of determining when a program meets its goals—whether the program is aimed at improving the educational experience of disadvantaged children as in the Bushell et al. paper, or whether it has been established to produce "quality" behavior modifiers in an attempt to deal with issues of certification.*

The definition of quality control. The adjective quality is an abstraction, a discriminative stimulus having many properties to which we make discriminated responses. As with any concept, a reinforcing community will agree on which specific discriminative stimuli are examples of the concept and which discriminative stimuli are not. A major goal of this conference, it would seem, must be a comprehensive list divided into these example and non-example stimuli. The best example of an approximation to this task has been the attempt by Professor Sulzer-Azaroff, at this conference, to specify competencies for behavior modifiers (Sulzer-Azaroff, 1975). She has satisfied at least one aspect of the above definition by soliciting the opinions of a single reinforcing community (the editorial board of the *Journal of Applied Behavior Analysis*) and by providing us a list of examples from which we might infer quality. Has a similar attempt been made to define quality control

---

* Bushell et al. also attempted to deal with this aspect of quality in their attempt to make the teachers in their project classrooms better teachers.

within behavior analysis programs? The Bushell et al. paper does contain specified procedures which attempt to circumscribe quality control. However, defining quality control as only a set of procedures is clearly inadequate. We must ask *what* procedures *and* whether or not the program can show that those procedures are responsible for the quality of its product. In the latter the allusion is to functional analysis.

What procedures constitute quality control? The best example of quality control I remember was Thom Verhave's inspector pigeons (Verhave, 1966).* These pigeons were trained to discriminate "skag" gelatin capsules in a demonstration project generated by Verhave for a pharmaceutical company. The pigeons had to detect various kinds of defects in gelatin capsules that passed before them. The industrial analogy of quality control—sampling a product to see how well it meets certain standards—seems implied in the use of the term in Bushell et al., and provides a good starting place. Our use of the term should carry similar meaning: we must be able to detect a substandard product.

In the present conference this means (1) detecting that a program fails to meet its objectives, or (2) detecting that a person who has experienced a particular program fails to meet the program's objectives. As in the industrial analogy, we can specify quality control procedures and these are presented in terms of the following questions: does the program being evaluated contain procedures for *rejecting* defective products? Are people who are products of the program evaluated objectively? When the individual or the program is found to be substandard, is it possible to *recycle* to bring the person or program up to standard? Are there systematic procedures for evaluating the program overall? Finally, we need a way to keep our program evaluators objective. Verhave suggested the agreement of another bird who might have been called the "External Validator." The implication is that outsiders should be asked to evaluate behavior analysis programs, and even perhaps to suggest measures by which programs may be evaluated. We may ask whether this last event has occurred before making a decision about quality control. When all of these things are accomplished, we could at least approximate quality control *operationally*. But is this sufficient? Operationally, it may be possible to describe procedures to manu-

* Verhave, T. The pigeon as a quality-control inspector. In R. Ulrich, T. Stachnik, and J. Mabry (eds.), *Control of human behavior, Vol. I.* Glenview, IL: Scott, Foresman, 1966.

facture an automobile; however well these procedures can be followed, the completed automobile may not run. Repeating the procedures (which we have *a priori* decided are quality-producing procedures) may simply result in more automobiles that don't work.

Necessity of functional analysis in determining quality control. Many of us get caught in the above trap. We think that because we have rigorously specified the operations involved in our procedures we are good applied scientists and professionals. Yet the very emphasis on operations so necessary to scientific procedure, and the important first step to quality control, can divert our attention from functional analysis where we need it the most. Bushell et al. have specified many programmatic operations and have taken that important first step, but the question must be raised about whether their program contains sufficient functional analysis to satisfy this second aspect of a complete definition of quality control.

An example may clarify what is meant by functional analysis. We must ask what gives a program its quality. This is a more complex question than it seems. Certainly our regular "applied behavior analysis" (ABA) is part of the answer on the level of teacher, teacher aide and student interactions. Bushell et al. do attempt behavior change in teachers, aides and parents in order to produce more adequate student behavior, and we are familiar with analyses of this type in our journals. Although Bushell et al. do not identify particular instances, it is a safe assumption that ABA on this level exists in this program. But the type of functional analysis I am referring to takes place not only at this level but at one level removed from this as well.

To have quality control, functional relationships between a priori *defined quality-control procedures and the outputs of the program must be identified.* In principle these considerations are simple, but practically, they are less so. The same research designs employed in applied behavior analysis obtain. If a procedure is important to quality, repeatedly inserting and removing the procedure should systematically affect the quality of the product that the program turns out. The training of Achievement Place parents presented at this conference (Braukmann, page 131) contains the beginnings of this type of analysis. Two parents were passed through a training program that did not contain some aspects of later training programs. Independently they received lower evaluations from their "children" than other parents who had experienced the later training programs. The two teaching parents were recycled through the revised training program and their evaluations increased to a level similar to other teaching parents who had experienced the more complete program. Although this type of feedback and recycling of teachers and aides is hinted at in the Bushell et al. program, a functional analysis of the effects of these procedures is not.

Furthermore, we might ask about the importance of the professional staff in the Bushell et al. program with respect to quality control. The procedures for supervisory staff are well specified. They called on the telephone, performed inservice training and so forth. But which, if any, of these behaviors (i.e., procedures) were crucial to the quality of the program? Without functional analysis we cannot know. Although improbable, it may just be that telephone calls from a supervisor are an aversive event suppressing desirable teacher behaviors preceding them. Or it may be that telephone calls are largely non-functional and therefore a waste of the supervisor's time. I submit that it is these latter aspects of a program that we need to analyze. If they are related to a program's quality, we need to know it. If they are not, we need to know that too so that procedures which are functional can be substituted.

Conclusions. In summary, quality control will be a meaningless phrase unless it is specifically defined for practitioners (and evaluators) of applied behavior analysis. A necessary part of this definition will be the listing of a great many examples and non-examples of the concept. These examples may be programmatic procedures such as those that reject inferior products reliably and validly, and procedures that foster recycling of inferior products. However many of these procedures are agreed on *a priori* as necessary for providing either a quality program or a quality behavior modifier, quality control is insufficiently defined until a functional analysis demonstrates a relationship between the program's procedures and its eventual outcomes. This bipartite analysis would bring meaning to the term quality control by defining it as the majority of concepts are defined in the experimental and applied analysis of behavior.

ACHIEVEMENT PLACE: THE TRAINING
AND CERTIFICATION OF TEACHING PARENTS

Curtis J. Braukmann, Dean L. Fixsen, Kathryn A. Kirigin,
Elaine A. Phillips, Elery L. Phillips, and Montrose M. Wolf

This paper will describe the development, dissemination, and ongoing quality control of a treatment model being utilized by a growing group of professionals. That model is the Teaching-Family Model of community-based, family-style treatment for predelinquent and delinquent youths. The dissemination of the model is occurring through the training provided to couples in a one-year, competency-based training program. The quality control of the treatment provided by the couples who operate Teaching-Family Model group homes is insured through contingent certification of those couples based on evaluations of their performance. These evaluations are by professional evaluators and, most importantly, by the consumers of the program services; e.g., youths in the program, their parents, and community agencies.

THE TEACHING-FAMILY MODEL
In April 1967, Elery (Lonnie) and Elaine Phillips became houseparents in a group home for 12 to 16-year-old boys in Lawrence, Kansas. The home was called Achievement Place. Under the direction of Lonnie and Elaine, Montrose Wolf and Dean Fixsen, Achievement Place became the focus of an effort to develop and refine a systematic and effective model for the family-style, community-based treatment of pre-
-delinquent and delinquent youths.

The model treatment program developed at Achievement Place is called the Teaching-Family Model. It has been described in detail in the *Teaching-Family Handbook* (Phillips et al., 1972) and is being replicated in group homes in other communities. Teaching-Family Model group homes are usually renovated older homes located in a residential area of the local community. One couple directs and carries out the treatment model in each of these small (6 to 8 youths), family-style settings. These couples are called teaching parents.*

The most important role of teaching parents is their teaching role. They educate their youths in a variety of social, academic, prevocational and self-help skills. Their goal is to equip each youth with an alternative, more adaptive skill repertoire and to thereby increase his chances of survival and success in his community. The family-style setting allows the teaching parents to tailor their teaching to the individual needs of each youth.

Teaching parents utilize a flexible motivation system to enhance their effectiveness as teachers. In that motivation system a youth earns points for learning and engaging in appropriate, adaptive behaviors and loses points for inappropriate, maladaptive behaviors. These points are exchanged by the youth at first on a daily, and later on a weekly, basis for privileges such as watching television, allowance, and returning to his natural home on the weekend. Success in the motivation system advances a youth to the merit system in which points are no longer required for privileges. If the youth maintains his appropriate behavior while on the merit system, he begins to spend more and more time with his natural or foster family before being released from the program.

The youths participate in the direction and operation of Teaching-Family Model treatment programs through the self-government mechanisms of the manager system and the family conference. In the manager system the youths exercise self-government through the daily democratic election of a peer to oversee and teach routine social and self-help skills (Phillips et al., 1973b). The youths and teaching par-

---

* Many dedicated and innovative people have made substantial contributions in the development of the treatment, training, and evaluation models described in this paper. A partial list of these people includes Hector and Jenny Ayala, Jon Bailey, Dick Baron, Willie and Linda Brown, Pam Daly, Joan Fixsen, Dennis and Margaret Ford, Bob Kifer, Denny and Karen Maloney, Neil and Bonnie Minkin, Dave and Sharon Russell, Gary and Barb Timbers, Diane Turnbough, and Alan Willner.

ents review the performance of the manager at the daily family conference that the family members democratically establish and review their guidelines for appropriate behavior, decide whether any behaviors that day were particularly inappropriate or appropriate, and determine the consequences of any such behaviors (Fixsen, Phillips, and Wolf, 1973). At the family conference the teaching parents teach the skills involved in constructive criticism, problem solving, and negotiation.

The community-based aspect of direct replications of the Teaching-Family Model permits a youth to continue to attend his local school and to return to his home on weekends, thus enabling the teaching parents to assist him in learning to deal with his problems in those settings. Being community based also allows the teaching parents to continue to monitor and, if necessary, to provide additional treatment for the youths after they graduate from the program.

The development and refinement of the treatment procedures used in the Teaching-Family Model have been facilitated by systematic procedural evaluations. For example, procedural evaluations have been conducted on such aspects of the model as the motivation system (Phillips, 1968; Phillips et al., 1971), the family conference (Fixsen, Phillips, and Wolf, 1973), and the teaching procedures (Ford et al., unpublished; Timbers et al., 1973). The model's treatment components have been and continue to be evaluated using the dual criteria of effectiveness of the procedures and youth preference for the procedures (see, for example, Phillips et al., 1973b).

The overall effectiveness of the model has been preliminarily evaluated at the program level (Phillips et al., 1973a). Pre- and post-treatment comparisons were made *post hoc* between the first 16 youths treated at Achievement Place and 28 similar youths, 13 of whom had been placed on probation; the other 15 had been placed in the state industrial school. Pre-treatment comparisons indicated all three groups of youths to be comparable on measures such as the number of police and court contacts, the percentage of youths in school, and the percentage of youths receiving passing grades. These same indexes indicated better post-treatment adjustment for the Achievement Place boys than for either of the other two groups. In addition, the Achievement Place youths had considerably lower recidivism (post-treatment institutionalization) than either of the other groups.

These preliminary program evaluation data were not based on random assignment to groups, and the positive findings may have been due in part or in whole to a population effect rather than treatment effect. Currently, when there are two or more youths meeting selection criteria and only one opening in the Achievement Place program, the selection decision is determined randomly. Comparisons will then be possible between those youths randomly selected and those not selected. Teaching parents operating other Teaching-Family Programs are also being encouraged to adopt the random selection procedure and several of them have. This procedure will allow for an evaluation of the model on a larger scale.

As of March 1974, there were 24 replication homes operated by couples in training, or trained in the model through the University of Kansas. Twelve of these homes were in Kansas and 12 were in 8 other states. Most of the replication homes were community controlled, thus insuring that those programs served the needs of, and corresponded to the goals and norms of, the local community. Such community control is exercised through a local board of directors, composed of community representatives. These boards review and adopt the Teaching-Family Model and handle the finances involved in setting up and operating the facility. It is the board's responsibility to determine the overall goals of the program. A member of the board, together with school, court, and welfare representatives and the teaching parents, participates in the selection of youths most in need of treatment. The board also selects and hires a couple and pays for their training in the model.

THE TEACHING-PARENT TRAINING PROGRAM
Our initial attempt three years ago at a strategy for training teaching parents to replicate the model involved a basically academically-oriented master's degree program. Several couples interested in replicating the Achievement Place program came to the University of Kansas and participated in course work emphasizing behavior modification principles and the applied analysis of behavior. They studied token economy systems and the Achievement Place procedures, and observed the successful program at Achievement Place. At the end of the one-year program, they went out and started their own programs.

The results of these early replication attempts indicate that we had failed to specify or to teach many of the necessary skills involved in operating the model. Apparently learning about the model and observing it in operation were insufficient to teach a variety of the necessary practical skills. On the basis of that feedback we modified the training program to increase its relevance and its effectiveness.

The current training program places greater emphasis on the practical skills involved in successfully directing and operating a Teaching-Family home. Trainee couples now participate in a one-year training sequence, the core of which is the supervised in-service practical experience the trainees obtain while actually operating a home. The first step in this training sequence is an intensive, 50-hour, one-week workshop at the University of Kansas. This initial workshop builds on the knowledge the teaching-parent trainees obtain by studying the *Teaching-Family Handbook,* and teaches them the basic skills required to establish and begin operating their treatment programs.

The first three months or so following the workshop constitute a practicum and evaluation period. During this time the trainees are operating programs in their respective communities and are in frequent telephone contact with the experienced teaching parents and training staff at the University of Kansas. This provides the trainees with direction, advice and feedback. At the end of this period, the program's consumers (e.g., youths, parents, personnel from the juvenile court, welfare department, schools, and the board of directors) complete rating scales asking them to describe their satisfaction with the teaching parents and the program. In addition to this consumer evaluation, a professional evaluator makes an on-site evaluation of the program. In a summary report, prepared by the training and evaluation staff, the couple is given detailed feedback on the results of the consumer and professional evaluations, and suggestions on how they might improve their performance in areas where they received a low evaluation. The feedback is given in a way that protects the anonymity of the individual consumers.

Following this first evaluation, the trainees participate in a second practicum and evaluation period that extends until the end of the year-long training sequence. During this period telephone consultation continues and a second evaluation is conducted covering those areas where the couple received low ratings. This evaluation provides feedback to the trainees and the training staff on how well the trainees are correcting those problems. Early in this second practicum and evaluation period the couple attends a second one-week workshop designed to extend and refine their skills.

At the end of the first year, the first in a series of annual evaluations is conducted. The results of this evaluation are made known not only to the teaching parents but also to the board of directors and the agencies involved in placing youths in the program and funding the program; i.e., the juvenile court and welfare department. The results of this annual evaluation determine whether or not the couple will be certified as professional teaching parents. Continued certification is contingent on continued high evaluations in subsequent annual evaluations.

A master's program is available to teaching parents with a bachelor's degree. The degree is contingent upon successfully completing the training and certification requirements, passing closely-monitored, self-instructional courses, and designing, carrying out, writing, and defending an experimental thesis. This training model is currently being replicated in North Carolina by Gary Timbers and Dennis and Karen Maloney, three Ph.D. graduates from the Departments of Human Development and Psychology at the University of Kansas who worked with the Achievement Place Research Project for several years. This team is currently establishing eight group homes in North Carolina based on the model.

The workshops. In the initial workshop the three to five couples who attend receive specific instructions and rationales concerning the use of important skills. These instructions are usually supplemented by live or video-taped examples of professional teaching parents modeling the skills. Wherever possible the trainees are given opportunities to rehearse the skills in simulated situations with the staff and their fellow trainees. During these rehearsals, they receive systematic, detailed feedback on their performance and continue to practice until they meet criterion performance for each skill. In this way the trainees practice and receive feedback on the competent skills involved in operating the motivation system, counseling, engaging in youth-preferred styles of interaction, conducting family conferences, engaging in effective teaching interactions, and working with parents and teachers.

During this first workshop, each trainee couple also visits one of the local Teaching-Family homes (e.g., Achievement Place for Boys or Achievement Place for Girls) for an afternoon and evening. This visit starts with a tour and conversations with the youths in the program. The couple then observes the experienced teaching parents handling both routine duties and staged incidents. The simulated incidents give the teaching parents an opportunity to model for the trainees how they would teach certain complex skills to the youths and handle various problems that might arise. The trainees are then asked to handle similar situations and, following each one, they receive feedback from both the teaching parents and the youths. The trainees then stay for dinner, observe a family conference, conduct a simulated family conference, and receive feedback on their overall performance.

The second workshop is designed to refine the trainee couple's skills in such areas as working with parents, using the motivation system and counseling; it also extends the couple's skills and knowledge to such areas as grant-writing, legal issues, and measurement and design. In addition, the trainees receive advice and feedback in individual and group problem-solving sessions conducted by experienced teaching parents.

The workshops continually evolve as we obtain feedback from the trainees. Each section of the workshops is followed by the trainee's evaluation that also gives suggestions on how the section might be improved. Several months after they have participated in a workshop, the trainees complete a questionnaire in which they are asked to provide feedback on how the workshop might have better prepared them for their responsibilities. The results of the consumer and professional evaluations also point out areas where training needs to be included or improved. With this continual feedback the workshops are continually evolving and becoming more relevant in meeting the needs of the trainees.

One aspect of the training program that has evolved considerably is the training given teaching parents in the skills involved in moment-by-moment interactions with their youths. At first we taught no skills in this area, emphasizing only point-transaction interactions. However, professional and consumer evaluations indicated that the youths in a couple of programs found interactions with their teaching parents unsatisfactory. In one program in particular the youths described the teaching parents as cold, uncaring, and unpleasant. The consumer evaluations by the youths were low, as well as the evaluations by every other group of consumers, each of whom had heard about the unpleasantness of the home environment. This feedback pointed out the need to specify and teach youth-preferred interaction components to trainees.

To specify what behaviors youths find pleasant in interactions with teaching parents, Alan Willner, a doctoral candidate in psychology at the University of Kansas, has been gathering data on the kind of interaction components youths prefer. These interaction behaviors seem to be: (1) using request rather than the demand forms of instruction; (2) providing reasons to a youth to explain why he should change specific forms of his behavior; (3) giving verbal recognition to a youth for his accomplishments. The trainees are now taught such youth-preferred interaction skills in the initial workshop in conjunction with the skills involved in effective teaching interactions (see Kirigin et al., in press). The consumer and professional evaluations provide feedback to the training staff on the adequacy of the training program. These evaluations also serve a variety of other feedback and quality control functions.

CONSUMER AND PROFESSIONAL EVALUATIONS

The main objectives of a Teaching-Family Model program are to help the youths and their parents and to serve the community. One way of obtaining information on how effectively these goals are being met by a program is through the use of control-group designs utilizing measures of later institutionalization, later job success, police and court contacts before and after treatment, and so on. However, this is slow feedback because these measures are of low frequency behaviors and because there is a long delay between the time a youth enters a program and the time he has been out of the program the necessary one or two years to allow a reasonable assessment of his post-release adjustment. In addition, because of the small number of youths in a program, it requires several years of program operation to obtain an n of sufficient magnitude to allow a meaningful analysis.

While such follow-up behavioral measures are essential, there is nevertheless a need for more immediate feedback on the extent to which the youths are being helped and to which the community is being served. The consumer evaluation procedures provide this more immediate feedback. It provides a formal means for such program consumers as the youths in the program, their parents, personnel in the juvenile court, welfare department and schools, and the board of directors, to indicate their degree of satisfaction with the service provided by the teaching parents and with the effectiveness of the teaching parents in correcting problems.

Except for the evaluation by the youths, the consumer evaluation process is conducted through mailed questionnaires which ask the consumer to rate the program on various dimensions using seven-point, bi-polar rating scales (Osgood, Suci, and Tannenbaum, 1957).* The consumer is also asked to comment on each dimension. The youth questionnaire is administered during the on-site professional evaluations conducted by one or two members of the training staff. The professional evaluation allows systematic, first-hand observation of a program and the skills of the teaching parents and the youths.

By providing feedback to the couples about their success in accomplishing their goals, the consumer and professional evaluations can help shape the couple's behavior by pointing out the strengths and weaknesses of their program. This feedback must be *formal* feedback. In early replications of the model, before the evaluation mechanisms were developed, couples were not always able to deal with weaknesses in their program because they were not always aware of them. Formal feedback allows a social service program such as a Teaching-Family program to be fully responsive to the people and agencies it is designed to serve.

The annual certification evaluations provide for the ongoing quality control of the emerging teaching-parent profession. Only

---

* In response to some difficulty in communicating what average rating figures obtained on the Osgood-type scales meant, and some complaints from raters about not understanding the Osgood-type scale, the 7-point Osgood-type rating scale used in the consumer and professional evaluations described in this paper has recently been replaced by a Likert-type 7-point rating scale. The Likert-type scale avoids the above-mentioned problems. Unlike the Osgood-type scale, which provides labels only at the poles (e.g., very satisfied . . . very unsatisfied), the Likert-type scale provides a label for each point (e.g., completely satisfied, satisfied, slightly satisfied, neither satisfied nor dissatisfied, slightly dissatisfied, dissatisfied, completely dissatisfied).

couples who continue to have evaluations and to operate highly rated programs continue as certified members of the profession. In this way the evaluations establish teaching parents as accountable professionals and allow members of the profession to operate programs that are fully responsive and acceptable to their consumers.

The consumer and professional evaluations serve to protect everyone involved with the program. For example, the evaluations protect the youths in the program. Through the youth evaluations, the youths have a chance to anonymously indicate to a third party their satisfaction with the program. Due to the public nature of the annual evaluation and the control of the third party over certification, the youths have access to a powerful means of counter control. While the openness of the homes to public scrutiny and the youths' continued participation and interaction in the local community with teachers, parents, etc., make serious abuses unlikely to occur or to go unreported, every reasonable safeguard for protecting the youths must be implemented. The need to protect them in social service programs is emphasized by recent cases of reported physical or psychological abuse in supposed behavior modification programs. See, for example, Risley's discussion of the abuses in a Florida institution for retarded adolescents ("Certify Procedures Not People," p. 159).

The evaluations also protect the agencies that place youths in the program. Through the annual evaluation report they have information on their community's satisfaction with the program. Only programs that have the evaluations can be considered genuine Teaching-Family programs. If a program neglects to carry out evaluations, it may indicate an attempt to hide failure or malpractice.

The results of a number of consumer and professional evaluations of Teaching-Family homes will now be presented in some detail. The description of these results will provide the reader with a more detailed description of the consumer and professional evaluation instruments and an account of the evolution of those instruments.

Figure 1, page 146, shows the results of an evaluation of a couple, here called the Allens, at a group home, here called Boys' Home. The names of the couple and home in this, and in all subsequent figures, are fictitious. The figure presents the average ratings by each group of consumers and by the professional evaluators. The figure is divided into two major sections: "I. Consumer evaluation" and

140

"II. Professional evaluation." The Consumer evaluation section has six subsections (A-F), one for each of the six groups of consumers. Within each subgroup the dimensions rated by that group of consumers are listed; e.g., "1. Correcting problems." As shown in the key at the bottom of the figure, the horizontal bars to the right of each of these dimensions represents the 7-point rating scales used in the evaluations. The hatched portion of each bar represents the average rating by the designated consumers on the dimension labeled to the left of each bar. The further to the right end of each bar the hatched area extends, the higher the rating. The darker vertical line within each bar represents the criterion line used to determine if the ratings are acceptable on that dimension. If the hatched area extends up to or beyond the dark line then the rating on that dimension is acceptable.

The position of the criterion line differs from dimension to dimension. After evaluation results had been collected on a number of programs, members of the training and evaluation staff individually judged which of the programs were, in their opinion, clearly acceptable. The lowest average rating in each category for those programs judged acceptable by all the staff became the criterion for that category.

The Allens were evaluated on their effectiveness in correcting problems and their level of cooperation by personnel in the juvenile court, the welfare department, the schools, and by the board of directors. The board also evaluated the couple on the extent to which they had followed the board's guidelines and rated the positive comments they had heard about the program from other community members.

The parents of the youths in the Allens' program rated the couple's effectiveness in correcting problems, their level of communication, and their effectiveness in using "home notes" (cards which provide feedback to the teaching parents concerning a youth's behavior in his natural home). The youths evaluated the couple's fairness, concern, effectiveness in correcting problems, and pleasantness. They also rated the degree to which the program had helped them improve their relationships with their parents, teachers, and peers. They also rated the overall quality of the program.

The professional evaluators rated the social skills demonstrated by the youths in interactions with the teaching parents, with each other, and with the evaluators. The evaluators also observed and rated the teaching skills of the couple and the condition of the home. They

141

also rated the overall quality of the program. As can be seen in Figure 1, the average ratings received by the Allens were at or above criterion on each dimension rated by the consumer and professional evaluators.

Figure 2, page 147, presents consumer satisfaction data on a program operated by a couple referred to as the Clarks at a home we will call Home A. Their program was the first attempted replication of the model and this evaluation was the first consumer evaluation that was conducted. The evaluation was conducted *post hoc* when the Clarks had been released by their board of directors. This failure to successfully replicate the model indicated a need for consumer evaluation measures as well as the need for a handbook carefully detailing the treatment procedures and a training program with more emphasis on practical skills.

The fact that the board fired the Clarks while giving them average ratings of 3 and 4 on the scales suggested that it did not take average ratings of 1 or 2 to indicate considerable dissatisfaction with a program. Like the board, the school and court gave the Clarks low ratings in correcting problems. In addition, the average rating by the court on level of cooperation was below criterion.

The Clarks were a dedicated couple and returned to the University of Kansas for further training. During the next six months, the training staff attempted to identify and teach the skills that had not been taught well enough or at all. The Clarks subsequently accepted another position with a home we will call Home B.

Figure 3, page 148, displays the results of the Clarks' certification evaluation in that new setting. Their ratings were uniformly high on both the consumer evaluation, which had been expanded, and the professional evaluation, which had been developed in the meantime. The Clarks are now certified teaching parents and continue to operate an extremely successful home. An initial failure had been transformed into a success and in the process a tremendous amount had been learned about replicating the Teaching-Family Model.

Figure 4, page 149, presents the results of the consumer evaluation of the second attempted replication of the Teaching-Family Model. The couple attempting that replication, the Glenns, had, like the Clarks, participated in the early, academically-oriented training program. They did very well in the training program, receiving A's in all their coursework. After finishing the program, they accepted positions at a group home, here referred to as Girls' Home. At that point in the training program we had not yet identified and specified the skills involved in effective teaching and in implementing a self-government system. Partly as a result of their lack of these skills, their Girls' Home program had many problems. The youths were often out of control, frequently ran away, and usually avoided the couple by staying up in their rooms. As can be seen in Figure 4, the average ratings by the parents and the board members were above criteria. On the other hand, the average ratings by the court, welfare and school personnel were considerably below criteria on effectiveness in correcting problems. The welfare rating on cooperation and the school ratings on communication and effective use of the school note (a feedback device similar to the home note; see Bailey, Wolf, and Phillips, 1970) were low.

The youth evaluation of the Girls' Home program was the first time a youth evaluation had been conducted. The youths rated the program below criterion in fairness and effectiveness although above criterion in pleasantness. The professional evaluation was not yet in use at the time of this evaluation. The development of the consumer evaluation came late in the course of the Glenns' stay at Girls' Home. Perhaps if we had been able to institute the consumer evaluation earlier, we may have been able to identify, and help them solve, their problems. As it was, the Glenns decided to leave the home for another profession.

Figure 5, page 150, like Figure 4, represents an evaluation of the Teaching-Family program at Girls' Home. After the Glenns left that position, the board hired another couple, the Martins. As is evident from Figure 5, the Martins' average ratings were at or above criterion level on all dimensions. The agencies responding to the consumer evaluation of the Martins' program were the same agencies that had responded in the Glenn evaluation. The high evaluations suggested that consumers are sensitive to variations in a program and that community satisfaction with a program is modifiable. The Martins became actively involved in the training program and were instrumental in developing the current model of training.

Figure 6, page 150, depicts the ratings of youths staying in a county detention home. Hector Ayala, Director of Achievement Place for Girls, was called in to consult with the program's staff. In an attempt to isolate some of the many problems facing that program he administered the youth evaluation scale. The average ratings by the youths were low on every dimension. These results, when compared to the youth satisfaction ratings obtained by the various Teaching-Family programs, demonstrate the range of ratings obtainable on the youth evaluation scale. As is the case in youth evaluations of Teaching-Family programs, the detention home staff was given feedback on the evaluation results and suggestions about ways to remedy the problems.

CONCLUSION

The Teaching-Family Model of group-home treatment for pre-delinquent and delinquent youths developed at Achievement Place is now being disseminated. A model has been developed for the training of teaching parents to operate treatment programs based on the Achievement Place program. The training model is a one-year training program which provides trainee couples with extensive, in-home, practical experience in operating a Teaching-Family treatment program. Initial and follow-up workshops concentrate on teaching and refining the basic skills critical to operating the model. Feedback on how well the trainees are performing their teaching-parent functions is obtained through consumer and professional evaluations which are conducted periodically. These evaluations serve a quality control function. They allow the training staff and trainee couples to determine problem areas and to take corrective action. Certification of a couple as professional teaching parents is contingent on high ratings on the first annual consumer and professional evaluation. Continued certification is contingent upon subsequent annual evaluations.

The procedures used in the Teaching-Family Model treatment program, in the Teaching-Parent Training Program, and in the consumer and professional evaluations are designed to facilitate the delivery of quality services to the consumers. The most direct quality control of the services provided by teaching parents is possible through public knowledge of the results of the annual evaluations and contingent certification based on those results.

It is important that certification of professionals be based on evaluation of the quality of the service actually provided for the consumers. Certification could be based on evaluation of the "quality of training" that a person received. For example, certification could be based on the completion of an accredited or certified training program.

On the other hand, people could be certified on the basis of their ability to demonstrate skills judged or shown to be important in providing quality treatment. This type of certification is based on a "quality of skill" evaluation. While this type of evaluation can reveal whether or not an individual has a certain skill, it does not follow that he will use the skill or that his use of the skill will result in quality; i.e., effective and preferred treatment. Certification on the basis of an evaluation of "quality of performance" provides for more direct quality control of treatment than does certification on the basis of an evaluation of "quality of training" or of "quality of skill." The latter two types of evaluations are indeed useful, but the evaluation of performance, such as that provided by consumer satisfaction measures, is necessary to *validate* the other evaluation measures.

Figure 1. Consumer and Professional Evaluation

TEACHING PARENTS:ALLENS
BOYS' HOME

I. CONSUMER EVALUATION

A. JUVENILE COURT
1. CORRECTING PROBLEMS
2. COOPERATION

E. SCHOOLS
1. CORRECTING PROBLEMS
2. COOPERATION

B. WELFARE DEPARTMENT
1. CORRECTING PROBLEMS
2. COOPERATION

F. YOUTHS
1. FAIRNESS
2. CONCERN
3. EFFECTIVENESS
4. PLEASANTNESS
5. IMPROVED RELATIONSHIPS
6. PROGRAM QUALITY

C. BOARD OF DIRECTORS
1. CORRECTING PROBLEMS
2. COOPERATION
3. FOLLOWING GUIDELINES
4. COMMUNITY COMMENTS

II. PROFESSIONAL EVALUATION
1. YOUTH SOCIAL SKILLS
2. COUPLE AS TEACHERS
3. CONDITION OF HOME
4. OVERALL PROGRAM

D. PARENTS
1. CORRECTING PROBLEMS
2. COMMUNICATION
3. HOMENOTES

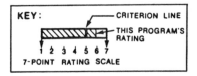

KEY:
CRITERION LINE
THIS PROGRAM'S RATING
1 2 3 4 5 6 7
7-POINT RATING SCALE

146

Figure 2. Consumer Evaluation

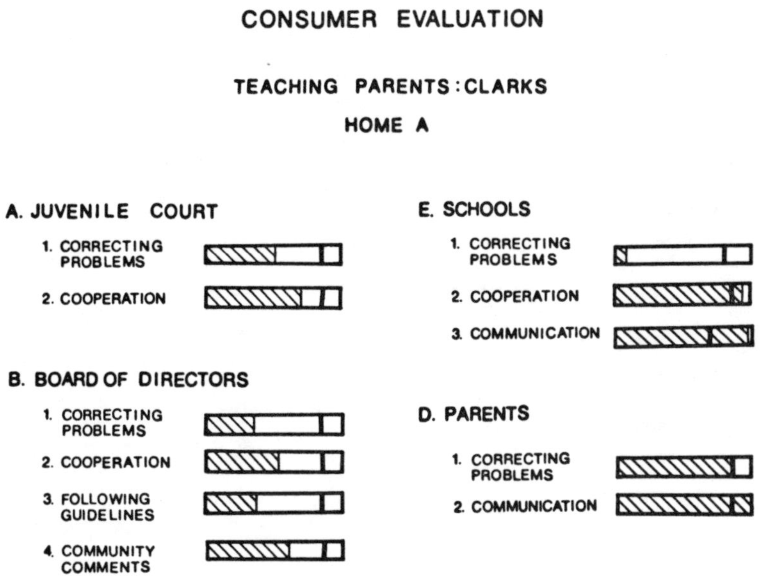

CONSUMER EVALUATION

TEACHING PARENTS : CLARKS
HOME A

A. JUVENILE COURT

1. CORRECTING PROBLEMS
2. COOPERATION

B. BOARD OF DIRECTORS

1. CORRECTING PROBLEMS
2. COOPERATION
3. FOLLOWING GUIDELINES
4. COMMUNITY COMMENTS

E. SCHOOLS

1. CORRECTING PROBLEMS
2. COOPERATION
3. COMMUNICATION

D. PARENTS

1. CORRECTING PROBLEMS
2. COMMUNICATION

Figure 3. Consumer and Professional Evaluation

TEACHING PARENTS:CLARKS

HOME B

I. CONSUMER EVALUATION

A. JUVENILE COURT

1. CORRECTING PROBLEMS
2. COOPERATION

B. BOARD OF DIRECTORS

1. CORRECTING PROBLEMS
2. COOPERATION
3. FOLLOWING GUIDELINES
4. COMMUNITY COMMENTS

C. YOUTHS

1. FAIRNESS
2. CONCERN
3. EFFECTIVENESS
4. PLEASANTNESS
5. IMPROVED RELATIONSHIPS
6. PROGRAM QUALITY

D. PARENTS

1. CORRECTING PROBLEMS
2. COMMUNICATION
3. HOMENOTES

E. SCHOOLS

1. CORRECTING PROBLEMS
2. COOPERATION
3. COMMUNICATION
4. SCHOOL NOTES

II. PROFESSIONAL EVALUATION

1. YOUTH SOCIAL SKILLS
2. COUPLE AS TEACHERS
3. CONDITION OF HOME
4. OVERALL PROGRAM

148

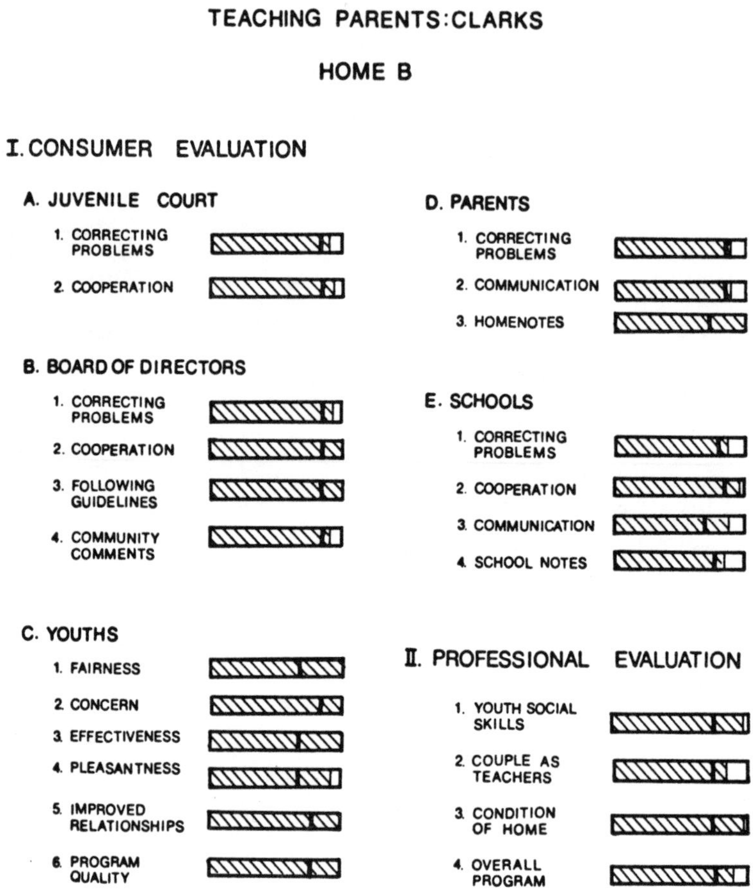

Figure 4. Consumer Evaluation

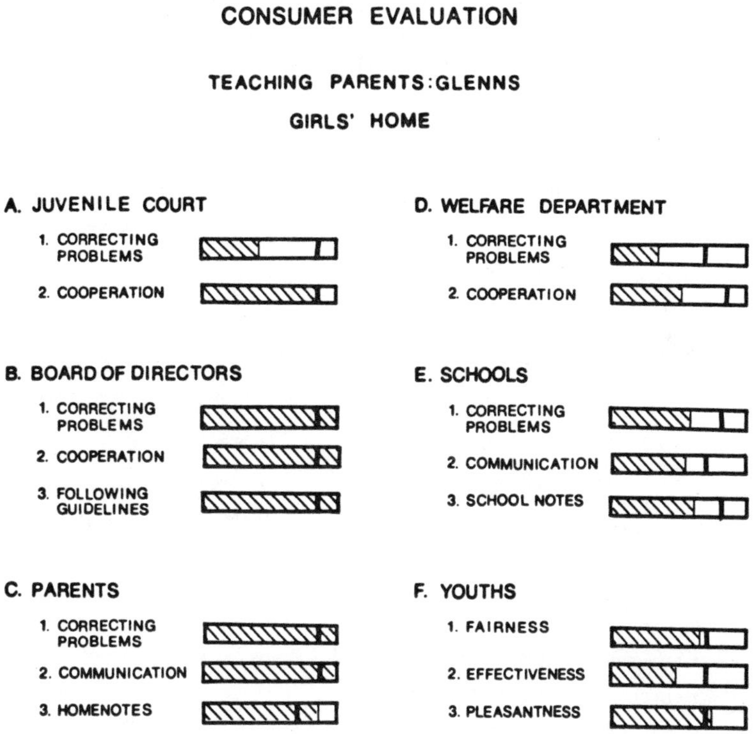

CONSUMER EVALUATION

TEACHING PARENTS:GLENNS
GIRLS' HOME

A. JUVENILE COURT

1. CORRECTING PROBLEMS
2. COOPERATION

B. BOARD OF DIRECTORS

1. CORRECTING PROBLEMS
2. COOPERATION
3. FOLLOWING GUIDELINES

C. PARENTS

1. CORRECTING PROBLEMS
2. COMMUNICATION
3. HOMENOTES

D. WELFARE DEPARTMENT

1. CORRECTING PROBLEMS
2. COOPERATION

E. SCHOOLS

1. CORRECTING PROBLEMS
2. COMMUNICATION
3. SCHOOL NOTES

F. YOUTHS

1. FAIRNESS
2. EFFECTIVENESS
3. PLEASANTNESS

Figure 5.   Consumer and Professional Evaluation

TEACHING PARENTS:MARTINS

GIRLS' HOME

I. CONSUMER EVALUATION

A. JUVENILE COURT

1. CORRECTING PROBLEMS
2. COOPERATION

D. WELFARE DEPARTMENT

1. CORRECTING PROBLEMS
2. COOPERATION

B. BOARD OF DIRECTORS

1. CORRECTING PROBLEMS
2. COOPERATION
3. FOLLOWING GUIDELINES
4. COMMUNITY COMMENTS

E. SCHOOLS

1. CORRECTING PROBLEMS
2. COOPERATION
3. COMMUNICATION
4. SCHOOL NOTES

C. YOUTHS

1. FAIRNESS
2. CONCERN
3. EFFECTIVENESS
4. PLEASANTNESS
5. IMPROVED RELATIONSHIPS
6. PROGRAM QUALITY

II. PROFESSIONAL EVALUATION

1. YOUTH SOCIAL SKILLS
2. COUPLE AS TEACHERS
3. CONDITION OF HOME
4. OVERALL PROGRAM

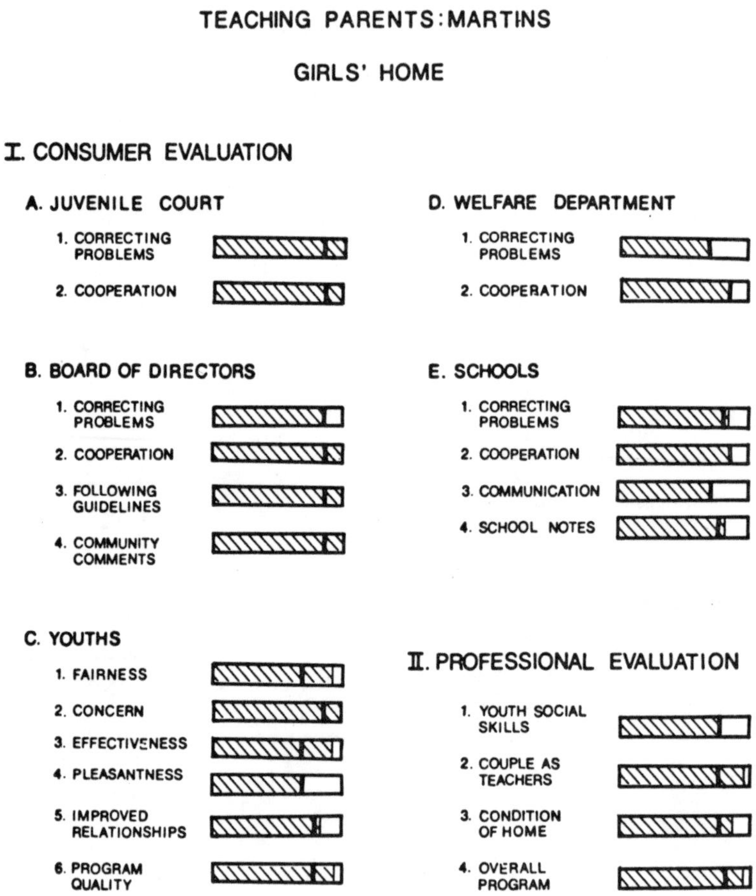

Figure 6.   Youth Evaluation

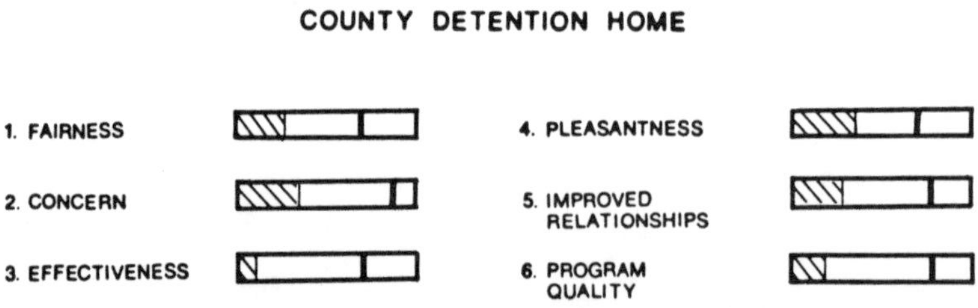

COUNTY DETENTION HOME

1. FAIRNESS
2. CONCERN
3. EFFECTIVENESS

4. PLEASANTNESS
5. IMPROVED RELATIONSHIPS
6. PROGRAM QUALITY

REFERENCES

Bailey, J. S., Wolf, M. M., and Phillips, E. L. Home-based reinforcement and modification of pre-delinquent's classroom behavior. *Journal of Applied Behavior Analysis*, 1970, *3*, 223-23.

Fixsen, D. L., Phillips, E. L., Phillips, E. A., and Wolf, M. M. Training teaching-parents to operate group home treatment programs. In M. E. Bernal (ed.), *Training in behavior modification*. New York: Brooks/Cole (In press).

Fixsen, D. L., Phillips, E. L., and Wolf, M. M. Achievement Place: Experiments in self-government with pre-delinquents. *Journal of Applied Behavior Analysis*, 1973, *6*, 31-47.

Ford, D., Christopherson, E. R., Fixsen, D. L., Phillips, E. L., and Wolf, M. M. Parent-child interaction in a token economy. Department of Human Development, University of Kansas, Lawrence, Kansas. Unpublished manuscript.

Kirigin, K. A., Ayala, H. E., Brown, W. G., Braukmann, C. J., Fixsen, D. L., Phillips, E. L., and Wolf, M. M. Training teaching-parents: An evaluation and analysis of workshop training procedures. In E. A. Ramp and G. Semb (eds.), *Behavior analysis: Areas of research and application*. Englewood Cliffs, NJ: Prentice-Hall, Inc. (In press).

Michael, J., Bailey, J., Born, D., Day, W., Hawkins, R. P., Sloane, H., and Wood, W. S. Panel discussion: Training behavior modifiers. In G. Semb (ed.), *Behavior analysis and education*, 1972. Lawrence, Kansas: The University of Kansas Support and Development Center for Follow Through, 1972.

Osgood, C. E., Suci, G. J., and Tannenbaum, P. H.. *The measurement of meanings*. Urbana, IL: University of Illinois Press, 1957.

Phillips, E. L. Achievement Place: Token reinforcement procedures in a home-style rehabilitation setting for "pre-delinquent" boys. *Journal of Applied Behavior Analysis*, 1968, *1*, 213-223.

Phillips, E. L., Phillips, E. A., Fixsen, D. L., and Wolf, M. M. Achievement Place: Modification of the behaviors of pre-delinquent boys within a token economy. *Journal of Applied Behavior Analysis*, 1971, *4*, 45-59.

Phillips, E. L., Phillips, E. A., Fixsen, D. L., and Wolf, M. M. Achievement Place: Behavior shaping works for delinquents. *Psychology Today*, June, 1973b.

Phillips, E. L., Phillips, E. A., Fixsen, D. L., and Wolf, M. M. *The teaching-family handbook*. Lawrence, KS: University of Kansas Printing Service, 1972.

Phillips, E. L., Phillips, E. A., Wolf, M. M., and Fixsen, D. L. Achievement Place: Development of the elected manager system. *Journal of Applied Behavior Analysis*, 1973a, *6*, 541-562.

Timbers, G. D., Timbers, B., Fixsen, D. L., Phillips, E. L., and Wolf, M. M. Achievement Place for Girls: Token reinforcement, social reinforcement and instructional procedures in a family-style treatment setting for "pre-delinquent" girls. Lawrence, KS: Department of Human Development, University of Kansas. Unpublished manuscript.

RESPONSE
Kenneth E. Lloyd

The Braukmann et al. paper illustrates many features of an applied analysis of behavior. A set of target responses have been objectively specified (the 7-point rating scale). These responses are observed at more than one point in time (not simply a pre- and post-test comparison), thus permitting both the teaching parents and the consumer to change their responses. The responses of single pairs of teaching parents are considered (not a group design). Finally, the analysis is experimental rather than statistical (low ratings are not compared to high ratings via chi square; instead, low ratings result in a behavioral analysis of what response to change). Some features of an applied analysis of behavior are lacking; e.g., a measure of the reliability of the ratings (inter-rater or intra-rater agreement), and the use of a reversal or multiple baseline design for demonstrating that the behavior of the teaching parents does indeed control the rating responses.

I have used standard criteria for evaluating this paper since I believe that there is no reason to change our methods or assumptions as we enter areas of professional issues, ethical or moral issues, or value judgments. Despite a traditional acceptance of these areas as somehow separate from a behavioral analysis they still represent a response by a responding individual. As responses they are part of the subject matter of psychology. Physicists, with atomic bombs, may not know what to do with the bombs. They can with justification ask the psychologist what to do. The psychologist, however, with a developed behavioral technology, must also deal with the behavior involved in the spread or restriction of this technology.

A frequently invoked controlling technique for a behavioral technology is counter-control (see *Walden II* or *Science and Human*

Behavior for early references). Two forms of counter-control are discussed: within Achievement Place (teaching parents interacting with youths in the manager system, or the family conference); and between Achievement Place and the consumers of the products of Achievement Place; that is, the youths, parents, juvenile court, welfare department, schools, and the board of directors. The latter form of counter control is the major topic here. The control is based on an open system. The program approaches a continuous feedback system from the consumers. The consumers are multiple and varied. The feedback is public!

The public nature of the feedback from the consumer to the program director is a readily accepted form of counter control within a behavioral system. In such a system the absence or lack of public notice could be unethical, unprofessional, immoral. This feature contrasts sharply with a traditional view of ethics or morality in our society in which the right of privacy of the individual holds a central position. Privacy or secrecy regarding the behavior of teaching parents would occupy a very low position in a hierarchy of values in Achievement Place.

As a professor I immediately think of the consumer analogy at a university. The consumers of the professor's responses are students, colleagues on and off campus, deans, vice presidents and the people in town. Student ratings of professors are commonplace, but often distrusted. That is, a professor with high student ratings may be viewed by his colleagues as an "easy grader." A question to be considered is whether or not the consumers of Achievement Place are "more trustworthy" than the professors' consumers. We need data to deal further with this question.

In summary, the paper presents a behavioral approach to notions of ethics or value judgments. The issue is not a search for an ethical person, but a search for certain responses. The unit being analyzed is much smaller than the traditional ethical unit. The appropriate unit is a response not a person. This is not yet a technology. There is still a need for research on the rating scales to consider the extent to which the rater's response is a function of the actual responses of the person being rated.

Dale A. General

The Teaching-Family Model presented by Braukmann et al. stands as a fine example of the development of an effective training, treatment program through the use of systematic evaluation. I would like to discuss implications of this sort of evaluation procedure for the assessment of behavior modification training and treatment programs on a broader scale, in terms of what I see as five major functions of consumer and professional evaluation.

The educational function. Behavior modifiers in many settings—especially recent graduates with little experience, or people starting out on a new project such as the one described in the Braukmann paper—often suffer from a lack of adequate feedback from other professionals. Outside professional evaluation as well as consumer feedback can serve to point out aspects of their procedures and outputs about which they may not have been previously aware. As pointed out in the paper, the consumer evaluation can bring out consumer difficulties and dissatisfactions that, for lack of a means of expression, were not previously made known. In this sense, then, this sort of evaluation serves an educational function for the person or group being evaluated.

If done frequently enough (as in the initial stages of the training program), such feedback could be used as a part of the program to shape the behavior (both therapeutic and political) of novice behavior modifiers. But even on a yearly or bi-yearly basis, this type of formal feedback can serve an important and useful informative function.

Training system feedback. As was mentioned in the paper, the teaching-parent training program has been fairly extensively revised on the basis of data concerning subsequent practical performances of its trainees. This appears to be an exceptionally useful function of evaluations in the design of training programs of all sorts. It seems that no matter how carefully plans are made and problems anticipated in advance in the design of systems, unforeseen deficits and difficulties arise that sometimes can only be detected by impartial evaluation. On a broader scale, it is certainly feasible that as behavior modification programs place more and more graduates in the field, performance evaluations of this sort will be useful as an empirical base for curriculum changes in undergraduate and graduate degree programs.

Basis for certification. If criteria were developed as a basis for certification of behavior modifiers, it is fairly certain that they would rely somewhat heavily on actual performances in the field. Evaluative data of the type being discussed would surely be helpful in providing information of this sort.

Quality-control data. Another function of the evaluation is a check on the quality of the services being provided by the program or the people being evaluated. For example, is the system serving the function it was designed to serve, or are services being offered that are, in fact, not being delivered? If the system is functioning up to par, such information could point to suggestions for further improvement and development.

Behavior-maintenance function. Finally, it also seems to be the case that, potentially, evaluations could serve to help maintain the behavior of the professional in the field. New graduates out on the job soon find that it is hard to be a hero unless their social environment supports such behavior. As evidenced by conferences of this sort (as well as casual observations in hospitality suites), behavior modifiers are, above all, not immune to the effects of social contingencies. Contact with and feedback from fellow professionals maintain a good deal of creative and productive behavior on the part of behavior modifiers.

Conclusion. It was said that such evaluation procedures can educate professionals who aren't afraid to be evaluated and who, indeed, may perhaps welcome the opportunity as a source of feedback. It's my feeling that this is an extremely healthy attitude, and perhaps a crucial one. I believe that it will prove to be beneficial both professionally, in terms of increasing the effectiveness of our training and treatment programs, as well as politically, in our relationships with the community around us and the public in general.

CERTIFY PROCEDURES NOT PEOPLE
Todd R. Risley

As the title of this paper indicates, I propose that we endeavor to certify specific procedures for use by therapeutic or educational practitioners. Furthermore, I propose that until we as a profession identify explicit procedures whose use we officially advocate and sanction, we cannot even begin to certify people rationally.

I will first present in some detail the three events which have led me to this position. Then I will briefly characterize the practical steps which can be taken to certify specific behavior modification procedures for use by practitioners in nonresearch settings.

THE FIRST EVENT

The first event was an official investigation of resident abuse focused upon a behavior modification program in a mental retardation insitution in a southern state. The investigation throughout April 1972 was made by a committee of professional and lay persons from that state and two outside experts appointed by the director of the state's division of retardation. I was one of the outside experts. Pending the outcome of our investigation, the state had suspended the superintendent of the institution, the director of cottage life, a staff psychologist (whom we will call Dr. X), a cottage supervisor, and three other cottage personnel. After receiving testimony from virtually every person associated with the behavior modification program in question, including cottage personnel, residents, parents, and from all of the professional and administration personnel of the institute; and after examining cottage log books, institution memoranda, diaries, personnel files; and after checking references and vita information by long distance telephone, the committee submitted a 32-page report to the director of the division of retardation. Let me quote from that report:

Abuse of residents
——It is the opinion of this Committee based upon the testimony given and documents examined that the punishment practices that have existed in . . . [this special program] are, in fact, abusive. The following incidents, all considered abusive, have been confirmed by eyewitness reports and entries in official records to have occurred in . . . [this program] during the period January 1, 1971 through January 25, 1972.

(a) Forced public masturbation.

(b) Forced public homosexual acts.

(c) Forced washing of mouth with soap and liquid detergent as punishment for lying, abusive or vulgar language, or, at times, for speaking at all.

(d) beating administered with wooden paddle ½ inch thick. Residents received "10 licks" as standard punishment for running away; one resident received "35 whacks" for cumulative bad behavior.

(e) Excessive and unnecessary use of leather or fabric restraints, and restrictions on personal freedom. One resident was restrained for more than 24 hours except for meals and bathroom; another was forced to sit in a bathtub for most of two days. These restraints were used as punishment and not for the purpose of preventing injury to self or others.

(f) Made to wear bizzare clothing—a boy was required to wear female underpants.

(g) Excessive use of seclusion. Although "time out" is an accepted technique for controlling certain types of disruptive behavior, it was often misused in . . . [this program]. Seclusions as long as four hours (much too long) were recorded. The seclusion rooms are barren and unpadded. Three residents testified that they were not permitted to leave seclusion to use the bathroom.

(h) Public shaming by forcing one resident to wear a sign proclaiming him to be "The Thief" and to be addressed by other residents and staff personnel as "The Thief."

(i) Withholding of food as punishment.

(j) Forced lack of sleep as punishment. In one case a boy was punished for sleeping while he was receiving several different sedatives which could be expected to cause drowsiness.

(k) Use of military disciplinary measures as punishment, specifically the "lean and rest" position (the "up" position of a push-up) and a squatting position. Also, residents required to confine themselves to a small square of floor or to a certain chair for excessive periods of time.

(l) Resident forbidden to speak, other than: "Yes, sir," "No, sir," "I have to potty," for an indefinite period of time.

(m) Resident required to hold feces-stained underwear under his nose for approximately 10 minutes as punishment for incontinence.

(n) Resident bathed with cleanser as punishment for fecal incontinence.

(o) Resident made to lie in urine-soaked sheets as punishment for repeated incontinence.

(p) Punishment of *all* residents for incidents such as finding an unexplained pill or theft of an object.

(q) Denial of visitation privileges.

The section on abuse of residents concluded with this statement:

——Although limitations of time did not permit the Committee to conduct an investigation in sufficient depth to reach a firm conclusion, it is the Committee's impression that abuse outside . . . [this program] is limited to random occurrences arising from occasional anger or the frustration of inadequately trained personnel, and that generally, limited corrective measures are taken promptly. Only within . . . [this program] did the Committee find "programmed abuse."

Evaluation of the [special] program
——The incidents of abuse described above . . . were largely prescribed by responsible personnel of the . . . [special program], and it is the Committee's opinion that they were no less abusive because conceived (however erroneously) to be "behavior shaping devices." A detailed examination of this program in both concept and application leads to the conclusion that what started out as an attempt to create a superb behavior modification program degenerated—with the best of intentions of those involved—into a bizarre, abusive, and ineffective system of punishment. These practices deviated from usual cases of abuse found in institutions of this type in the following respects:

(a) They were systematically applied as part of a total "program."

(b) They were condoned—and in some cases encouraged—by some supervisory and professional staff.

(c) They were regularly recorded in daily living unit logs.

(d) They included unusual practices, such as forced public sexual displays.

162

——The token program on the ... [special] cottages was a combination of at least two established token reinforcement systems. The definitions of appropriate and inappropriate behaviors and the approximate magnitude of tokens gained or lost for each were adapted from the token economy program for trainable retarded girls operated by Dr. James Lent at Parsons, Kansas. The overall system was organized and operated similar to the program for juvenile delinquents at the National Training School for Boys operated by Harold Cohen. Both of these programs are established, successful, and have been used as models for similar programs in many institutions throughout the country. However, in actual operation, Dr. X's program lacked one vital element of these and most other successful token systems: precise and current monitoring of the improvement of each resident's individual problem behaviors. It appears that the overriding goal of the program was research into some rather esoteric questions of statistical models for economic analysis. (It should be noted that there is nothing wrong in pursuing such research goals. However, such goals were irrelevant to the pressing problems which were continuously present in these cottages.) Consequently, little time and attention was devoted to the collection and analysis of information on particular behaviors.

——In operation, it appears that Dr. X's token program had one even more serious deficit in its structure: its organization into separate "phases." In Phase Two the resident could exchange his tokens for a large and diverse menu of items and privileges. Thus in this phase, by earning sufficient tokens, a resident could participate in a relatively rich and varied life both in and out of the cottage. However, when a resident became "out of control," or when he initially entered the program (usually because he was "out of control" in his previous cottage), he would be placed in Phase One in which no items or privileges could be purchased with tokens. Thus, during the very time when a resident would need the strongest and most immediate reinforcement to control his behaviors, he would be placed in the Phase One program which had few immediate reinforcers. In fact, it is only after the resident's behavior had been well under control for a considerable period of time—such that he accumulated a large number of tokens—that he was allowed back into the Phase Two program where those tokens could become "meaningful" through the opportunity to use them to purchase various items and privileges.

——In summary, it is almost inevitable that this token economy program would be plagued with frequent problem behaviors from residents in the Phase One program. In addition to this (or in recognition of this), some residents were even completely removed from the token economy program. Thus, many residents required . . . [unique prescriptions] when their problem behaviors could not be adequately handled by the (poorly designed) general token economy program in the . . . [special] cottages. (It should be noted that the flaws in this token program were present in the token system in use on these cottages at the time Dr. X assumed responsibility. He did not, however, change these aspects during the 16 months of his direction of the program.)

——The . . . [unique prescriptions] instituted for particular residents of the . . . [special] cottages are the focal point of this investigation. In dealing with the recurrent behavior problems which were not adequately remediated by the token economy the attendants were . . . [indoctrinated by Dr. X to] three general guidelines: (a) . . . [The first guideline was] *to emphasize the natural consequences of the behavior* in responding to the deviant behavior of the residents. (b) . . . [The second guideline was that they were not to delay but] were to *devise their own immediate response* to problem behaviors for which specific instructions had not been provided them. (c) And finally, they were instructed that they were to *follow through on every contingency* (promise or threat) that they verbalized to the residents. The incidents which lead to this inquiry evolved almost inevitably out of this method of devising . . . [unique prescriptions] for problem residents.

——From examining the log entries for the . . . [special] cottages, and from the interviews with the parties involved, we have determined that unusual procedures were being used in these cottages; that these unusual procedures, although infrequent, were systematically employed and even within the context of the problems and settings of these cottages, these procedures were, in most cases, unnecessary, unwarranted, probably ineffective, and completely unjustified. The use of such procedures as the "lean and rest" position, spanks, prolonged seclusion, prolonged physical restraints, "washing the mouth" with soap; public humiliation by forcing residents to wear special attire or [forcing them to] engage in public masturbation or other sexual acts are not normal therapeutic or educational procedures. They have neither been suggested, researched, nor promoted in behavior modification literature or in the literature of any other modern therapeutic or educational methodology.

—On the . . . [special] cottages, these unusual procedures were *not* instances of random cruelty, but neither were they the result of a prescriptive program derived from a body of literature. They were the result of well meaning, but poorly trained personnel attempting to deal with problems which they perceived as dangerous in a situation totally isolated from outside monitoring, guidance, and intervention. It appears that in each case mild forms of these unusual procedures were initiated by the cottage parents from their own imagination or from the precedent set by the covert use of some level of these procedures on these cottages in the past. In most cases, the use of each procedure was dutifully logged and probably otherwise reported to . . . Dr. X. If the unusual procedure appeared to follow the three general guidelines for dealing with unique problem behaviors, they were either actively approved—and instituted as a general pattern for dealing consistently with that behavior problem for that resident by Dr. X—or were at least passively accepted. What appeared to result then was that on the next instance of the behavior, the staff member would employ a slightly more extreme form of the special procedure which would, in turn, receive approval or acceptance. In this way, quite extreme procedures evolved in gradual steps from the spontaneous initiation of less extreme procedures by the cottage staff until, by the latter part of 1971, a pattern had been established of dealing with recurrent problems by escalating the intensity of whatever procedures happened to be in use for a particular resident. This designation of how these incidents came to arise in these . . . [special] cottages should not be interpreted as an attempt to condone or justify their use, but to relate their occurrence to the problems in the administration and staffing arrangements in these cottages and in the institution.

—The evolution of these procedures could only have occurred in the complete absence of monitoring, guidance, and intervention by the administration and professional personnel in . . . [the institution]. The cottage staff could implement these procedures in good faith—under the assumption that they were beneficial to the residents and acceptable to society at large—only because they were isolated from professional interaction with other personnel in the institution. The absence of a serious program of orienting and training new employees and the

165

lack of regular in-service training sessions were a contributing factor to this situation. In spite of the apparent religious entry of most of these events in cottage log books, it appears that Dr. X and . . . the rest of the staff rather systematically discouraged communication about their program with other institutional personnel and with the outside professional consultants employed by the institution. The question remains, however, in spite of this, of how . . . [the superintendent] could have allowed such nearly total isolation to have developed. Thus, the apparently incompatible facts of abusive procedures being used by a staff apparently dedicated to the welfare of the residents could occur because of the lack of formal procedures for training and monitoring of the staff by persons outside the little world of the . . . [special] cottages.

——In October of 1971, Dr. X was given responsibility for the program and management of the . . . [special] cottages. In December of 1971, he was also made responsible for the nursery and semi-ambulatory cottages. These were (and are) the most troublesome divisions within the institution. Dr. X had little experience with—and certainly no training in—dealing with the type of resident present in the . . . [special] cottages [large adult residents with potentially dangerous problem behaviors]. Although he now admits to this, it has become apparent from our interviews that such humility is uncharacteristic of him, and, in fact, was not evident when he was offered the responsibility of . . . [special] cottages. It seems Dr. X's verbal skills and tendency to exaggeration resulted in his being given a level of responsibility inappropriate to either his maturity or his training. He isolated himself from his previous professional mentors and from local professional peers. He was able to functionally isolate his activities, plans, and research goals from other professionals at . . . [the institution]. Thus, he was given responsibility for which he was unprepared, and allowed to operate in the absence of any peer review from his profession or from his superiors in the institution . . . .

Let me point out that Dr. X received his doctorate from a well-known university; his professors were people of some repute in behavior modification work; he was a disciple of one of the great charismatic leaders of the field; he spent a year as a post-doctoral fellow at a very reputable behavioral program in a retardation center associated with a prestigious university; he had systematically visited the laboratories and applied research programs of several other senior members of our field, and could claim their acquaintance. In sum, I think you would be hard pressed to devise certification criteria that he could not meet. Yet in an enthusiastic attempt to apply the principals of behavior (and some other "rules-of-thumb" given him by great men) he inflicted bizarre and abusive procedures on the retarded residents in his care.

The committee made recommendations regarding specific personnel and procedures of the institution. However, the major thrust of its recommendations to the state were to implement measures to prevent such abuse to residents in all state institutions. The preventive measures recommended focused solely upon increased monitoring, information gathering, and advocacy procedures to bring potentially abusive practices to the attention of state, lay, and professional groups. —It is noted that the . . . [State] Association for Retarded Children . . . and the [State] Division of Retardation have already developed the machinery to establish a statewide advocacy program . . . for the retarded. This program will rely heavily on volunteer manpower but will be coordinated by paid staff at local and state levels. Funding is to be via federal monies. It is recommended that the Director of the Division of Retardation proceed immediately to negotiate with . . . [the Association for Retarded Children] the framework within which this program will monitor for abusive practices. This framework *should* include the following features:

1. Unannounced as well as announced visits to institutions.

2. Free access to records.

3. Required periodic interviews of key personnel.

4. Ability to receive privileged testimony from retarded individuals, parents, employees of the Division of Retardation, and other concerned citizens.

—The Division should emphasize and clarify to all current and future employees at all levels that a superintendent's responsibility for monitoring and guiding programs *includes* even those programs which are *outside* the domains of his formal training.

—. . . [State] Child Abuse laws should be revised to include mentally retarded and mentally ill persons over the age of 17 years.

—There should be professional peer review of all programs which includes documentation in professional literature that the procedures used are not experimental. Any new or experimental programs shall be subject to the rules of human experimentation as set forth in present divisional guidelines.

—The Committee recognizes great value in the content of the exit interview procedure. It is recommended that they be considered a major tool for the identification of abuse as well as other problem areas. It is further recommended that these data be supplemented by a similar questionnaire to be given to each employee at the time of his semi-annual evaluation and that these questionnaires also be sent directly to the Division Central Office. These reports should also be made available to the State Advocacy Program director.

Recommendations such as these are (happily) in current vogue throughout the country. However, to increase exposure of behavior modifiers to scrutiny and criticism by persons unfamiliar—and often unsympathetic—to their procedures is less than a complete solution to the problem.

THE SECOND EVENT

The second event was an official review of the general programs, including a large behavior modification component, of another retardation center in the same state during October 1972.

In response to complaints from parents of residents, a five-member review panel was formed by the Director of the State Division of Retardation. I was again on that panel as an outside expert. For 2 days the panel reviewed documents and heard testimony from 6 parents and 13 staff members. Some of the findings of that panel concerning the behavior modification program are given below:

Alleged "death in the closet" incident

—Parents' testified to hearing that a resident died because he had been placed in a closet as part of the Behavior Modification Program and that no autopsy had been performed. Parents indicated that the chaplain could furnish the identity of the resident and the names of other employees who had knowledge of the incident. The chaplain was consulted and identified the resident as . . . [Bobby Jones]. Extensive investigation of this incident, including a review of the autopsy report with the medical director, determined that a resident, . . . [Bobby Jones] died on . . . [April 1, 1972] from aspiration.

—Several other staff members were questioned regarding this incident. The Review Panel determined that . . . [Bobby Jones] had been placed in time out during the day of his death but this was not the time out "box" or the closet.

—The Review Panel found that he . . . had in fact been placed in a pedi-crib in full view of attending personnel. He was removed from this confinement several hours before his death and had eaten his supper. It was noted that he was attended by a physician at his death.

—. . . [Bobby Jones'] death was in no way related to time out procedure; furthermore, the rumor pertaining to his death was distorted, inaccurate and misleading. The autopsy stated the condition at the time of death as well as the cause of death was aspiration and associated severe medical problems.

—It was further determined that the chaplain and other employees failed to comply with existing policies and procedures of the Division of Retardation regarding resident abuse reporting.

—The chaplain played a key role in transmitting false information relating to this death to parents as well as other staff even though her information was gained through hearsay by her own admission.

Recommendation

—— The Review Panel recommends that disciplinary action be taken against the chaplain for her part in this highly volatile, deleterious situation.

Behavior modification program

—The Review Panel found the basic Behavior Modification Program . . . [the] hospital to be procedurally excellent, well designed and appropriately administered. The degree of its integration into the entire hospital program, the positive regard (with the exception of "Time Out Boxes") in which it is held by parents and other staff, the cooperation between department heads . . . and most importantly, the observable effects of the program are rare indeed. . . . The Review Panel noted, however, that there was considerable misunderstanding surrounding use of time out. This was attributed to not providing an adequate explanation [of the time out procedures to the staff, and to] the [unfortunate] use of the . . . [term] "box." It was determined that the time out "box" was a misnomer and that its use was misunderstood and exaggerated. The time out "box" was, in fact, a cubicle, open at the top and bottom allowing proper ventilation and light. Use of the [term] "box" has led to parent and staff confusion . . . . It is the opinion of the Review Panel that the time out . . . [procedure] was an extremely benign and acceptable treatment modality but because of the misunderstanding and exaggeration it has taken on a negative connotation.

Recommendation

— With this in view, it is recommended that time out cubicles as presently used be dismantled and discontinued but that time out procedures be continued with revisions that include graduated steps and a final back up of a multi-purpose cubicle [also used] for various [other] functions including positive learning and recreational activites. It is also recommended that a letter of explanation concerning time out procedures, and other behavioral techniques, be sent to all parents with children in the program.

Here is a case of well-established behavior modification procedures being properly used by a well-trained specialist. However, although the time out procedures were humane, the staff did not "market" them as humane procedures: they called this free-standing, open-topped wooden screen arrangement a "time-out box" and followed the old-fashioned behavior-mod rule: never "explain or reason with" the child when placing him in T O. Therefore, the only verbal description the staff had for the procedure was "putting the kid in the box." This was the description they used with the residents, with other staff and even, unthinkingly, with parents. And parents don't want their children put in boxes.

There was a high level of involvement in this program by various professionals within the institution and by behavior modification experts and graduate students from a nearby university. The procedures were conducted in open wards subject to the scrutiny of parents and other resident-advocates. However, the very openness of this program to public scrutiny made it susceptible to unfounded public criticism. The criticism was instigated by the chaplain who personally disliked some of the staff and who philosophically disagreed with behavior modification. This criticism was amplified by parents who did not understand the procedures and whose contacts with the program were too brief to allow them to become informed.

THE THIRD EVENT

The third event was a request by the Director of the Division of Retardation that I systematically visit all eight institution and regional centers in the state to review their behavior modification programs, and to propose some general guidelines for the state regarding behavior modification in their retardation institution—particularly their methods of dealing with behavior problems.

I began with enthusiasm. On the first trip in February 1973, I spent a day at each of two institutions going over their behavior modification programs and providing lots of free advice.

My first visit was to the hospital which was the subject of the official review the preceding October. Although the crisis had passed, the behavior modification programs were disrupted. The staff hesitated to proceed in the face of the possibility of public criticism. In my advice to the Director of Programs and Services, I tried to suggest how such criticisms could be avoided.

——Two general problem areas which seem to have arisen in the behavioral programs at . . . [your Institution] revolve around the determination of appropriate requirements for the independent display of self-help skills; and the appropriate forms of sanctions for undesirable and socially disruptive behavior.

——I recommended that you address yourself to the complaints that you are requiring too much independent self-help behavior from specific residents by taking the time at each instance of formal or informal complaint to specify, in writing, the professional judgment formulating the program for that individual resident. For example, for complaints that you were requiring self-feeding from children who "are not able to feed themselves"; you should define the criterion test for self-feeding skills used to determine that the resident can feed himself. You should also specify the criteria which you would use to indicate that the resident had regressed and "lost" the ability to feed himself so that he would no longer be able to adequately exercise a choice in the foods he consumes or doesn't consume. Thus, if a resident had eaten without assistance a number of meals which included a variety of foods and a variety of eating utensils, you would formally consider that resident a "self feeder" and therefore able to exercise his own choice about which and how much of the various foods available to him at a meal he would consume. At this point his choice in foods and diets would not be contravened, by spoon feeding or nutritional supplements, except when explicit medical evidence indicated that continuing to allow free choice was detrimental to his health. Thus your procedures, rather than emphasizing "requirements," would emphasize "normalization," once a resident has demonstrated the skills that would allow him to choose responsibly what happens to him, he is allowed to exercise that choice, to the extent that it is not detrimental to his well-being.

—The complaints which arose about the time-out procedures on several of your wards were generated not by the procedure itself, but by the unfortunate terminology which was associated with it (i.e., calling the partitions a time-out "box"), and by the rather callous discussion of time out which was allowed to develop on the wards and was consequently transmitted to the parents.

—The review panel recommendations in October were that the cubicles then in use be discontinued and dismantled and time-out procedures be continued with revisions, including graduated steps and a final backup of a multi-purpose cubicle which was used for various functions other than time out. I further recommend that the staff be instructed in the explicit statements to make to each child as each step of the time-out procedure is employed. This is to insure that the procedure is clearly interpreted to the child, which will be of some benefit to verbal children. This will insure that the staff will be able to describe clearly the reasons for those procedures, not only to the child, but to each other and to parents and visitors.

My second visit was to an institution that had not been involved in any recent scandal and that had several well-trained behavior modifiers on its staff. Here again I found behavior modification programs at a standstill and a "gun-shy" staff. Again I tried to encourage them to proceed and suggested how they might avoid criticism for their efforts.

—Your procedures for dealing with the socially disruptive and inappropriate behaviors of most of your residents—primarily the restriction of extra privileges—appear to be well within the normal and accepted procedures of our society. My major concern is that some of those procedures have never been documented as being particularly effective in formal studies in the professional literature, with either retarded or normal people. Although the restriction of the privilege of a Friday movie for an offense which occurs on Monday is indeed a normal procedure in our society, one wonders whether it is an effective one for reducing offenses of normal children. If you have a continuing level of minor problems, you might consider other equally normal techniques which have been professionally demonstrated to be effective.

—Of course there are procedures which have been thoroughly and repeatedly demonstrated to be effective, but which are unusual and unfamiliar to our society, such as electric shock. In my opinion, you have children for whom electric shock may be the only possible way to enable an educational program to begin for them. Unfortunately, they must for the moment remain untreated. I only hope that the conditions necessary to allow this form of treatment for those few children for whom it is the last resort can be established somewhere in the state in the future. In the meantime, I'm afraid you will be able to do little for those children who are so profoundly self-stimulatory that there is no other way to reach them, or so self-destructive or aggressive that they must be managed in special environments or kept in restraint.

—Regarding special environments: I am impressed with the apparent success of your program on T cottage. This program is apparently functioning as it was designed to function, that is, it receives the residents from other cottages who are, or who have become, unmanageable, works with them for a limited period of time, and transfers them back to their home cottages. Thus it successfully serves as a holding program for residents who are temporarily unmanageable and a training program for those residents who have never been manageable. The only drawback to this program appears to be in the "public relations" efforts surrounding it. The time-out rooms, although apparently used properly, look like jail cells. This simply means that any visitor is going to require a great deal of explanation and convincing to be assured that the program is primarily to habilitate—rather than incarcerate—the residents. It did not appear to me that the staff was prepared to provide such an explanation. My suggestion was that the appearance of those rooms be changed; that they be deliberately used primarily for purposes other than seclusion, such as individual tutoring or small group lessons, etc., and that they be used only to back up milder forms of time out, such as in a chair away from the ongoing activities. The staff should be given detailed training in the verbal rationale for each step of the time-out procedure and they should be instructed to provide that rationale to the resident as they are implementing the procedure. This will assure that the resident will have every chance to understand the relationship between his behavior and the time-out procedure and that the staff will have an adequate rationale for the procedure to provide to parents and visitors. I am enclosing a model of such a rationale that we use in day-care programs for normal children. You will note that it nowhere mentions punishment but rather emphasizes the social learning that is expected to occur in the procedure. I hope you find this helpful when you are considering ways of rationalizing your own time-out procedure in T cottage.

—Your use of noise to eliminate the self-stimulatory and self-destructive behaviors appears to be an important, humane, and apparently effective approach to these problems. Enough is known about the physiological effects of noise that the possibility of any physical harm can be eliminated (as you were so careful to do). However, you must understand that this remains an experimental procedure until it has been replicated by a sufficient number of people to enable a general picture to emerge of its efficiency, its effectiveness, and the potential problems arising from its use. I would anticipate that after four or five publications on its use have appeared by several different authors, it would be considered a standard therapeutic procedure ready for general use in clinical settings. Until that time it must be considered an experimental procedure and each occasion of its use must be subject to all the checks and reviews of any human experimentation. Thus far you have exercised a great deal of responsibility in providing such a review. My suggestion is that you include professionals who are not otherwise involved in the Center or the research on the review committee. I would especially urge you to include several parents of retarded children on such a panel. I do not urge you to allow the extra response cost of providing this review discourage you from actively pursuing further research in this treatment for self-stimulatory and self-destructive behaviors. It appears to be an important, effective, and humane way of dealing with the problem.

As I progressed on my itinerary through the state my rate of giving such advice diminished. It was in the third institution, I think, that I was asked for a reference about where to find details of the procedures I was recommending. Since those details were spread among several different articles in the literature, I could not be of much concrete assistance. I could advise them on some strategy, some general tactics, refer them to many research articles which contain bits of the technology they would need and encourage them to keep trying. I could not, however, give them what a member of a practicing profession must have: an immediately useable technology; a professional sanction and protection for their legitimate efforts to use that technology.

After participating in two agonizing reviews of behavioral programs in the state, where behavior modifiers had been called on the carpet (and in one case even fired) for attempting to implement behavioral programs in good faith, I could not assure them that they would not also come to grief in trying to implement my general suggestions.

I *especially* could not assure them that other behavior modifiers would rally to their support if they were criticized by the public. Indeed, the pattern seems to be that although behavior modifiers seldom cast the first stone, they tend to join the rock-throwing crowd quickly whenever another behavior modifier is singled out for public criticism.

In this state it seemed that behavior modifiers in the Division of Retardation were becoming afraid to practice their technology.* And, partially as a result of our investigations, Human Rights and Resident Advocating Committees were being expanded—these committees'

---

* As a result of these observations and similar incidents in other states, a great deal of activity is underway to establish clearer "ground rules" for the use of behavior modification procedures, some of which are presented in other chapters of this book. One such effort in the state of Florida, where a task force of experts in behavioral procedures, the law, and retardation was assembled, has culminated in a comprehensive document, "Florida Guidelines for the Use of Behavioral Procedures in State Programs for the Retarded." A limited number of copies of these guidelines is available from the co-chairmen of that task force: Jack May, Department of Psychology, Florida State University, Tallahassee, Florida 32306; and Todd Risley, Department of Human Development, The University of Kansas, Lawrence, Kansas 66045.

175

unfocused reviews and mini-investigations functioned to suppress further any active, therapeutic efforts to modify residents' behaviors. It also appears to be a national trend.

A profession's most important function is first to train, and thereafter to support and regulate, members in their application of legitimate professional procedures. Behavior modification is not a profession because it has no mechanism for specifying its legitimate professional procedures. Training, professional or otherwise, can have meaning only in the context of specific skills or procedures. The growing diversity of populations, settings, and problems in behavior modification research and practice has made obsolete the concept of a behavior modification "generalist" who has been trained in the "principles of behavior" and thereafter applies them to solve any behavioral problem. Both research and practice are becoming increasingly specialized and behavior modification practitioners can only be expected to be proficient in a finite number of specific procedures for use with certain populations in particular settings. Behavior modification has only recently begun to develop a penumbra of non-research practitioners around its experimental core. These practitioners are members of diverse professional fields—speech pathology, special education, social work, recreation, music therapy, psychiatry, experimental psychology, home economics, business administration, clinical psychology, sociology, elementary education, developmental psychology, physical therapy, linguistics, architecture, etc., and many are not active participants in any professional organization. The only common denominator is that behavior modification practitioners profess to employ behavior modification procedures in their practice. To support and regulate the practice of behavior modification will require a new professional organization centered around the one common denominator which exists: not professional training programs and not existing professions, but behavior modification procedures themselves. This conference and other recent activity indicates that we are finally ready (indeed required) to form a profession.

Accordingly, I have considered how we might establish a continuing system for specifying and making officially legitimate professional procedures for our practitioners.

176

CERTIFYING BEHAVIOR MODIFICATION PROCEDURES

Behavior modification must be a continuing system so that our procedures are continually evolving and expanding. It must be closely related to our research systems so that the transition from an experimental procedure to an officially sanctioned therapeutic or educational procedure is smooth and efficient. The process of legitimizing a procedure must involve empirical evaluation and peer review, for what else is the hallmark of our field.

With this in mind, I have considered our most established and durable professional structure—our peer-reviewed research journals—as the possible vehicles for such a system. In my (perhaps biased) judgment the routine peer-reviewing activities of professional journals represent the only organized, data-based professional system in our field of activity; and certainly the only system which continuously functions every day without requiring external support and continuous prompting.

In spite of their names, the most central journals in our field—*Behavior Research and Therapy, Journal of Applied Behavior Analysis, Behavior Therapy,* and *Behavior Therapy and Experimental Psychiatry*—are not primarily oriented to practitioners. Their articles are written for other investigators; they are reviewed by other investigators, and they are read primarily by other investigators. The *Journal of Applied Behavior Analysis (JABA),* which has the most elaborate peer-reviewing system and has published research on the most varied areas of behavioral problems, is perhaps the least practitioner-oriented of the four. However, even *JABA* can easily include the function of specifying and certifying procedures for behavior modification practitioners into its existing operations with only minor revisions.

There are three issues which must be resolved in certifying a procedure for general use by practitioners: (1) Is the procedure still experimental or can it be considered an established therapeutic or educational technique? (2) Is the procedure sufficiently specified to enable its use without error by practitioners and to enable the accuracy of its implementation to be judged by professional or lay monitors? (3) Is the procedure unusual or is it within the normal practices of society?

The first two issues can be handled easily within our present journal-reviewing systems, with only minor revisions in our instructions to reviewers. The peer-review systems of our professional journals already distinguish between new and established procedures. After a certain number of systematic replications of a procedure, reviewers tend to reject further displays of that procedure as contributing nothing new. The existence of a body of research attesting to the effectiveness of variants of a procedure and analyzing some of its internal workings, should, I feel, be an absolute prerequisite to certifying a procedure. However, saying that a procedure has been clearly and repeatedly shown to be effective is not the same as recommending its general use for nonresearch practitioners. For this step the procedure should be "packaged" in cookbook detail for implementation by practitioners in the field. The package should describe the training required, the monitoring which should accompany it, and the precautions to be taken. The adequacy of the packaging would be formally evaluated by "product testing" with many practitioners, with systematic data collected on practitioners' accuracy in implementing the package, and on the resultant behavior changes in their clients. This evaluation would then be submitted for peer review. The review would utilize the usual researchers. But several practitioners or administrators who could critique the content of the procedures according to their probable acceptability in their own service setting would also review the package.

Effectiveness and acceptability are not necessarily correlated. For example, many of the procedures normally used by parents, and accepted by society, such as scolding, delayed restriction of privileges, etc., are often ineffective. Conversely, time out in a bare, locked closet, or electric shock, may be quite effective but are rarely publicly acceptable; people cannot relate these procedures to their own experiences or to familiar methods of child rearing, and may confuse them with child abuse.

When behavioral procedures are recommended for unsupervised use in private practice or in public settings such as institutions for the retarded, more than their effectiveness is at issue. The procedures must be acceptable to the general public. It must be possible to describe them in terms of common experiences and common practice. They must sound familiar and allow people to feel comfortable about their use. Furthermore, the people who implement them must be able to understand and describe what they are doing, and the resulting benefits to the residents, so that they can convey this information to lay observers in a way which will avoid misunderstanding.

There is nothing intrinsic in the principals of behavior which require that their application must take forms which are outside the range of procedures commonly used in our society. Heretofore there has been little emphasis in behavior modification research on developing procedures which are also familiar and acceptable to the general public (indeed, it appears that the emphasis has been in the other direction). I propose that we should (indeed must) supply that emphasis in the process of certifying behavior modification procedures for use by nonresearch practitioners.

The third issue—the public familiarity and acceptability of procedures—will require some expansion of the reviewing systems of our journals. Parents, client-rights advocates, and other concerned citizens should be solicited to review the content of "packaged" procedures at the same time that professional peers are reviewing the data on the formal testing of the package.

An excellent recent example of behavioral procedures deliberately developed to be familiar and acceptable to the general public—and packaged for effective use by pracititoners—is the toilet training book by Azrin and Foxx (1974).* (The presence of that book on the best-seller list indicates that the procedures are, in fact, immediately acceptable to the general public.) In the system I am proposing, an experimental demonstration of the effectiveness of that book in instructing parents (the intended users) in the procedure and enabling them to toilet train their children would be submitted to a journal. The adequacy of the evaluation would be judged by professional peers while the "lay" reviewers would review the book itself to judge the humaneness and acceptability of its procedures.

If both sets of reviews were acceptable, the evaluation report (not the book itself, just the procedures and results of the evaluation) would be published, and would thereby be certified on an interim basis. After several replications of the evaluation by independent investigators, the book would become a formally certified procedure in behavior modification. Such evaluated packages should then become the goal and ultimate final product of all other work reported in our applied research journals.

---

* Azrin, N. H. and Foxx, R. M. *Toilet training in less than a day.* New York: Simon & Schuster, 1974.

However, some effective procedures will not be found publicly acceptable. If no alternative acceptable procedures are available which will produce effective treatment, the lay reviewers might be persuaded, if the packaged procedures specify sufficient safeguards, that individuals who could benefit from the procedures would not be deprived of them but their use would not become the occasion for abuse or widespread misunderstanding. For example, a packaged procedure involving electrical stimulation for eliminating self-destructive behavior of institutionalized retarded residents might specify that the procedures be implemented only within a specially established treatment unit; that the unit be staffed by a team of therapists and supervised by a professional who has been formally trained in the therapeutic use of electrical stimulation; that only a member of the treatment team could use electrical stimulation outside the unit to generalize the treatment; and that the procedures be thoroughly explained to any other staff who might observe them. The treatment package might also specify that the special treatment unit be closely monitored by a public committee of representatives from community organizations as well as parents of the retarded who would become informed of the details and rationale of the procedures used on the unit; who would serve as the admissions committee and make the final decision on whether or not a resident needed to be admitted to the unit; and who would periodically observe the electrical stimulation procedures and be able to explain them to the concerned public. With such specifications the package might be judged acceptable and be certified on an interim basis until such time as more normal procedures could be found which were effective in eliminating severe self-destructive behavior.

Innovations—whether they be experimental or anecdotal, and whether they be called behavior modification or go by any other labels—must be subject to the prior review and informed consent guidelines for human experimentation. To be considered an established therapeutic or educational practice, rather than an experimental effort, both the effectiveness and the public acceptability of a procedure and the conditions of its use must be explicitly established. I propose that this can best be accomplished by incorporating into the reviewing process of our professional journals representatives of the concerned public who can certify the acceptability of a packaged procedure while professional peers are certifying its effectiveness and usability.

I leave you with one final thought on certifying procedures rather than people. Clinical psychology, psychiatry, social work, etc., have long had systems for certifying people. Were we to apply the criteria I am proposing to the procedures these practitioners now use every day, then how many of these officially certified people would be left with nothing at all to do?

RESPONSE

Garry L. Martin

In a nutshell. Dr. Risley appears to be in agreement with the view that behavior modifiers require their own professional organization. However, he suggests that rather than following the usual practices of developing professional guidelines around training programs and certification criteria for members of the profession, a behavior modification professional organization must be centered around certified behavior modification procedures. He has further outlined a plausible system for establishing a continuing mechanism for specifying officially legitimate professional procedures for behavior modification practitioners. Accordingly, the variants of a procedure should be researched and analyzed according to its internal workings. The procedures should then be "packaged" in cookbook detail for implementation by practitioners in the field. The package itself should then be field tested and the results submitted for peer review, as well as for review by practitioners and administrators who may utilize the package. If both professional peers and "lay" reviewers judge the package acceptable, then the package would be certified on an interim basis. After several replications of field tests by independent investigators, the package would become a formally certified procedure in behavior modification. The only example cited by Dr. Risley of such a behavioral package (that he considers excellent) is the toilet training book by Azrin and Foxx (1974). The general tone of Dr. Risley's comments seems to imply that certifying procedures is all that is really necessary to overcome the problems facing behavior modification as a profession (this implication is especially obvious in the last paragraph). My first reaction is to applaud Dr. Risley for his very insightful suggestions. Packaged procedures of the sort that he has described would undoubtedly be a tremendous boon for behavior modification practitioners and may alleviate some of the problems that he described in the earlier portion of his paper.

A problem: we need to certify procedures to certify procedures. My second reaction, however, is one of skepticism of the possibility of certifying very many of our procedures in the way that he has described. I am skeptical for several reasons. First, the example of the excellent behavioral package that he cited, namely, the toilet training program of Azrin and Foxx, is one that includes a widely acceptable target behavior (namely, successful toileting) as a part of the program package. Does this mean that behavior modifiers will always certify procedures that specify the target behaviors? If the answer is yes, then behavior modifiers seem to be setting themselves up as the judges for what is "good and right" in our society. This is obviously another "can of worms" that many behavior modifiers do not want to open. If the answer is no, then certifying procedures will not solve many of the problems that Risley cited in the first part of his paper that relate to the application of procedures to questionable target behaviors. Second, I am not as convinced as Dr. Risley about the adequacy of our present journal reviewing systems for reviewing the packages as he has suggested. Which journal would be used? Although he suggested that the most central journals in our field—*Behavior Research and Therapy, Journal of Applied Behavior Analysis (JABA), Behavior Therapy*, and *Behavior Therapy and Experimental Psychiatry*—are not primarily oriented to practitioners, I believe the data suggests otherwise for all the journals except *JABA*. For example, Agras (1973) surveyed three of these journals and reported that only *JABA* published the majority of its articles as controlled experiments (82% as compared to 48% for *Behavior Therapy* and 29% for *Behavior Therapy and Experimental Psychiatry*). If *JABA* is the appropriate journal for reviewing the procedures, then I question Dr. Risley's suggestion that the peer review system readily distinguishes between new and established procedures. He has suggested that "after a certain number of systematic replications of a procedure, reviewers tend to reject further displays of that procedure as contributing nothing new" as though the reviewers are quite consistent within and across procedures. In my view, there is a great deal of variability in the peer review system. I would suggest that if behavior modifiers are to certify procedures for practitioners, they should first more clearly certify procedures to be followed by the certifiers (i.e., the peer reviewers). For example, in an editorial article in the very first issue of *JABA*, Baer, Risley, and Wolf (1968) outlined seven dimensions of an analytical behavioral application. However, comparison of articles within any issue or across several issues of *JABA* indicates a tremendous amount of variability with which the published articles meet one or more of these dimensions to any given degree. In short, certification of procedures is a very worthy undertaking, but an exceptionally difficult task.

Another problem: certifying procedures is not enough. Even if it were possible to pursue the task of certifying procedures with some degree of success, that is only one of three major tasks facing us, and perhaps the easiest of the three. In addition to certifying procedures, we cannot ignore the problem of selecting target behaviors to which the procedures will be applied. In addition we must be concerned with the development of contingencies to maintain proper application of the procedures by the practitioners to the particular target behaviors. I believe it would be a mistake to concentrate only on the certification of procedures as though that is going to solve all our problems. Although excellent procedures might be made available, they could be applied to develop questionable target behaviors, or not applied at all.

Another problem: what about the nonprofessionals? My final reaction is that Dr. Risley seems to be concerned primarily with practitioners who are members of diverse professional fields, citing speech pathology, special education, social work, and several others. However, we cannot be concerned just with practitioners who are also members of other professional fields. Nonprofessionals in various walks of life are coming into contact with behavior modification from such sources as newspaper columns, mini-workshops, parent training programs, word of mouth, and so forth. As behavior modifiers we must also be concerned with the chosen target behaviors, the procedures applied, and the long-term maintenance of those procedures by nonprofessionals as well.

Grassroots behavior modification associations: a complement to certifying procedures. A positive approach that is compatible with the certification of positive prescriptive guidelines by academic behavior modifiers, and that will help solve the problems of identifying target behaviors, developing contingencies to maintain application of positive prescriptive procedures, and minimizing abuses of behavior modification and bad publicity, is the development of grassroots behavior modification associations. Such an association was founded in the Province of Manitoba in June 1973. The Manitoba Behavior Modification Association (MBMA) is concerned with providing information about behavior modification and its possible application to any interested persons in the province. Membership is open to anyone who ascribes to the goals of promoting behavior modification, abides by the ethical statement in the by-laws, and pays a nominal membership fee. Members include parents, psychiatric nurses, psychologists, social workers, high school students, etc. The major thrust for organizing (and maintaining) the association came from a core of behavioral staff and students from the Universities of Manitoba, Winnipeg, and Brandon. MBMA provides its members with a local journal (*Barefoot Behavior modification*), a monthly newsletter, an annual two-day behavior modification conference at which time various people from the province describe their projects and one or two guest speakers of some reknown make formal presentations, and an information service concerning ongoing behavioral programs around the province. The association is organized on a committee basis with elected committee chairpersons and members serving on committees for clerical services, conference organization, ethics and membership, publications, nominations, legal and by-laws, financial and public relations. Thus far the association has proven highly popular and successful. Moreover, at the 1974 annual Canadian Psychological Conference, a "Behavior Modification in Canada" interest group met and people from each province in Canada resolved to develop local associations in each province with the potential goal of tying such associations together in a national organization in the future.

Thus far it seems that our grassroots association has been able to provide information to a number of interested individuals in the province, and has developed many friends for behavior modification in Manitoba who can be counted on if various bad publicity and erroneous pieces of information concerning behavior modification are presented via the media or other means. It is our belief that more and more behavior modification will be done at the grassroots level. It would therefore seem essential to have an effective mechanism for reaching such people to ensure that positive program packages of the sort envisaged by Dr. Risley are consistently applied to develop target behaviors that are acceptable to a great many concerned people.*

* For further information concerning the MBMA, write to the Manitoba Behavior Modification Association, Box 189, Winnipeg, Manitoba, Canada.

QUALITY CONTROL IN A PROFESSION
Jack L. Michael

Until the late Sixties, most people who would have identified themselves as "behavior modifiers," in the sense of applied behavior analysis, were either academicians whose main responsibility was to a university department, or applied professionals with a Ph.D. in clinical psychology, counseling and guidance, or a related field. If these professionals performed so as to bring criticism upon themselves and thus upon their profession, those who trained them in behavior analysis would not generally have been singled out as responsible since behavior analysis was only a small part of their training. Criticism by laymen or professionals in other fields would reflect simply on their performance as psychologist, educator, academician, etc.

Another factor protecting us from blame and thus from a keen sense of responsibility for any ineffectiveness in our trainees is the general difficulty of detecting ineffectiveness in such areas as clinical psychology, college teaching, counseling and guidance, etc. Either outcomes have not been specified clearly or they are expected to occur over a long time period. The incidence of unprofessional or "unethical" behavior was not frequent since most people with doctoral degrees in applied areas had received a good deal of deliberate or inadvertent instruction in professional problems; also, they had usually served a relatively long apprenticeship in their field.

It appears that the technology we are promoting is, indeed, a useful supplement to existing approaches if the number of practitioners is any indication. Many doctoral programs in clinical psychology, counseling and guidance, educational psychology, and others are now offering courses in applied behavior analysis; some offer a specialty in this area. There are even a few doctoral programs whose main focus is applied behavior analysis. The graduates of these advanced programs are still likely to function primarily in academic settings where outcomes are only vaguely specified or long delayed, making detection of ineffectiveness unlikely. But they are increasingly likely to be identified as specialists in behavior analysis, and any unprofessional conduct or bad judgment is now more likely than before to be considered evidence of defects in their behavioral training program or in behavioral programs in general.

In addition to this increasing identifiability of a profession concerned with behavior analysis, and so labeled, the appearance of behavioral specialists at the sub-doctoral level further adds to our sense of responsibility for the effectiveness of our training programs. These people generally function in settings where outcomes are somewhat more assessable than is the case with most Ph.D. positions. They begin their function as behavior analysts soon after they receive their professional training, which renders the training program more clearly responsible for any ineffectiveness, bad judgment, or unprofessional conduct. Since their apprenticeship is two or three years shorter than the practitioner's with a doctoral degree, such undesirable behavior is generally more likely.

As a result of this "success," we are feeling the effects of a form of accountability. Most of us are convinced that a person with no more maturity and general wisdom than that required by a bachelor's degree from an accredited college, coupled with the equivalent of 45 to 60 hours of effective training in applied behavior analysis, will be able to make a valuable contribution to any problem involving the control of human behavior. (The possible contribution of the "behavior technician" with only a bachelor's degree, or the graduate of a two-year community college program in behavior analysis, will be discussed later.) However, we face the same problem as all the other professional specialties—dentistry, medicine, occupational therapy, nursing, etc. That is, how to assure and maintain the professional quality of the product of the training program; put in other terms, how do we protect the consumer and thus, in the long run, ourselves as producers? Failure to maintain such quality will result in harm to people or institutions who are disadvantaged by the ineffectiveness, bad judgment, or unprofessional conduct of poorly trained behavior analysts; in turn, the profession and its related science will suffer.

If it were not for one complicating factor, the solution to this problem would be relatively straightforward, namely, development of a quality-control system like those in other professional fields. Such systems have essentially two basic aspects: accreditation of training programs by a state or national organization of the particular profession; licensing or registration of only those graduates of such accredited programs who, in addition, pass some form of examination, usually constructed and monitored by the national organization.

Such a system would not be difficult to develop. At first, the national organization could be based on the existing rudiments of organizational membership available in the *JABA* editorial board, Division 25 of the APA, and members of the most relevant existing academic training programs. Once such a national organization is formed, one of its main functions would be to accredit sub-doctoral training programs in behavior analysis. After this process had been in existence for a few years, it would be possible to develop examining procedures which function as a further guarantee of the person's competence, and as a form of ongoing quality control of previously accredited programs. Naturally the accreditation of programs and the examination of participants would be on the level of minimal requirements; every effort would be made to prevent such procedures from stifling new developments. Such a stifling effect is not too likely, however, if the experience of other professions is any guide; furthermore, extensive recognition for innovation and discovery can counteract any such effect.

The above procedures involving a national organization, accreditation of training programs, and certification of graduates of such programs are, in general, a manageable and reasonably successful way of dealing with the problem of quality control within a profession. The details of such a system would have to be worked out for the unique characteristics of our particular profession, and would be expected to differ in various ways from those systems currently in effect. We can anticipate a few years of argument, false starts, trial and error, before arriving at a generally satisfactory system. In fact, increas-

189

ingly frequent symposia and conferences dealing with this general topic can be viewed as the early stages of this development.

In our case, however, there is one major problem which makes such a development more than just ordinarily difficult. What many of us see as a new profession—applied behavior analysis—has considerable overlap in concepts, technology, personnel, and training institutions with a number of other professions. Already graduates of established programs offering the master's degree in clinical psychology, counseling and guidance, and other related areas compete, in a sense, in roughly the same job market. Any attempt on our part to determine the adequacy of training programs and their graduates according to *our* notion of a minimal professional repertoire will undoubtedly be seen as an unjustified attempt to force our idiosyncrasies and prejudices about theory and method on other professionals who are already doing an excellent job. Furthermore, our notion of what constitutes minimal requirements will most certainly be seen as deficient to the degree that we omit certain subject matters and skills thought important by those who direct these other programs.

Still, there seems no acceptable alternative but to go ahead and form a national organization and to develop a system for accrediting programs and licensing people. Future employers will, at least temporarily, continue to have a variety of professionals to consider for some of their positions. Thus, in order to direct a training program for retarded teenagers, one might consider hiring a person with a master's degree either in clinical psychology, educational leadership, counseling and guidance, or applied behavior analysis. Among the credentials of this last person would be his graduation from a program accredited by the National Association of Applied Behavior Analysis, and that he has taken and passed the licensing examination given by that organization. If this system of quality control is ultimately effective, and if we are correct in our understanding of the value of this science and technology, this person, other things being equal, will be the best one for the job; to the extent that the profession has earned a good reputation, he will get the job. Other professions in competition for the same types of positions will either require approximately the same kinds of programs and then merge with the NAABA, or compete openly with different kinds of programs. If they compete successfully, a possibility I consider unlikely, there may emerge alternative but different professional approaches to the same practical problems, or a more refined way of classifying the practical problems. In any case, now is the time to begin, and if this competitive attitude seems undignified, the alternatives are even less satisfactory.

Addendum. For professional levels below the master's degree, it is reasonable to suppose that the graduate of a well-designed bachelor's degree program with a major in applied behavior analysis, or even of a two-year community college program, will be able to make a valuable contribution to our society with its increasing emphasis on human services. However, it appears easier for us to begin at the master's degree level where the acceptability of a profession in applied behavior analysis seems quite high, and work down as we become more experienced and as our profession becomes better known and more organized. This does not mean that we should wait for the establishment of a national organization and its accreditation machinery before initiating programs below the master's degree level, but only that we should postpone formal attempts to regulate and monitor them until we have the master's degree system well in hand.

SECTION III:
Accountability and Ethics

WHO DECIDED THAT WAS THE PROBLEM? TWO STAGES OF RESPONSIBILITY FOR APPLIED BEHAVIOR ANALYSTS

Robert P. Hawkins

Recently I was vividly reminded of a problem in applied behavior analysis that I believe has plagued us for years, and one that we need to recognize if we are to conduct ourselves responsibly in the various human services we are trying to perform. A bright, conscientious graduate student was interested in doing his thesis in a program for severely maladjusted children. He wanted to teach cursive writing to a rather bizarre and retarded child. I knew something about the child and was rather surprised that he selected cursive writing skills since the child could not read (except his name), print, or even reliably identify all the letters of the alphabet. I asked "Who decided *that* was the problem to work on next?"

That problem had been selected in a three-way conference between the child's teacher, a behavior modifier with several years' experience in the program; my graduate student, who certainly must be considered a behavior analyst; and a psychologist in the program who was also trained as a behavior analyst in our department, and had been employed as a behavior analyst for two or three years. I do not know the processes they went through to determine what problem should be attacked next, but their rationale for choosing the skill deficit of cursive writing was that they thought, "It would be neat if he could write." They felt it would be efficient to omit the step of teaching him manuscript writing, though there was no mention of any research showing that this omission is an efficiency.

When I questioned their selection of cursive writing, I inquired about skills the boy had in various areas of development. I found that he could not color within boundaries proficiently, could not draw easily recognizable pictures, could not tie his shoes; he spoke in complete sentences only if prompted, could not carry on even simple conversations, never initiated play with peers, never engaged in cooperative play although he did engage in parallel play occasionally if others initiated it, and could imitate a few gross motor acts accurately. I doubted that the child had the prerequisite skills to learn cursive writing; and if he learned to write, I doubted that it would be a functional skill for him (except in a very restricted sense).

In addition, I felt uneasy about cursive writing as the next behavioral objective because, in general, it seems wise to program the development of children's (or retarded people's) skills so that they keep approximately the same profile, across the various social and physical skills, as is typical of most children's development unless one is systematically investigating alternative sequences of development. To attempt to teach this particular child cursive writing now appears to run two risks in this regard. It might make an already unusual child even more unusual (somewhat like the "idiot savant" who has one remarkably well developed skill and is otherwise developmentally retarded) so that he would likely be less socially acceptable to others; and it would likely result in others expecting too much of the child in some areas of his development, and thus possibly failing to teach him important skills.

I felt chagrined that we had not done a better job of training the two behavior analysts involved. The student's thesis will involve gross motor imitation, not cursive writing.

The problem I wish to illustrate is also evidenced clearly in another true story.* A behavior analyst was given responsibility for the case of a young man with a Ph.D. in biology who had developed hysterical blindness and had lost his university teaching position. The behavior analyst was particularly interested in studying the aversive control of behavior, so he constructed some laboratory apparatus with which he could make electric shock contingent upon the young man's failure to make an avoidance response that required a gross visual dis-

---

* The specific facts have been changed to avoid embarrassment with friends whose work I generally admire.

crimination. Then as the subject became proficient at avoiding the shock under one discrimination problem, the problem was made more subtle and complex.

This may sound reasonable until we look at the facts of the case. The biologist had great difficulty getting through graduate school; the teaching job he had lost was his first position; he had held it only a few months when he became "blind"; he had demonstrated a high level of anxiety about his work, and he had always shown an unusual amount of dependent behavior. It would seem that the man's problem was much more than hysterical blindness, and involved such things as his job competency, his own evaluation of his job performance, the achievement goals he set for himself, and certain kinds of dependent behavior under stress. Most clinical practitioners, upon finding that such a case was dealt with by only addressing the blindness (particularly with an aversive control procedure, in which the man could either avoid work or avoid shock, but not both, except by termination of the treatment), would probably ask, "Who decided *that* was the problem?" Unfortunately for the young biologist, he became increasingly anxious as his visual discrimination improved, and he rather suddenly terminated the treatment. That was the end of the behavior analyst's involvement, and I do not know the ultimate outcome of the case.

THE GENERAL PROBLEM
The problem has to do not only with what skills and knowledge the behavior analyst brings to his applied work, but also with his sense of responsibility for the different steps of the process in which he is involved. All education and therapy could be described by the following 4 Steps:

1. *Setting of Behavioral Objectives.* This is a determination of what behaviors (and whose, which is not always as it seems) need establishing, strengthening, maintaining, weakening, or eliminating. This step might include, as sub-steps, determination of what kind of information is needed and how best to get it; arranging for opportunities to get the relevant information (e.g., observing, interviewing, testing, referring to other experts); getting the information (as described by Kanfer and

Saslow, 1969); watching for unexpected or otherwise significant information; and integrating the information into a set of
behavioral objectives.*

2. *Design of a Program for Achieving the Objectives.* This is a
determination of how to achieve the behavioral objectives
effectively, economically and humanely. This step might
include, as sub-steps, selection or designing of a setting for
learning, selection or designing of tasks and materials; sequenc-
ing of tasks and materials; determination of consequence contingencies; determination of who will implement aspects of
this program; and determination of how its effects will be
evaluated.

3. *Implementation of the Program.*

4. *Evaluation of the Program's Effects.* This includes returning to
Steps 1 and 2, as needed. The evaluation is best done continuously during the program, not as a distinct fourth step
after the program is over (or even at infrequent times).†

The problem being highlighted in the present analysis is that we behavior analysts, though generally outstanding at Steps 2 through 4, often
do not seem to appreciate the importance of Step 1. It appears that we
frequently lack the skills to perform Step 1 ourselves and yet sense too

---

* Any of these may overlap in time, and it is common for behavior analysts
to carry out Step 4 continuously during Step 3 and even 2.

† A step preliminary to Step 1 has been omitted, because it is usually a diffuse,
implicit process that would be difficult to describe as "a step" in education
or therapy though it governs all education and therapy. It is the assumption of
certain kinds of behavior to be culturally or personally desirable, and others to
be less desirable. Thus, before one elects to strengthen, say, independent,
rational thinking on the part of a child or adolescent, one must assume that a
society functions better, overall, if its members are relatively rational and
independent in their thought. In some nations this assumption would not be
made. This example is extreme, but subtler assumptions about what is "good
mental health" and the like would not be so universally accepted among professionals or in the society at large. One can readily think of examples in the areas
of sexual behavior, drug consumption, and reliance on scientific data.

little responsibility to see that someone else does the job competently.

A competent, responsible performance of Step 1 appears to require that a professional have most or all of the following characteristics as they apply to the particular type of behavior he is dealing with:

(1) A sense of responsibility for the learner's overall, long-term welfare, including his safety, comfort, happiness, freedom and self-satisfaction.

(2) A similar sense of responsibility to protect and promote the welfare of society while dealing with the target individual(s).

(3) Knowledge or hypotheses regarding what behaviors "should" be present (presumably those within his discipline's purview that will promote Steps 1 and 2 above). Different human service professions vary greatly in the objectivity of the bases for their respective bodies of lore regarding what behaviors are desirable and in what order they might best be taught. This will be discussed further, below, under research implications.

(4) Skill at sensitive, well-directed observation and at creating situations (including interviews, tests, etc.) in which potentially significant behavior will be emitted for observation.

But development of these characteristics requires training, and characteristics (2) and (3) are likely to be developed only through training in some specialty *other* than applied behavior analysis, specialities such as speech pathology, orthopedic rehabilitation, marital therapy, school psychology, and those very general specialties: clinical psychology, social work and psychiatry.* And when the characteristics have been developed, there must still be the necessary discriminative stimuli and incentives for exhibiting the characteristics in one's professional work. However, these cues and consequences tend to be minimal

* An exception may be the behavior analyst whose only applied work is training others in behavior analysis. His specialty might be considered to be behavior analysis alone. However, he may be likely to promote in his students the attitude that behavior analysis is all they need to know, which would perpetuate the problem presented in this paper.

among behavior analysts, probably as a natural outcome of the unique historical development of applied behavior analysis.

HISTORICAL ROOTS OF THE PROBLEM

Applied behavior analysis had its origins in the laboratory. Many basic principles describing how behavior is controlled, and numerous techniques for controlling behavior, were discovered and elaborated on laboratory research with lower animals and humans. These principles and techniques were then applied to changing more significant human behavior in non-laboratory settings.

This laboratory background has been a source of considerable strength to applied behavior analysis. First, it gives the behavior analyst a conceptual scheme (called learning theory or behavioral principles) that allows him to think of behavior and its causes in a much more valid way than his predecessors,* thus making it more likely that he will succeed in his attempts to engineer behavior (e.g., Allen et al., 1964; Williams, 1965; Haughton and Ayllon, 1965; Madsen et al., 1968; Hawkins and Hayes, in press). Second, the technology developed in the laboratory for engineering behavior often has proved directly applicable to significant human behavior so that the behavior analyst has ready-made tools for effecting behavior change. One of the more notable examples might be shaping, a technique that has been used to reestablish speech in psychotics who were mute for decades (Sherman, 1965); to develop sociability in a withdrawn nursery school child (Allen et al., 1964); to increase the volume of a shy sixth grader's speech (Schwarz and Hawkins, 1970); and to solve many other problems that had resisted change. A third advantage of having roots in the laboratory is that the behavior analyst tends to be optimistic about his

---

* The relativity of this statement should be noted. I do not believe we can say that the behavioral scheme *is valid* and others *not valid*. It is more likely the case that the behavioral principles discovered to date from experimental research in the laboratory constitute a very sizeable *improvement* in validity over other theoretical frameworks, at least in conceptualizing most behavior. This higher level of validity seems to be an outcome of a "natural science," a theoretical approach to the study of behavior (Skinner, 1954; Bijou and Baer, 1961; Bijou, 1963). Such an approach also appears to promise a continuously increasing validity of our understanding of "how behavior works," as opposed to a succession of fads in theory, treatment methods, and other educational methods.

ability to engineer behavior, being accustomed to having relatively complete control over the environment, and even the total experimental history, of his laboratory animal. Finally, the laboratory background results in the likelihood that the behavior analyst will objectively measure the dependent variables he is interested in. And, further, he is likely to carry out his environmental manipulations in a manner that allows him to verify whether or not these manipulations are really the cause of whatever behavioral changes occur (Baer, Wolf and Risley, 1968). This kind of empiricism and accountability promises to result in continuously improving behavioral technology (Risley, 1969) and constitutes a monumental improvement over the practices of others in the helping professions.

But the laboratory origins of applied behavior analysis may also have certain disadvantages. In most laboratory research the experimenter is interested in investigating the effects of certain environmental factors on behavior; not on a *certain* behavior, but just on "behavior." The particular response measured is selected not for its high social value, its facilitating of further learning, or its maladaptive character. The response is selected on the basis of its being easy to measure, easy to condition (in that particular species), and perhaps having the potential of occurring at a high rate. Thus the experimenter in the laboratory has a strong interest in particular independent variables but is less likely to have an interest in particular dependent variables. For example, Thorndike and others have studied the learning of nonsense syllables in humans; Hull and others have studied maze-running in rats; Skinner and others have studied bar-pressing in rats and key-pecking in pigeons. Even when human subjects are used, the response is likely to be something like marble dropping or lever pressing. Those responses are all selected largely for reasons of expediency rather than because of their significance to the species in its natural environment. This is as it should be, for only through such an approach has it been possible for us to learn so much about how behavior, in general, "works."

As behavior analysts left the laboratory to deal with significant human behavior, they brought their expertise with them. Their outstanding ability to manipulate relevant environmental variables has already resulted in remarkable achievements in a wide variety of endeavors involving human behavior. They might be characterized as experts on the independent variables involved in human behavior (or at least on a number of powerful ones). But it may be time for behavior analysts to consider their expertise on the dependent variables, and their ability to determine what behavior is needed by various learners in various settings.

When anyone in a human service profession decides to change a particular behavior it is, of course, because some person or some process has led him to that particular behavior as the target. But when that professional is a behavior analyst it is likely that he had little involvement in the process that determined what behavior was desirable and adaptive. For example, in offering training in behavior modification to groups of parents, a behavior analyst may take the attitude that it is solely the parents' responsibility to determine the behavioral goals for their child (Walder, Cohen and Daston, 1967). Such an attitude certainly makes the job of group training easier because the analyst can concentrate on behavioral theory or technology alone.

But it is important that behavior analysts at least appreciate the significance of Step 1 in the behavior change process, and realize the skill and humane considerations that are frequently involved. Would it be appropriate, for example, to offer training in behavior modification to an unselected group of prison guards who are then never monitored by the behavior analyst; or would the behavior analyst sense a certain lack of sophistication on the part of the guards in selecting appropriate behavioral objectives? Should the same question be raised regarding training mental hospital attendants who then go unmonitored? Even in the case of parents, who certainly have no systematic training for this very important job (Hawkins, 1971 and 1972; McIntire, 1973), behavior modification training might be questioned.

Certainly behavior analysts must at least recognize the limitations inherent in such programs as the group training of parents. Parents have little or no systematic training regarding either desirable behavioral objectives for their offspring or methods for achieving those objectives. When given training only in how to modify behavior, with no guidance whatever regarding slection of behavioral objectives (an infrequent approach, I suspect, because behavior analysts tend to be humanitarian, unlike the illusion conjured up by their detractors), it is likely that parents will select only obvious target behaviors that they find annoying or embarrassing. There is some support for this prediction in Berkowitz' and Graziano's (1972) observation that results from most parent-training programs in behavior modification emphasize the reduction of excessive behaviors (especially aggression, hyperactivity and disobedience) rather than the remediation of behavioral deficiencies.

The issue raised recently by Winett and Winkler (1972) is relevant here. Although teachers and school administrators have extensive training for their work (training that particularly emphasizes the philosophy and purposes of education), when given training in applied behavior analysis, they often apply their new technology only to the achievement of relatively trivial and perhaps even counterproductive objectives, such as sitting still, being quiet and being obedient to the teacher's every whim. As Winett and Winkler suggest, behavior analysts have a genuine responsibility in the process of selecting objectives, even in the context of a system that should be competent in selecting its own objectives wisely, with appropriate priorities.

PROBABLE IMPLICATIONS OF THE PRESENT ANALYSIS

So what am I advocating? A return to "the good old days" of psychological and psychiatric diagnoses? Of course not. We don't need the Rorschach, the TAT and the Bender-Gestalt. We don't need the assessments conducted in offices instead of the real world. We don't need the long descriptions of irrelevant personality traits, impulses, wishes, conflicts, anxieties, latent tendencies, hostile feelings, guilt feelings and the like, that somehow said nearly the same thing about everyone and never said what John Doe's problem was or what might be done about it. What I believe we do need is first to recognize our limitations, and then to work to see that we and those we train do become more competent and responsible regarding Step 1, (Setting of Behavioral Objectives) in the educational or therapeutic process. The means for achieving this can be found in our professional conduct as applied behavior analysts, in our training programs, in our research efforts, and in the content and format of our professional literature. These implications will be discussed in that order.

Professional conduct. The first implication I see for our professional conduct is that it probably is advisable for each applied behavior analyst to ally himself with one or more professional groups *besides* his fellow behavior analysts. That is, I suspect each of us should consider himself a school psychologist, clinical psychologist, special educator, speech pathologist, retardation expert, or the like. Like Horowitz (1973), I believe we should read other literature besides behavior analysis literature and listen to other people besides behavior analysts.

Behavior does not occur in the abstract, it comes from a particular person in a particular setting. If we isolate ourselves from consideration of the issues, awareness of the technology and knowledge of the values extant among the non-behavior analysts in the fields where we are doing our work, I think we limit our own individual development and limit the speed with which an empirical approach to planning and problem-solving will be accepted and adopted.

The second professional implication is more complex. It has to do with two different levels of responsibility in our professional work, one of which we often ignore. It is possible for a behavior analyst to be a kind of free-lance generalist, on occasion applying his conceptual skills and technological knowledge to a wide variety of setting-learner-behavior combinations. Many of us have had experience at serving as a consultant (or researcher) in some area that we know very little about, and some of us even get full-time jobs in such areas. Perhaps because we bring with us an empirically-based conception of human behavior that is so much more valid than other conceptions, and because we also have the empirical attitude and experimental skills to continue discovering further information about behavior, we have often managed to be of considerable value in these "foreign lands." But in these "foreign lands" we are typically valuable only in a reactive way. If someone else tells us what they see as the problem, we can sometimes react with ingenious solutions. But they must identify the problem; they know much better than we what behavior "should be" exhibited by the learner.

It is important that we recognize the two stages of responsibility involved here, and recognize further that we are accepting only one of them. There is the responsibility for Step 1, which is being carried by the on-site expert; and there is responsibility for Step 2, which is being carried by the behavior analyst. Once we have recognized the two responsibilities, we can attempt to assess the following three factors realistically:

1. The on-site expert's competence for Step 1, including his ethical values about what behavioral objectives are desirable.

2. Our own competence for Step 1.

3. The amount of responsibility we are willing to accept for Step 1.

After deciding on the responsibilities an analyst has the competence for, and which ones he is willing to accept, there is the obligation to assure that all other parties have approximately the same view of each person's responsibilities. Typically this can be done by simply making it clear what aspects of these steps we are addressing ourselves to, and reminding others about what aspects are still their responsibilities. For example, in a parent training group one might point out to parents that neither the child nor his natural environment will be observed, and thus that sensitive observation and priority-setting by the parents (and perhaps the child) will be the primary means of accomplishing Step 1. The behavior analyst could then point out that he will make some general suggestions to guide the parents, such as the suggestion that they consider whether their expectations are reasonable or the suggestion that they look for skill deficits as well as behavioral excesses; and he will occasionally try to raise pertinent questions about their goals (or, better, encourage other parents to raise them), but also realize that most of the responsibility for setting goals will continue to be theirs.

TRAINING

Admissions. It is my subjective impression that many of the best behavior analysts (most responsible, most effective in the applied setting, and possibly most likely to do significant applied research) coming out of our program at Western Michigan University are people who had previous training in some area other than applied behavior analysis, be it speech pathology, clinical psychology, early education, social work, or one of the many other human-service disciplines. These people have often already acquired the four characteristics indicated above as important in assessment of behavior, though much of their knowledge about what behavior is desirable can be improved in objectivity and precision. And those with clinical psychology, counseling, and social

205

work backgrounds usually have a great quantity of vague, misleading and erroneous concepts about behavior that they have to sort through and largely discard (but they still tend to have characteristics 1, 2, and 4). We should probably continue to encourage people with strong backgrounds in these other disciplines to bring their expertise with them, evaluate it in the light of the natural science concepts they learn with us, and add our behavioral engineering technology to their expertise.

Program content. An alternate way of phrasing the main thrust of the argument in this paper is to say that training in behavior analysis is not enough. One does not analyze or engineer behavior in the abstract, there is always a *setting*, a *learner*, and a certain *behavior*. Various combinations of setting, learner and behavior constitute the basis for the various human service professions and certain academic disciplines, such as physical therapy, counseling, elementary education, human development, speech pathology and therapy, community psychiatry, family therapy, school psychology, psychiatric social work, or blind rehabilitation. Each discipline implies certain settings, learners with certain characteristics, and focusing on certain kinds of behavior (though some discipline titles are much more definitive than others).

It is questionable whether there ever should be a program that claims to train people in applied behavior analysis alone; because either that leaves the trainee with no expertise for work in a particular setting with a particular type of subject or particular kinds of behavior, or else it attempts to train him as a behavior analysis generalist, who knows something about several (certainly not nearly all) settings, types of subjects, and kinds of behavior, but does not know much about any of them. In addition, he does not seem to acquire the needed sense of responsibility (characteristics 1 and 2, above) or the sensitive observing skills (characteristic 4) necessary for identifying behavioral objectives. As a final product, he is likely to be deficient in all four of the above characteristics.*

What are the alternatives? A few are obvious. First, the training in applied behavior analysis can take place wholly within a depart-

---

* To a large extent, this is probably what Horowitz (1973) was saying in her plea for less isolation of behavior analysis from other disciplines. Krantz' (1971) article on the isolation of operant conditioners is also relevant, but was not as oriented toward issues of an applied nature.

ment organized around a particular discipline. Of course many training programs believe they are accomplishing this when they have their token behavior modifier who teaches one or two courses in behavior modification and then sends the student on to others who teach him an eclectic potpourri of sense and nonsense. But there are programs seriously working at adopting a behavior analysis view throughout, yet without discarding the valid (or at least reasonable) knowledge and skills already available in their discipline.*

Second, a department as a whole can have a behavior analysis orientation and have within it two or more programs of training oriented toward particular types of setting-learner-behavior combinations. For example, a behavior analysis psychology department might have within it a school psychology program, a retardation program, and a community psychology program. Of course the four characteristics of a professional who is competent in assessment, listed earlier, will be developed in the trainees only if such training is taken seriously, and in a field as inclusive as community psychology, particularly, this would be a substantial task.

Finally, a department offering excellent training in behavior analysis, but having too few resources to also offer good training in certain disciplines where the behavior analysis knowledge might be applied, could arrange a joint training program with another department. For example, a joint program of parenthood education might be arranged between a psychology department and a department of child development, or a joint program in aging might be arranged between two or three departments.

Research. It is often asserted that behavior modification or behavior analysis does not tell us *what* behavior to modify, but only how to modify it. Unfortunately, this may imply to many people that behavior analysis *cannot* tell us what behaviors are desirable. This appears questionable. For example, take Ayllon's and Azrin's (1968) "relevance of behavior rule," which states that one should teach behavior that will be functional for the individual after he leaves the institution, school, clinic, or other formal training situation. While this is simply a logical

---

* The Special Education Department at California State College, California, Pennsylvania, uses this approach.

207

assertion on the part of these two behavior analysts, and perhaps not an empirically verified fact, experimental analyses could readily be conducted to verify that assertion. One could experimentally determine what specific behaviors were highly relevant in the natural environment and what their function was, with the result that the setting of behavioral objectives in educational and therapeutic programs would be based on an experimental analysis rather than on educational, mental health, and management theory or guesswork. At that point behavior analysis would certainly be telling us *what* behavior should be learned, not just how it can be learned.

This may seem like a monumental task, but if we look carefully we find that many of our studies already have told us much about what behaviors parents, teachers and therapists should *not* emit (e.g., Harris et al., 1964; Williams, 1965; Allen and Harris, 1966; Madsen et al., 1968; Hawkins and Hayes, in press) and even more about behavior that they can emit to increase their effectiveness. What we are almost totally lacking is empirical data on what these parents, teachers, and therapists should be teaching their children, students and clients. But such data can and should be obtained.

Several other kinds of research related to setting behavioral objectives are probably needed. One kind has to do with the interrelationship between various responses. An example of this type is a study by Sajwaj, Twardosz, and Burke (1972), in which they monitored several different behaviors while modifying one. They discovered that responses one would expect to be unrelated actually were functionally related, which might suggest that we should not be as confident as we typically are about the likely or unlikely side effects of our interventions. A second example is a study by Nordquist (1971), in which he showed that eliminating the oppositional behavior of a child during the day resulted also in elimination of bedwetting at night. It is possible that with many children who are enuretic, the bedwetting is simply one form of oppositional behavior (a result that, if true, would surprise few non-operant clinicians). But much more research would be required before any such conclusion could be drawn, and even then it would be helpful to obtain the actuarial data that would permit prediction of the treatment's success based on that hypothesis.

This suggests a second type of research on the dependent variables of applied behavior analysis. Some behavior-change efforts are very expensive, and as cost-effectiveness analyses become more common over the next few decades, it will become more important for us to be able to predict the effectiveness of proposed programs. But reasonably accurate prediction is only possible if one has discovered predictor variables that correlate highly with outcomes from the type of behavior-change program proposed. Thus, in order to set behavioral objectives and priorities realistically, it will be helpful to state the probability of our success, given a particular budget and time frame. This requires extensive correlational research.

As a third type of research, we need normative studies like that of Johnson et al. (1973) which will allow us to objectively answer such seemingly simple questions as "How many eight-year-old boys still wet their beds two or more times per month?" And thus, should a boy's parents be upset that he wets his bed twice a month? "What conversational behaviors tend to keep people interested in talking with someone?" And thus, perhaps, what might I teach a withdrawn, depressed person; or what behavior might I assess for and teach school children? Or, "How frequently do adults use algebraic concepts or procedures in their daily lives?" And thus, how important is it to teach algebra to all school children? In the absence of data, such questions continue to be answered by hypothesis and simple assertion, sometimes at considerable financial or human expense.

The final type of research needed on the dependent variables is the experimental study of prerequisite skills. This would be an experimental analysis of the efficiency of a person's learning skill H when skills E, F, and G, which logically appear to be prerequisites to H, have not been learned. Through this and related types of studies we not only discover much about which sequence of learning will be most efficient but also about the nature and function of some skills that we do not understand very well.

Professional literature. Comparison of the contents of the *Journal of Applied Behavior Analysis* (*JABA*) with the contents of other behavioral journals dealing with applied work suggests that the other journals devote more space to problems involved in Step 1 of the educational model presented on page 197. In particular, the other journals contain a modest number of articles presenting possible conceptual analyses and assessment tools that have been found useful in determining the nature of a particular type of problem. For example, Hersen (1973) presents a critical review of several measures of fearfulness and the research relating to them; Carter and Thomas (1973) present an interesting system for determining the specific deficits and excesses in the interaction between a husband and wife; and Holland (1970) presents an outline useful in interviewing parents of children with adjustment problems. It might be argued that any one of these articles would be of interest to only a small fraction of the readers of *JABA*. This may be true, but it may be as much a limitation in the nature of *JABA* as it is in the nature of the articles.

JABA is a general journal presenting developments in work with the retarded in institutions, work with parents of essentially normal children, work with speech problems of cleft palate children, work with adults who are out of jobs, work with institutionalized psychotics, work with teachers in general education, and an unlimited number of other possibilities. This kind of journal is needed because methods developed in one field of application are often at least partially generalizable to other fields; but it appears that such a journal inevitably encourages primary interest in independent variables, as though behavior occurred in the abstract. In addition to developing greater expertise with independent variables, behavior analysts need to be encouraged to conduct research oriented toward better understanding of dependent variables (as suggested above), to develop tools for assessing behavioral needs (including tests, which are simply planned, standard, stimulus situations), and to raise ethical, professional and programmatic issues regarding work in a particular type of setting or with a particular type of population. This calls for special interest journals, and I propose that any further journals established by behavior analysts be of this type.*

---

* There is considerable validity in arguing instead for behavior analysts publishing in existing special interest journals. This could help to interest others in a more empirical approach to their area of interest, and it would certainly increase the behavior analyst's exposure to the research, thought, and other activities of non-operant professionals—an outcome which many of us, in our less arrogant moments, admit would improve our own competence.

SUMMARY

It has often been asserted that behavior analysis is a conceptual framework and a technology that tells us much about how behavior is learned and how it can be taught, but little about *what* behavior should be learned. While it may be true that behavior *analysis* tells us little about what should be taught, this does not mean that the behavior *analyst* has no responsibility regarding the issue of what should be taught.

Four steps involved in all education and therapy were outlined, the first having to do with determining what behaviors are needed, and the other three having to do with the planning, implementation and evaluation of behavior change procedures. It was suggested that applied behavior analysts, perhaps because of the laboratory origins of their approach to problems, have often ignored the processes and issues involved in setting behavioral objectives and accepted no responsibility for them. While this is an appropriate mode of professional conduct in some contexts, it was suggested that the behavior analyst at least has the obligation to recognize the limits he is setting on his responsibilities and to be sure that others recognize and accept them.

Suggestions were also made regarding how behavior analysts, as a group, can come to be more knowledgeable, skilled, and responsible in Step 1 of the educational or therapeutic process. These suggestions dealt with our professional identification, our training programs, our research, and our professional literature.

To the extent that behavior analysts limit their responsibility and interest to independent variables, they open themselves to criticism of irresponsibility and superficiality. While the kind of preoccupation with "diagnosis" that has characterized much educational and therapeutic endeavor would not be a healthy change (and is unlikely in any group that has a powerful technology for changing behavior and the methodology for continuously improving that technology), a greater interest in this aspect of our work appears to be needed.

REFERENCES

Allen, K. E. and Harris, F. R. Elimination of a child's excessive scratching by training the mother in reinforcement procedures. *Behavior Research and Therapy*, 1966, *4*, 79-84.

Allen, K. E., Hart, B. M., Buell, J. C., Harris, F. R., and Wolf, M. M. Effects of social reinforcement on isolate behavior of a nursery school child. *Child Development,* 1964, *35,* 511-518.

Ayllon, T. and Azrin, N. *The token economy: A motivational system for therapy and rehabilitation.* New York: Appleton-Century-Crofts, 1968.

Baer, D. M., Wolf, M. M., and Risley, T. R. Some current dimensions of applied behavior analysis. *Journal of Applied Behavior Analysis,* 1968, *1,* 91-97.

Berkowitz, B. P. and Graziano, A. M. Training parents as behavior therapists: A review. *Behavior Research and Therapy,* 1972, *10,* 297-317.

Bijou, S. W. and Baer, D. M. *Child development: A systematic and empirical theory.* New York: Appleton-Century-Crofts, 1961.

Bijou, S. W. Theory and research in mental (developmental) retardation. *The Psychological Record,* 1963, *13,* 95-110.

Carter, R. D. and Thomas, E. J. Modification of problematic marital communication using corrective feedback and instruction. *Behavior Therapy,* 1973, *4,* 100-109.

Harris, F. R., Johnston, M. K., Kelly, C. S., and Wolf, M. M. Effects of positive social reinforcement on regressed crawling of a nursery school child. *Journal of Educational Psychology,* 1964, *55,* 35-41.

Haughton, E. and Ayllon, T. Production and elimination of symptomatic behavior. In L. P. Ullmann and L. Krasner (ed.), *Case studies in behavior modification.* New York: Holt, Rinehart and Winston, 1965.

Hawkins, R. P. It's time we taught the young how to be good parents (And don't you wish we'd started a long time ago?). *Psychology Today,* 1972, *6,* 28ff.

Hawkins, R. P. Universal parenthood training: A laboratory approach for teaching every parent how to rear children. *Educational Technology,* 1971, *11,* 28-31.

Hawkins, R. P. and Hayes, J. E. The School Adjustment Program: A model program for treatment of severely maladjusted children in the public schools. In R. Ulrich, T. Stachnik, and J. Mabry (eds.), *Control of human behavior: Behavior modification in education. Vol. III.* Glenview, IL: Scott, Foresman, 1974.

Hersen, M. Self-assessment of fear. *Behavior Therapy,* 1973, *4,* 241-257.

Holland, C. J. An interview guide for behavioral counseling with parents. *Behavior Therapy*, 1970, *1*, 70-79.

Horowitz, F. D. Living among the ABA's: Retrospect and prospect. Paper presented at 4th annual Conference on Behavior Analysis in Education, Lawrence, KS, April-May, 1973.

Johnson, S. M., Wahl, G., Martin, S., and Johansson, S. How deviant is the normal child? A behavioral analysis of the preschool child and his family. In Rubin, Brady and Henderson (eds.), *Advances in behavior therapy. Vol. 4*. New York: Academic Press, 1973.

Kanfer, F. H. and Saslow, G. Behavioral diagnosis. In C. M. Franks (Ed.) *Behavior therapy: Appraisal and status*. New York: McGraw-Hill, 1969.

Krantz, D. L. The separate worlds of operant and non-operant psychology. *Journal of Applied Behavior Analysis*, 1971, *4*, 61-70.

Madsen, C. M., Becker, W. C., Thomas, D. R., Koser, L., and Plager, E. An analysis of the reinforcing function of "Sit down" commands. In R. K. Parker (ed.), *Readings in educational psychology*. Boston: Allyn & Bacon, 1968.

McIntire, R. W. Parenthood training or mandatory birth control: Take your choice. *Psychology Today*, 1973, *7*, 34ff.

Nordquist, V. M. The modification of a child's enuresis: Some response-response relationships. *Journal of Applied Behavior Analysis*, 1971, *4*, 241-247.

Risley, T. R. Behavior modification: An experimental-therapeutic endeavor. Presented at Banff Conference on Behavior Modification, Banff, Alberta, Canada, March 1969.

Sajwaj, T., Twardosz, S., and Burke, M. Side effects of extinction procedures in a remedial preschool. *Journal of Applied Behavior Analysis*, 1972, *5*, 163-175.

Schwarz, M. L. and Hawkins, R. P. Application of delayed reinforcement procedures to the behavior problems of an elementary school child. *Journal of Applied Behavior Analysis*, 1970, *3*, 85-96.

Sherman, J. A. Use of reinforcement and imitation to reinstate verbal behavior in mute psychotics. *Journal of Abnormal Psychology*, 1965, *70*, 155-164.

Skinner, B. F. *Science and human behavior*. New York: Macmillan and Company, 1953.

Walder, L. O., Cohen, S. I., and Daston, P. G. Teaching parents and others principles of behavior control for modifying the behavior of children. Progress report, U. S. Office of Education, 32-31-7515-5024.

Williams, C. D. The elimination of tantrum behavior by extinction procedures. *Journal of Abnormal and Social Psychology,* 1959, *59,* 269.

Winett, R. A. and Winkler, R. C. Current behavior modification in the classroom: Be still, be quiet, be docile. *Journal of Applied Behavior Analysis,* 1972, *5,* 499-504.

RESPONSE
Jayme S. Whitehead

I readily agree with Dr. Hawkins' identification of an important deficit which may exist in many of the professional training programs for applied behavior analysts. Behavior analysts may not be receiving systematic training in "taking the responsibility" for selecting or even examining the behavioral objectives of educational or therapeutic projects to insure that they are justifiable, as well as ethically and legally acceptable, through relevant research findings in behavior analysis or other fields of study. Dr. Hawkins also emphasized the historical roots of this problem by tracing applied behavior analysis to its laboratory origins and the interest in independent, not dependent, variables. But it should be pointed out that our professional community may be maintaining this emphasis on independent variables. Currently, professional prestige is likely to be assigned to our colleagues based primarily on their methodological or technological expertise. Emphasis on methodology is potentially dangerous to behavior analysis, however, because it narrows our definition of what constitutes a competent behavior analyst; it also influences the direction of our professional training programs.

It is becoming increasingly important for us to train behavior analysts who are both willing and capable of taking the responsibility for selecting behavioral objectives that are based on a knowledge of behavior analysis and other related fields of study. The importance of this training is more obvious now than ever before because of two major changes that are occurring in the field of applied behavior analysis (Miller and Lies, 1974). First, the populations that behavior analysts work with have shifted from being exclusively populations with pro-

215

found and easily identified behavioral deficits, populations such as the developmentally disabled or the severely emotionally disturbed, to include populations for which desirable objectives are less obvious and more difficult to specify or sequence. The second change in the field involves a shift from being primarily a reactive, problem-solving applied discipline to a discipline involved in program design in a wide variety of non-problem areas. Miller's and Feallock's (1973) work in the development of an experimental, group-living program for college students provides an excellent example of this. No longer is it the case that a behavior analyst is called in only when there is a "crisis" or a problem situation with a readily identifiable objective for intervention procedures. These extensions of our applied work to new populations, new settings, and new situations are making the difficulties involved in the determination of behavioral objectives, and the need for a broader background in other related fields of study, more clearly recognizable.

Another area of change that is occurring in our society, and which has direct relevance for the applied analysis of behavior, is the increased expectation and, in fact, legally supported demand for adequate and accountable educational or therapeutic programming that does not violate the basic human rights of the person institutionalized or seeking psychological treatment. This situation is resulting in the formulation of new ethical and legal guidelines for behavioral programming, another area in which our professional training programs may not be providing satisfactory training. An increased emphasis in training programs on the ethical and legal requirements in the selection of behavioral objectives for educational or therapeutic programming is definitely needed.

While I agree completely with Dr. Hawkins' identification of the problem, I cannot agree with his suggested solution, his call for training in a specialized field in conjunction with any training in the applied analysis of behavior. I firmly believe that the deficits mentioned above can easily be remedied in our current training programs. I do not see training in a specialized field as a prerequisite to expertise in the specification of behavioral objectives. The next step would be to examine closely the role of our professional environment in encouraging the individual behavior analyst to take the responsibilities which Dr. Hawkins is urging. We may find that we want to be more careful in making our professional reinforcers, like prestige, financial gain and publications (Wood, page 23), contingent upon demonstration of expertise in all four of the phases which Dr. Hawkins describes as representing the behavior analysis model.

The last point I would like to discuss is Dr. Hawkins' statement:

> It is questionable whether there should be a program that claims to train people in applied behavior analysis alone. . . or else attempts to train him as a behavior analyst generalist, who knows something about several (certainly, not nearly all) settings, types of subjects, and kinds of behavior, but does not know much about any of them. . . . (The behavior analyst generalist) does not seem to acquire the needed sense of responsibility. . . . As a final product, he is likely to be deficit in all four of the above characteristics.

These are strong statements which are based on Dr. Hawkins' impressions, not data. I would suggest that the effectiveness and contribution of graduates from various applied analysis of behavior training programs should be determined before making any assumptions about the efficacy of alternative training approaches.

Here at Drake we are developing a questionnaire to look at this issue for the graduates of our applied analysis of behavior program, a program which would fit the model described by Dr. Hawkins as a training program for behavior analyst generalists. The questionnaire will ask, quite specifically, what our graduates are doing and how effectively they are doing it. I do not think that Dr. Hawkins really expects to find that behavior analyst generalists are truly as ineffective or as deficit in skills as his statement above implies. In fact, Dr. Hawkins states earlier in his paper that behavior analysts with no specialized training in other fields have, in the past, been of "considerable value" in areas in which they were not expert because they brought with them "an empirically based conception of human behavior which is so much more valid than other conceptions. . . and the empirical attitudes and experimental skills to continue discovering further information about behavior."

In addition to obtaining data on the effectiveness of current professional training programs, I think we should also look very closely at the possible implications which specialization might have for the field of applied behavior analysis. We would probably want to know first whether or not current practitioners in the field identify with or specialize in certain areas. Are those who specialize more effective in their positions than those who do not? Do those who specialize contribute more to the field of behavior analysis in terms of research, training, or applications? Is the specialist or the generalist more likely to make significant contributions to society?

If we were considering specialization, we would also want to know how that training would affect the "employability" of the graduates, either directly after graduation or later in their careers. For instance, what would happen to the behavior analyst specialist when the agency which employs him begins to work with new populations or in new situations? Could he continue to work effectively in his position? Certainly our professional training programs have a responsibility to train behavior analysts so that they will be able to find and hold positions. It should also be mentioned that it is important for us to begin identifying service agency and consumer "needs" which our graduates will be filling, a recommendation from the Vail Conference, and to train behavior analysts to be effective in these areas.

Based on our experience with Drake's master's degree candidates, I think we will find that professional behavior analysts are employed as program designers and program administrators, not as direct treatment personnel. Therefore, perhaps we should be thinking more in terms of training not in specialized treatment areas as Dr. Hawkins recommends, but more in terms of strengthening our training programs in the areas mentioned above, by providing more background in public and business administration, in the organization of state and federal social service agencies, and in systems analysis, accountability and cost-effectiveness models. I think that we may find that these additions may be more crucial in strengthening the field of applied behavior analysis and increasing its contributions to society than specialization in our professional training.

REFERENCES

Miller, L. K. and Feallock, R. A behavioral system for group living. In E. Ramp and G. Semb (eds.), *Behavior Analysis in Education.* New York: Appleton-Century-Croft, 1973.

Miller, L. K. and Lies, A. A. Everyday behavior analysis: A new direction for applied behavior analysis. *The Behavioral Voice*, 1974, *2*, 1.

ACCOUNTABILITY FOR BEHAVIORAL ENGINEERS
Jon E. Krapfl

Accountability is more hope and promise than it is contemporary fact. In trying to articulate an accountable position for behavioral engineers, I will not describe current conditions, but conditions that are likely to develop. There can be no question that the demand for accountability will continue to grow. People are becoming as unhappy with the quality of services provided as they are with the quality of products produced. A more educated population is not so easily fooled or mollified as a less sophisticated one. There was a time, not long ago, when it seemed sufficient to "be of good cheer," but those days are rapidly passing. Still, the ultimate aim of accountability, to produce social good at low cost, will probably continue to elude us for some time since we have serious difficulties in defining "social good." In the near future we are more likely to develop accountability models which evaluate intermediate effects, assumed to be related to the ultimate production of social good. For example, we may be held accountable for securing a discharge from a mental hospital for a person when we do not know whether or not he is really better off outside of the institution.

Yet this intermediate form of accountability seems desirable in relationship to the current situation where many undesirable practices are tolerated. While we may have some difficulty identifying which results ought to be produced, we can at least determine whether or not the promised results are delivered. Further, it is likely that a strong accountability will tolerate less politicalization and corruption in the human services area than currently exists. The vaguer our standards, the more likely they can be violated for personal or political gain.

The process of developing accountable models for human service professions will be a gradual one. It will require new behaviors for those conducting the review as well as for those providing services. Clearly the less than ideal conditions of political influence and toleration of bad practices, which currently exist, will continue for some time, although they will dissipate as accountable practices develop.

The point of this initial statement is that the implementation of a sophisticated accountability model is not just around the corner. We have started in this direction, but the demand for accountable practices will grow, and the reality of the immediate future will still tolerate some poor practices and poor review of those practices.

There are three basic objectives for this paper: (1) to understand the meaning of the term "accountability" for our profession; (2) to show how we are currently confused about our status as an accountable discipline; (3) to suggest possible remedies.

In order to appreciate my perspective on the overall current status of the field, I should like to draw an analogy between behavior analysis and coal-gasification. My reason for choosing this unusual or unseemly analogy is that the two seem to be in approximately the same stage of development. As you know, the current gasoline shortage has resulted in considerable public demand for fuel. One of the potential sources of that fuel is coal. Furthermore, the technology is already available for gasification of coal, and coal-gasification research centers have developed or are being developed throughout the nation.

This, of course, is similar to our own position. There is a heavy demand for effective human services. We have already available a technology to provide many of those services, and there are behavioral centers opening all over the country. All analogies break down if pushed too far, but one more analogous point needs to be raised. Virtually none of our current gas needs are being met through coal-gasification. The reason is that we currently lack the skill to produce gas from coal on a sufficiently large scale or in a cost-effective manner. These conditions precisely characterize our own field. Given that we are a very young profession, not yet rigid in our professional roles, and

220

given that accountability will eventually be demanded of us, I would like to devote the paper to an analysis of the following points:

1. Accountability principally defines our relationship to our culture, not to other members of our profession. It is important, then, for us to consider our relationship to the culture. Some behaviorists think they already do but, I submit, they usually do not.

2. Accountability, when viewed from a behavioral perspective, provides a functional account which more clearly explicates the relationship between the person held accountable and the person conducting the review.

3. A behavioral view of accountability for our field requires a distinction between those operants referred to as behavior analysis and those referred to as behavioral engineering.

4. The behavioral engineer can take steps to make himself more accountable.

THE ACCOUNTABILITY RELATIONSHIP TO THE CULTURE

Applied behavior analysts are referred to in many terms that are less than desirable; mechanical, nonhumanistic, narrow, and arrogant are common examples. Some of the name-calling may be deserved (e.g., narrow or arrogant), but others seem decidedly less appropriate (e.g., mechanical, nonhumanistic). However, the applied behavior analyst has been bothered very little by the attachment of these labels to him or to his practices.

Recently a far more serious charge has been lodged against applied behavioral practices. Wexler (1973, pp. 19-21) has referred to us as relatively ineffective. That such a charge could ever be made is startling to behavior analysts. After all, we are always supported by "the data." When behavior analysts make decisions, design, implement, or evaluate intervention programs, they always do so on the basis of data, don't they? Furthermore, other applied psychologists, though supposedly trained as scientists and evaluators, expend most of their efforts on process rather than on outcome evaluations so that, in comparison, the behavior analyst should look good, shouldn't he?

It seems that Wexler's arguments should be wrong for two principle reasons. First, relative to other human intervention specialists, the behaviorists are the "most hard nosed," and the most concerned about "proving" their effectiveness. Second, behavior analysts put themselves under the control of the data, and should thus be protected by a built-in corrective feedback procedure. If we are not succeeding, the data will inform us.

How is it possible, then, for Wexler to compare us unfavorably with another intervention specialist? The answer to this question is not simple and should not be dealt with trivially through the employment of a verbal expletive as we sometimes do. However, much of Wexler's argument can and should stand as an ominous warning to our profession. Currently, we spend little time analyzing our own professional behaviors, their variables, or the effects they produce. Consequently, we are sometimes vague, sometimes mistaken about the relevance, importance, or correctness of certain practices. Failure to undertake and to act upon the necessary self analysis may result in a limitation of our contribution to the culture and a consequent, and deserved, setback to our profession.

No one disagrees with the validity of the data which we are currently gathering. We are not being challenged in the sense that people find our studies poorly designed or our results illusory. If I may revert again to the coal-gasification analogy, an important distinction must be drawn between the capability to do something and actually doing it on a reasonably large scale with reasonably low costs. We can change behavior in a variety of socially relevant settings, but can we do it outside the guise of a demonstration or research project with their extra rich staff and monetary ratios? Further, are we changing the behaviors which are important for the culture? Accountability to the culture has nothing to do with the correctness of our experimental designs, reversals, multiple-baselines, or correct statistical analyses. It has only to do with the extent of positive impact on the culture. Of course research has a great deal to do with the extent of the profession's impact, but it is only the impact which has importance for the culture, not the research through which the impact was developed.

222

WHAT IS ACCOUNTABILITY?

I would like to turn now to a discussion of the nature of accountability, a process which calls for a review of the results which have been promised by a profession or bureaucracy. As defined by Lessinger (1971), this review must be independent, continuous, and publicly reported. Further, those responsible for the review must be outside of the profession or bureaucracy which conducts the activities.

There are several noteworthy features of this definition. First, the results are reviewed, not the practices. The outcome is of special interest, not how it was achieved. (This is not entirely true, of course, since violations of certain ethical or social standards clearly can result in the imposition of controls from outside the profession. Behavior modifiers have had some special problems in this regard, but they are solvable and, in the long run, are not likely to be as critical to the field as the results we produce.)

But it is these results which are evaluated in the accountability process. Further, the definition calls for these results to be specified in advance by the professional(s) involved. Recognition of the "promise" in "promised results" is important because it implies that the human interventionist will be held accountable on two occasions during the intervention process. The first occasion is an analysis of the promised results prior to intervention. At that time, the reviewing body must be convinced of the efficacy or worth of the promised results, and must be convinced that those results will be worth the expenditures of time and money required to achieve them. The second occasion for review is the comparison of quantitative and qualitative features of the promised results with those actually produced.

There are other critical elements in the definition of accountability. Again, the review must be independent, and must be conducted by someone outside of the profession or bureaucracy reviewed. Thus, the review calls for an open system in which the review is conducted by others, not a closed system in which the profession or bureaucracy reviews itself. This has critical implications for what is labelled a "successful result," since the profession no longer retains sole definining rights.

That the review must be continuous poses no major difficulties. All that is implied here is that professionals are not held accountable for the development of principles or abstract proofs, but for the production of specific outputs under specific circumstances. Thus accountability does not apply to the demonstration or proof that a law or principle such as reinforcement works, or to the fact that social approval used in a specifically contingent manner usually produces certain desirable effects on some behaviors. Rather, it is concerned with the fact that specific effects were attained in specific instances, irrespective of the principles, laws, methods, etc., which were used to produce them.

Finally, the results must be publicly reported. Thus, accountability is a term which implies responsibility, ultimately, to the public, though the extent to which they must be involved directly in the evaluation remains unclear.

A BEHAVIORAL VIEW OF ACCOUNTABILITY

The act of reviewing the results produced by others is itself a behavior and can, therefore, be subjected to a behavioral or contingency analysis. Such an analysis might prove useful in establishing accountable practices within the field. Therefore, I should like to view the problem of accountability from a behavioral perspective, and then discuss the implications of that view for current practices.

To say that we are going to hold a behavior modifier accountable for the results of his professional activities is to reflect a set of contingencies which hold between the production of a certain set of outcomes and the consequences provided for those outcomes by reviewers. Through the identification of the contingencies governing the reviewer's behavior it might be possible to predict what sort of controlling stimuli he is likely to provide and for what behavior.

Assuming that a system can be arranged in such a way that it is unnecessary to deal with serious instances of graft and corruption (an assumption which admittedly flies in the face of current data, at least at the highest levels of government), we can probably safely say that at least the following features will characterize the behavior of the reviewer.

Since the bulk of human intervention services are offered directly by governmental agencies or through their support systems, the reviewer will be a public representative, often a public employee. Assuming that he, too, will be held accountable for his reviewing activities, the reviewer's judgments will be influenced by the three following specifications, though there may be many more.

First, he will judge according to directives, guidelines and priorities established by the governmental or public agency he represents. Second, he will judge according to the greatest amount of good for the least cost which will accrue to the public or to that segment of the public which he represents. Third, and unfortunately, his judgments will be favorably influenced by events which are found to be most striking and most pleasing to the public rather than to the direct beneficiary of services.

Of course, none of these judgments is necessarily incompatible with each other. Under ideal circumstances all would be precisely the same. Each of them relates to the consequences which are likely to be provided for performing the reviewing task. These three controlling specifications are not exhaustive nor will any one of them necessarily be among the primary considerations involved in a judgment by a reviewer. Rather, they are examples, highly probable ones, that must be considered later when reviewing the interlocking features of the reviewer-behavior modifier relationship.

The contingencies governing the professional behaviors of the behavior modifiers also require some specification. If we look at the controlling relations specified in the definition of accountability, we can see that the behavior modifier is reinforced for producing results. Further, these results are not selected solely by him. They require the approval of a reviewer in an accountability relationship. Therefore, the selection of behaviors for change is partially under reviewer control. Further, the behavior modifier will be concerned either with the delivery of the best outcome for available resources or with the achievement of an outcome for the smallest expenditure of resources. The behavior modifier is less concerned with the precise identification of variables that produce an outcome in a particular instance than in achieving a successful result in that instance.

In addition, there are clear reciprocal effects in the relationship between reviewer and intervener. The reviewer or those who support him can be conceptualized as the controller, while the behavior modifier is controlled in this relationship. But, as in all controlling relationships, the controlling effects are exerted in both directions. The behavior modifier is likely to influence the reviewer in his selection of criteria to measure success as well as in the selection of the measurement system itself, just as the reviewer is likely to influence the behavior modifier's conception of a "successful program." Further, just as the behavior modifier may be influenced by the public's notions of good effects, so he will influence the public's conceptualization.

IMPLICATION OF
A BEHAVIORAL VIEW OF ACCOUNTABILITY

But do the activities just described characterize behavior analysts as we currently know them? No! They do not! A detailed analysis of the likely effects of the introduction of an accountability model leads both logically and behaviorally to the requirement that we draw a distinction between the practices of a behavioral engineer and those of a behavior analyst.

Some of you will find this upsetting. You bring to this situation a scientific heritage, a respect for data, and a belief that scientific principles are a requirement for an orderly explanation of human behavior and you are, in fact, the personification of the Boulder Model of Clinical Training, the scientist professional model that clinical psychology never achieved except on paper. But, I would ask that you hear me through. Any individual may be either behavioral engineer or behavior analyst, or both simultaneously, depending upon his behaviors and the consequences maintaining them at any moment in time. These categories are no more mutually exclusive than are those distinctions drawn between experimental and applied behavior analysts. Further, the relationship between behavioral engineering practices and applied behavior analytic practices is likely to be closer than that between the applied and the experimental behavior analyst.

Behavior analysts and behavioral engineers have much in common. The notion of control is implicit in the activities of both, as is a predisposition to look to the environment for controlling conditions. Selecting a dependent variable to be measured and accounting for change through the manipulation of observable independent variables is an inherent part of a functional analysis. Since there are only infrequent instances in which we can achieve effective control without data, it also follows that both groups will have great respect for data, and will design programs which will generate data upon which reasonable judgments can be made.

The importance of the relationship between behavior analysts and behavioral engineering can be seen in this reliance on a functional analysis to achieve control. While the demonstration of the effect of one variable on another is the cardinal feature of behavior analysis, the incorporation of these scientific advances into the applied technology assures greater practical impact (Skinner, 1953, p. 207). Thus, while the impact of the behavioral engineers provides the justification for the existence of the behavior analyst, improvements in the effectiveness of the behavioral engineer are, in turn, largely influenced by continuing analytic research of behavior.

Further, both behavior analyst and behavioral engineer show an interest in objectivity, not so much in shared rules or procedure, but objectivity as defined by Sidman (1960, p. 43) which consists principally in the self-corrective nature of the scientific process. We try to arrange an evaluation of our activities in order to minimize the effects of personal whim on our judgment.

While there are many shared characteristics, there are also distinctions which must be drawn between behavioral engineers and behavior analysts. Actually some of these distinctions were anticipated some time ago by Skinner (1961) and Sidman (1960). Skinner's article, The Design of Culture (1961), suggests a major reason for a distinction between analyst (scientist) and engineer (social technologist):

> The scientist is usually concerned with the control of nature apart from his personal aggrandizement. He is perhaps not wholly "pure," but he seeks control mainly for its own sake or for the sake of furthering other scientific activity. There are practical as well as ethical reasons for this: as technology becomes more complex, for example, the scientist himself is less and less able to pursue the practical implications of his work. There is very little personal reimbursement for the most profitable ideas of modern science. As a result, a new idea may yield immediate technological improvements without bringing the scientist under suspicion of plotting a personal coup. But social technology has not yet reached this stage. A disinterested consideration of cultural practices from which suggestions for improvement may emerge is still often regarded as impossible. This is the price we pay for the fact that men (1) have so often improved their control of other men for purposes of exploitation, (2) have had to bolster their social practices with spurious justifications and (3) have so seldom shared the attitudes of the basic scientist.

Sidman (1960) points out that behavioral engineers must deal with variability in a way which differs from that of the behavior analyst. On the one hand, the behavior analyst's function is to track down sources of variability, thus explaining variable data; but the behavioral engineer must take variability as he finds it, eliminate it if he can, or make some compromise with it; e.g., making a guess about optimal conditions for dealing with variability. But the behavioral engineer seldom has the time or the facilities required to eliminate variability in a given problem. The behavior analyst may refine his conditions until they bear little resemblance to the typical world in order to control variability, but the behavioral engineer cannot work in the abstract condition. His efforts must be carried out, and will be evaluated for effect, in the world to which we are all normally exposed.

Distinction between behavioral engineer and behavior analyst can be drawn on a number of other dimensions. The selection of the targeted behavior by the behavior analyst can be a function of a number of factors, but among them are likely to be such things as the relationship to previous research, the preciseness with which the problem can be identified and measured, the kinds of laboratory facilities available, the particular research question to be answered, and so forth. The behavioral engineer, on the other hand, may not even select his problem. It may be presented to him by another. When he does select a problem, it is likely to be based on the belief that an effective outcome can be secured for the client or that achievement of the objective would have cultural value. Like the behavior analyst, the behavioral engineer is concerned with the precise specification of the targeted behavior but, unlike the behavior analyst, he will not change the target for the sake of precision if such a change would result in a targeted behavior of less interest to his client.

The same features characterize the measuring and counting responses of the behavior analyst and engineer respectively. The analyst is evaluated by the adequacy of his measuring and counting procedures. Consequently they are of central importance to him. The behavioral engineer will strive to be as precise as the analyst in his measuring and counting responses, but will sacrifice that precision if necessary to deal with what he considers an important problem. For example, the behavioral engineer is less likely to have reliability checks on his data, or he may have a subject counting private events.

The selection of the intervention strategy is also likely to be somewhat different for the engineer and analyst. The engineer must consider the dollar and time costs of a project compared to others in which he might become involved, and he must consider public reaction to his activities. The analyst is relatively independent of these influences. Not only the nature of the intervention strategy, but also the length of time it is tested will differ. The engineer cannot afford to wait for long periods of time to make a judgment about effects as the analyst does. He will have less stringent criteria for judging stable performance, for example. Thus, he is more likely to make early judgments and, unfortunately, more likely to make bad judgments.

A behavior analyst's decision to terminate projects is principally a function of his having gathered the data he needs; the behavioral engineer must make certain that an effective social outcome has been achieved. If the data are good, but the permanent solution has not been found, the engineer has failed.

A major distinction might be drawn in the area of program design. The behavior analyst is principally defined by his use of reversal or multiple baseline designs, and most of us support the use of these designs whenever possible. The behavioral engineer, however, often uses the AB design, since the final outcome in the B condition is more interesting to him than the isolation of the true controlling condition(s). In addition, the behavioral engineer is likely to ask questions which are not of a "control" type. For example, he may ask questions which seek to compare different programs in order to assess their relative effects. Such questions are clearly a more traditional, statistical sort.

This list can be continued extensively, but let me quickly identify a few additional distinctions which can be drawn:

1. The use to which each puts the *Journal of Applied Behavior Analysis.* The analyst relates publications to his research; the engineer adds to his repertoire of techniques.

2. The preparation of grant proposals, in which the engineer is principally concerned with service benefits, the analyst with scientific benefit.

3. The use of the term "effective program," where the engineer is impressed by social impact, the analyst by data generated, and the identification of the controlling relation between variables.

4. Self-descriptive statements of interest in which the engineer is more likely to express concern for effective practices, the analyst for good research.

Obviously, I have not dealt with these distinctions in any detail. Hopefully sufficient evidence has been presented to justify the claim of a functional distinction between behavioral engineering practices and behavior analytic practices. While the same individual may at times be engineer, at times analyst, at times both, the point is that different controls exercised by different groups result in different professional behaviors on the part of behaviorists. These distinctions are being drawn, not in the interest of separation and fractionation, but to illustrate the difficulties from our current failure or refusal to acknowledge that these differences can and do exist.

Behavior analytic practices may be good practices (as judged by peers), but that does not mean they are accountable practices (as judged by the culture). The extent to which our practices are both at any one time is the extent to which a person is functioning as both engineer and analyst at the same time.

A further point is that the practices of the behavior analyst have been well delineated, principally by *JABA*'s publishing practices or in papers by its editors, but behavioral engineering practices are not well delineated. In fact, many people believe, and will continue to insist, that they are the same, and that they are both behavior analysis. I submit that they are not, and that the failure to recognize the distinction weakens the science and retards the culture's adoption or approval of the practices.

ACCOUNTABLE PRACTICES
FOR THE BEHAVIORAL ENGINEER

Behavioral engineers and behavior analysts should seek to maintain close relationships. Indeed, most applied behaviorists will continue to be trained in both behavior analysis and behavioral engineering, as is currently the case. But for the behavioral engineer to become account-able, he needs both to analyze and to alter some of his own behaviors and to influence the behaviors of those who will hold him accountable.

With respect to analyzing and changing his own behavior, behavior modifiers are principally identified as individuals who use certain techniques. These techniques are typically employed with populations that have little or no potential for counter control: chil-dren, the aged, the mentally ill, the mentally retarded, or prisoners. Thus, there has been little pressure on behavioral engineers to analyze what it is that they are doing, who is benefiting, how much they are benefiting, and at what cost. Further, except in rare cases, there has been little attempt to analyze the behavior of anyone other than the immediate client.

One way to remedy this situation is to deal with a much more significant portion of our professional environment from a behavioral perspective. We can stop thinking about behavior modification solely as a "treatment technique" to solve problems of enuresis, stuttering, etc., and start using what we know to analyze other elements of the system. How can we use behavioral principles to enlist staff support, to make administrators more effective, to improve relationshps between those within the profession and those outside of it? An administrator admini-strating, a reviewer reviewing, a behaviorist modifying, a psychiatric aid reinforcing, a parent complaining—all are people behaving, and their behavior can be analyzed to produce the most important effects for the culture. In the early days of our program at Drake, Scott Wood and I often heard students say that they could make a program work, but they couldn't get staff cooperation. We eventually realized that our students were working on the wrong problems because we were in-structing them in the wrong things. We were only teaching them methods and techniques to get a retarded person to talk, for example, when, in addition, we should have been teaching them to get staff to cooperate with them in effecting treatment programs. We should have been teaching them to consider the contingencies governing the decision-making behavior of administrators, rather than allowing derision of adminstrators for being too conservative or for providing them an opportunity to design a meaningful program.

There must be a deliberate effort on our part to identify and become sensitive to the controlling elements of the culture which affects us. We must come to recognize all of our interactions with others as reciprocal reinforcing relationships which can be subjected to the same sort of functional analysis as those which we currently investigate.

We must recognize that our current practices give rise to concern among the general public, some of it justified, some not. We use words like "control" and "behavior modification" which frighten people. Yet we all know that these words only imply that we do the things which mental health specialists, educators, and human interventionists have claimed to be able to do for some time. But to the general public, "control" is synonymous with "aversive control." We have seen the public reaction to *Beyond Freedom and Dignity* which illustrates the point nicely. Many people are worried about who controls the controller, but they neglect to ask who controls him now. Again, we know that the controller is not a single individual. He is the teacher, the businessman, the parent, and so forth, but the public doesn't understand this and we must help them to understand.

There are, in the meantime, other things we can do to work out an accountable relationship with the culture:

1. The most important thing we can do is to analyze the relationship of input to output variables within a systems framework. To elaborate on the already completed work in behavior analysis, it will be necessary for us to design procedures for analyzing the time and dollar costs of achieving whatever benefits we desire. Part of our future efforts will be devoted to producing a benefit for less cost or producing more benefit for the same cost.

2. It will be necessary for us to develop criteria for evaluating the ethics of our practice, just as we evaluate the ethics of our research. Unlike the behavior analyst, the behavioral engineer should alter the normal environment as little as possible to achieve an effect. A behavior typically maintained by praise in the culture ought to be developed by using praise contingently, if praise proves to be an effective reinforcer. This situation is analogous to the physician who does not resort to surgery when pills will do.

232

Achievement of a result is inadequate if the result dissipates over time or fails to occur under all necessary stimulus conditions. To the extent that either of the latter effects is true, we should look to poor or inadequate programming. We ought to make certain that, once a behavior is changed, it will be maintained or will continue to develop even further in a desirable direction. We ought to institute some sort of special controls over the use of aversive procedures. Many of us know personally of instances in which aversive controls have been improperly used, or instances in which little thought was devoted to the justification for such procedures. Most of these cases involved untrained behavioral practitioners.

Almost all graduate programs now have a course in behavior modification, as though that somehow qualified one to practice. Some cases, however, involve trained behavior modifiers. For them to engage in such practices is inexcusable, and we, as a group, must do something to stop it. I would suggest, as a beginning, that behaviorists exhaust all other viable alternatives prior to the use of an escape, avoidance, or punishment paradigm. Further, any case involving the use of any sort of aversive controls should be subject to some sort of public review prior to its inception.

3. A further accountable step would be for us to analyze our selection of target behaviors and intervention strategies more carefully. A behavioral engineer must justify his selection of both target and strategy on the basis of positive improvement in a client's behavior. Ethical considerations are the only additional concern, and no other.

4. It is important for all behaviorists to recognize that behaviorism can make important contributions to the culture outside of the research framework. That is to say, the implementation of research findings on a broader and cost-effective scale is also a contribution. Again, I am not advocating doing away with the science or relegating it to secondary importance. But the behavioral engineer can have an empirical, scien-

tific orientation, yet not engage in research, at least as it has been traditionally defined. We should support deliberate, perhaps cautious, attempts to go beyond the research realm into the engineering realm.

5. It is necessary to broaden our perspective to make use of non-behavior, analytic research. This is especially true in various content areas. Behavior analytic research has been methodologically rich, but has contributed little to our understanding of what methods should be used to teach. We need curricula for children in schools, hospitalized people, the aged and so forth.

Another concern of major importance in developing accountability is the arrangement of counter controlling practices by the culture. There are several ways in which we might contribute to the development of these counter controlling practices:

1. Train the public in the use of behavioral principles and practices. No man can be more free than the one who knows the variables of which his behavior is a function. Organizing the elementary school curricula is not as unreasonable as it might seem.

2. Support and design mechanisms for public review of efforts and effects. This model could be patterned directly on the model described by Lessinger, and would basically entail advance review of proposed practices and *post hoc* analysis of effectiveness by a body representative of the general public. Groups could be established at institutional, local, or state levels as needed, and a national clearinghouse could also be established which might provide information about who has done what in the past and with what results.

3. A final step would be to train these reviewers so that they could make disinterested, objective, but worthwhile evaluations of behavioral programs.

These suggestions for making ourselves accountable are by no means exhaustive. Others will be presented during this conference, and still others will result from deliberate attempts on our part to behave in accountable ways. Our history gives us every reason to believe that an analysis of our own behavior, and attempts to control it toward achieving accountable objectives, will be successful. We do not lack methodological sophistication. It is simply that we need to direct some of our effort to new problems.

A final comment on the relationship of accountability to licensing and certification is in order. Several years ago, after hearing a federal official discussing his difficulties in evaluating proposed programs labelled as behavioral, I was convinced that licensing was necessary for behavior modifiers as a way of maintaining the integrity of the discipline. Basically I thought licensing would make us accountable. I was wrong. I am currently in the process of being licensed as a psychologist in West Virginia. The process is not a serious one. All that is assessed is the extent to which I can recall material from my introductory psychology course. The exam is not related to my expertise in human intervention. And this test is the one recommended by the APA. In viewing what is currently done to license physicians, lawyers, and psychologists, no one can seriously maintain that licensing protects the public in more than a superficial manner. The general process of licensing people in broad areas of supposed competence bears no practical relationship to accountability.

I do not believe that making better tests will solve this problem either. There is no way that performance in the verbal domain can adequately reflect a person's skill as a practitioner. Therefore, I would reject licensing on the basis of written performance as altogether unsatisfactory.

It is possible to observe behavior modifiers at work and make objective judgments about their skills. The principle objection to this approach, however, is that it would tend to rigidify or instutitonalize practices. The only other seriously viable alternative is to certify the outcomes produced by people. There has been a truism in psychology for some time that past behavior is the best predictor of future behavior. Records of past behavior, as evaluated by public review committees in an accountability model, might very well be substituted for a licensing plan. Such records would fulfill most of the requirements for protecting the public and the profession from bad practices because they would be based on results, not practices. They would be under the control of the public. They would be confined to a particular skill area, and not to all behavior modification practices. The mold would be something like a credit bureau for human services, except that it would be under public control, and its information would likely be based on tighter evaluations. Local reviewing groups could simply make available a professional's record that would indicate the kinds of activities in which he had engaged, the populations he had worked with, and a summary of an outside evaluative review of that work. Local review boards could make their findings available nationwide through a national clearinghouse, much in the credit bureau model. I believe such a model would satisfy accountability requirements and would avoid many of the problems associated with licensing.

Accountability will be with us for some time, perhaps forever. It will provide thorny problems for us, but in the long run it will serve both the public and profession well. And, whatever current difficulties it presents us, a behavior analytic method is likely to fare well in the accountability process.

REFERENCES

Krapfl, J. and Ives, W. R. On the potential contribution of Wexler to applied behavioral psychology. West Virginia University. Unpublished manuscript.

Lessinger, L. M. Robbing Dr. Peter to pay Paul: Accounting for our stewardship of public education. *Educational Technology*, 1971, 1, *11*, 11-14.

Sidman, M. *Tactics of scientific research*. New York: Basic Books, Inc., 1960.

Skinner, B. F. *Science and human behavior*. New York: The Macmillan Company, 1953.

Skinner, B. F. The design of cultures. *Daedalus*, 1961, 534-536.

Wexler, D. B. Token and taboo: Behavior modification, token economies, and the law. *California Law Review*, 1973, *61*, 81-109.

RESPONSE

Stephen I. Sulzbacher

I believe that Jon is quite right in pointing out that the demand for accountability in our society will certainly grow and that accountability defines our relationship to our culture and clients, and not necessarily to other members of our profession. I was particularly impressed with his insightful distinction between the accountability process for behavior analysts as distinct from that which would be applied to behavioral engineers. I further agree that the behavioral engineer can take steps to make himself more accountable but I am not sure that I, personally, am inclined to take steps to make *myself* more accountable.

I certainly agree that licensing has never been, and holds no future promise to be, a viable procedure for insuring high standards of practice for behavioral engineers or any other profession. It is my position that accountability is more rightfully achieved through consumer education. In my practice, I expect to be fully accountable to my client who has the right to ask, *a priori*, "What exactly is it you plan to do and how can I tell whether it has worked or not?" The client is then in a position to subsequently ask, "Did he do what he said he'd do, and did it work?" I can see only one situation which justifies the creation of independent review boards as the instrument of accountability; that is, the situation where the third party is contracting for behavioral engineering services on behalf of a client who is either being coerced into changing his behavior (e.g., a prisoner or someone who is involuntarily institutionalized), or someone who is felt to be incapable of making a judgment (e.g., a child or someone who is mentally retarded). Even in these situations, however, I believe it is the objectives of the

237

contracting agent rather than the methods of the behavioral engineer which should be subjected to accountability.

However, our society is a long way from coming to grips with the ethical problem of clarifying whom we are to be accountable to. I have often found myself in the position of prescribing treatment for a child at the behest of his parents and teachers. Sometimes I would be paid for these services by the school district or the state and, at other times, by a federal or private insurance company. A fifth party to these treatment plans is often the court, which is charged with looking out for the interests of society as well as those of the individual client. Clearly the goals and perhaps the methods of my treatment would vary depending upon which of these five agencies I feel the most accountable to (child, parent, teacher, state government, or court system representative). It has been difficult, on occasion, for me to remain loyal to the child in the face of persuasive argument to the contrary by the other four parties.

Finally, whereas I agree with Jon that the behavior analytic method is by the nature of its data base highly compatible with the concept of accountability, and that we would fare quite well in any comparison with other methods, I am seriously concerned that behavior modification not be singled out among the social and health sciences as a set of procedures requiring more careful scrutiny. I believe it would be a serious error if we agreed to be more accountable than any of our other colleagues in psychology, psychiatry or social work.

ETHICAL ISSUES IN
RESEARCH ON BEHAVIOR THERAPY

Stephanie B. Stolz

The Department of Health, Education, and Welfare (DHEW) has had for some time an official policy on procedures for the protection of human subjects who participate in projects funded by the Department. This policy is implemented by the individual researcher, by a committee at the researcher's institution, by peer review committees working for government agencies, and by government staff.*

According to the DHEW policy, review of proposed research procedures by these various individuals and committees should

> determine that the rights and welfare of the subjects involved are adequately protected, that the risks to an individual are outweighed by the potential benefits to him or by the importance of the knowledge to be gained, and that informed consent is to be obtained by methods that are adequate and appropriate .... An individual is considered to be "at risk" if he may be exposed to the possibility of harm—physical, psychological, sociological, or other—as a consequence of any activity which goes beyond the application of those established and accepted methods necessary to meet his needs (Department of Health, Education, and Welfare, 1971, 1-2).

* I thank Drs. W. S. Agras, G. C. Davison, M. Hare, P. London, K. D. O'Leary, and R. B. Stuart for their helpful comments on earlier versions of this paper.

This policy is meant to be flexible. In each case, the reviewers must weigh the benefits to the subjects and the importance of the knowledge to be gained against their evaluation of possible risks.

However, stating a policy is much easier than implementing one. Judgments about subject protection procedures would be simple indeed to make, if the risk-to-benefit ratio could be quantified, or even if all of us could just agree on what the risks and potential benefits are for a given study.

Since such agreement is generally difficult to obtain in the behavioral sciences (Schwitzgebel and Kolb, 1974), quantification of risk and benefit is not now possible. Instead, various segments of society often have different views about the risks and benefits involved in a behavioral research project because each segment sees the practice in a different context. Thus, peer reviewers and behavioral researchers may find a technique acceptable because it produces rapid improvement in seriously maladaptive behavior, while civil libertarians might object to that same technique because it violates the client's rights or restricts his freedom, however briefly, and regardless of ensuing benefits. As another example, legal rulings may define as unacceptable a procedure generally used in mental health settings, such as paying patients tokens for working at off-ward jobs, or charging them tokens for the use of a television set (Wexler, 1973). To complicate matters even further, the definitions of risk and benefit change over time as customs, knowledge, and values change.

Despite these complexities, decisions must be made about the acceptability of procedures for the protection of subjects in proposed studies. For applications considered by the National Institutes of Health and the National Institute of Mental Health, this is done through the consensus of a succession of reviews by the investigator, the university ethics committee, the scientific peer review committee, the national advisory council, and the responsible program staff. The hope is that the many people involved will bring to bear sufficiently disparate points of view that a fair consideration may be given to the ethical issues.

Decisions are made for each individual case; the DHEW policy itself does not include detailed rules about what are acceptable or unacceptable professional practices or professional ethics. Rather, the aim of the policy is to sensitize people to the difficulties of balancing ethical and scientific goals in evaluating the appropriateness of the procedures proposed in a research project. Beyond that, evaluators are expected to use their common sense and professional judgment in interpreting the policy's general standards.

DATA BASE OF THIS REPORT

In this paper, I will confine myself to one segment of the chain of review procedures for the protection of human subjects; i.e., the evaluations made by members of the peer review panels. Since this conference is specifically concerned with applied behavior analysis, I will further restrict my examples to applications proposing research in this area. The material for my examples comes from the Summary Statements, or as they are referred to more familiarly, the "pink sheets"; these are the official reports that summarize the review committee's discussion of each application.

Limitations of the data. The material in a Summary Statement is not a verbatim transcript of a review committee's discussion. Rather, it is an edited version of that discussion, covering its main points. During the time period from which I drew my sample of reports—fiscal years 1971, 1972, and 1973—review committee members were not explicitly required to discuss the procedures for protection of human subjects in each application, a requirement that has since been put into effect. Thus, while I do have some numbers on the proportion of behavior modification applications that included comments on subject protection, the numbers themselves have questionable validity. Ethical problems may have been important in an application, but the review committee members may not have discussed them because of other, even more important difficulties with the project; or, the staff member who wrote the Summary Statement may, for any of a variety of reasons, not have felt it was necessary to include whatever discussion did occur.

My analysis includes reports from only three of the review committees of the National Institute of Mental Health (NIMH). These three committees generally consider a large number of behavior modification applications. In the three-year period I chose, two of these committees reviewed about 45 behavior modification applications each; the third committee reviewed 21 such applications.

Another limitation of my data is that I could not get good comparisons from projects not proposing behavior modification research, primarily because I was not able to define a suitable comparison population. It was easy to go through summaries of research projects and identify those that I would call behavior modification projects. My criterion for inclusion was any applied research that would not seem out of place in any of the four behavior modification journals. Thus, I included research on behavior therapy, behavior modification, biofeedback, attempts to develop behavioral treatments for alcoholism and drug abuse, and similar projects. However, what should I have taken as comparison projects? All other therapy research, as well as all other classroom research, and all other approaches to alcoholism, drug abuse, delinquency, asthma, depression, insomnia. . .? I gave up. In the end, I decided to make two kinds of comparisons. One is between the behavior therapy applications reviewed by one of the committees, and the psychotherapy applications reviewed by that same committee. This sample, however, covers a much more restricted range of topics than the total group of applications. A second comparison is between all the behavior modification applications reviewed by these three NIMH committees during my three-year sample period and all applications submitted to a different agency, the National Institutes of Health (NIH).

THE EXTENT OF THE PROBLEM

Behavior modification projects are rather frequently singled out for special discussion of their subject protection procedures. In my National Institute of Mental Health (NIMH)* sample, between 15 and 20 percent of the Summary Statements on behavior modification projects include a critical comment about subject protection procedures. However, among the applications reviewed by one committee, roughly the same proportion of psychotherapy and behavior therapy projects was criticized for their ethics. At NIH, in contrast, only about one percent of the nearly 40,000 grant applications on all topics appeared to have

---

* The National Institute of Mental Health (NIMH) was renamed the Alcohol, Drug Abuse, and Mental Health Administration (ADAMHA) in September, 1973. In this paper, the older name is used: it was the name of the agency at the time the reviews discussed were conducted.

problems involving the protection of human subjects. Thus, while the absolute number of grant proposals in behavior modification with problems in the protection of human subjects is small, the proportion of behavior modification projects that have such problems is much greater than the corresponding proportion among research proposals in general. Contrary to what you might expect, however, the proportion of behavior therapy applications singled out because of ethical problems is no greater than the proportion of psychotherapy applications with ethical problems. Thus, these data show that ethical problems in research on therapy are not restricted to behavior therapy.

THE ETHICAL ISSUES

At first glance, the ethics of therapy appear clear and straightforward: therapy should provide the maximum benefit to the patient and to society, with careful consideration and resolution of conflicts when they occur (Miron, 1968). Or, as London (1969) has put it, therapy and other behavioral influence procedures should strike a balance between personal liberty and the public interest. However, the high proportion of therapy applications where reviewers felt there were ethical problems is testimony to the fact that such considerations and balances are easier to state in the abstract than to observe in practice.

In this paper, I will draw from actual grant applications to illustrate the kinds of ethical issues that arise in research on behavior modification. These issues include the questions of who decides whether and how the client's behavior should be modified, issues of informed consent, problems arising from experimental designs involving the use of reversals or control groups, risks associated with the use of novel therapeutic procedures, and the general issue of aversive techniques.

While I have tried to disguise the identity of the researchers, it will be necessary to give some details about the question being asked, the setting, and the procedures. Therapeutic techniques or research designs are not, in themselves, ethical or unethical (Begelman, 1971). Rather, the evaluation of the adequacy of the protection of subjects needs to be made in terms of the risk-to-benefit ratio that characterizes the research as a whole.

243

The definition of deviance. Who decides that the client's behavior should be modified and in what direction it should be modified? This decision can be made by society's representatives, teachers or policemen, by the researcher, or by the client or his agent. I mention this general issue first in order to emphasize that the most basic decisions made by the behavioral researcher—whether to modify and which response to modify—involve value judgments (Krasner, 1962; Begelman, 1973). In practice, behavioral professionals often let society's representatives define deviance by telling the professional which behavior needs changing. The professional generally proceeds as though the deviance resides in the environment, or in the client's learning history as a product of his environment. The behavioral program is then set up either to alter the environmental contingencies to shape different behavior, or to give the individual new learning experiences, again to shape different behavior. Implicit in this approach are the assumptions that it is appropriate for society at large to define deviance, and that those who do not conform to that definition should change. Krasner and Ullmann (1965, p. 363), for example, say that "the ultimate source of values is . . . the requirements of the society" in which the patient and therapist live.

Winett and Winkler (1972), however, have eloquently argued the other side of this issue. Noting that behavior modifiers have typically worked to adjust people to existing institutions and social systems, they suggest that behavioral researchers must also consider creating new environments and changing the social system. According to this view, the deviance is not necessarily within the individual; it may be that the social system itself is inappropriate and in need of treatment.

Although I didn't happen to find a grant application in my sample that dealt with the treatment of homosexuals, that topic comes immediately to mind when this issue is discussed. Gay liberationists have argued that they should not be required to adjust to the existing system, and that others do not have the right to define them as deviant (cf. Wilson and Davison, 1974). Similar problems arise whenever conventional norms are undergoing change (Bandura, 1969). Ideally, it seems to me, the client's preferences should be the deciding factor in determining whether there should be treatment, and, if so, what the behavioral goal should be.

An illustration of this general issue comes from an application that proposed behavioral treatment for shy, withdrawn children. These children were to be referred to the treatment program by teachers and parents. The review committee considering this project strongly questioned the appropriateness of the implied definition of deviance. For one thing, it seemed clear that the children to be selected would not be pathologically shy. According to the investigator, children would be given treatment only if they were functioning reasonably well in school, had stable homes, and had never received psychotherapy. In short, the children could be characterized as exhibiting only relatively mild withdrawal and social isolation. The reviewers noted that studies of creative adults suggest that an appreciable portion of them were shy, detached, introverted children. Thus, the committee was concerned that while the children's behavior might be defined as mildly deviant in grade school, there was a reasonable probability that these same children would, under normal circumstances, become contributing members of society as adults, and that this normal development might even be inhibited if the children were made less "deviant." Thus, the overall risk to the children and to society appeared to outweigh the potential immediate benefits. I agree with O'Leary's statement that "the behavior modifier . . . must seriously question whether the behavior he is being asked to help change should really be changed" (1972, p. 509).

Justification of the intervention. Sometimes research projects in applied behavior analysis are criticized because the researchers propose to "control the behavior of the child." This issue arose in connection with a proposal that is not, strictly speaking, part of my sample because the study was laboratory research rather than applied work. I include it, however, because the issue is an important one.

In this study, children were to be trained in the laboratory to engage in an analogue of a significant real-life behavior. In the course of the study, the newly learned behavior was extinguished, an analogue of socially inappropriate behavior was taught, and there were further conditions involving training and extinction. One response the experimenter made to the reviewers' criticism about control was that, after all, parents and teachers affect children's behavior all the time, so that the researcher was doing only what other people were doing. This is a rejoinder that many of us have probably made at one time or another.

245

Nonetheless, those evaluating this application did not feel that this was adequate justification for the experimental intervention. The reviewers argued that parents and teachers have a special relationship to the child, a relationship that the experimenter does not have. The parents are responsible for the child's behavior, and education is compulsory under the law, but there is no legal relationship or position of responsibility between experimenter and child. Eventually the investigator persuaded the reviewers that the children would be adequately protected in this study, and that they probably would learn very little, if anything, in the experiment anyway.

This example has a more general message, however, about how a researcher can justify an intervention. It seems to me that it is pertinent to ask who will benefit from the "control" that results from the intervention. Is the child's behavior being changed for the benefit of the school, of the parent, of the experimenter, or of the child? I myself feel that the child's benefit should be considered foremost. Control can be justified when the interventions will benefit the children, or whoever the clients are, in some way that they or their guardians want them to benefit, other things being equal. The study I have just described was a laboratory study, so the primary benefit was to the experimenter and to science. The children were taught an artificial response, of no use to them in the real world. Thus, in my opinion, the questions raised by the reviewers were quite appropriate; if some behavior had been involved that was more significant in the life of the children, the control of their behavior would have been even more acceptable.

Informed consent. In some research studies in applied behavior analysis investigators have been criticized for proposing to conduct research without first obtaining permission from those whose behavior is to be modified or from those responsible for them. The DHEW policy on the protection of human subjects is detailed and explicit in this regard. According to the policy,

> the basic elements of informed consent are: (1) a fair explanation of the procedures to be followed, including an identification of those which are experimental; (2) a description of the attendant discomforts and risks; (3) a description of the benefits to be expected; (4) a disclosure of appropriate alternative procedures that would be advantageous for the subject;

(5) an offer to answer any inquiries concerning the procedures; (6) an instruction that the subject is free to withdraw his consent and to discontinue participation in the project or activity at any time (DHEW, 1971, p. 7).

As applied to research on behavior therapy, this policy means that the clients or their representatives should be told that the clients will be getting therapy; what the therapeutic procedures will involve; what problems might arise, if any; what the goal of the therapy is; and that the clients should feel free to drop out of the study at any time. Not mentioned in the guidelines, but, in my opinion, essential whenever possible, is that the client should cooperate with the therapist in specifying the way in which he wishes to be changed.

Several proposals in my sample involved procedures inconsistent with some aspects of the policy on informed consent. For example, in two proposed studies, the persons participating in the research were not to have been told that they were getting therapy. In one case, a new type of assertive training was to be tried on subjects who volunteered from an introductory psychology class. The subjects were to be told merely that they would be participating in an experiment on social behavior, although in actual fact they would be receiving an experimental therapeutic procedure. Moreover, it was not clear that the subjects would even have any need for that sort of therapy. Because the benefit to the subjects thus appeared minimal, the risk from the lack of informed consent assumed greater importance.

Another application with this problem involved behavior therapy for aggressive children. In this case, the experimenter proposed a cover story to tell the children and their parents, namely, that the children were to be hired to work on a research project. In actual fact, the "work" was participation in a behavior intervention with the goal of reducing the child's inappropriate behavior. The reviewers were concerned that when the parents and children discovered they had been deceived into accepting therapy, it might possibly anger the parents and alienate them and their children from research and therapy, and potentially from the school as well. The researcher did not give a strong explanation of why this risk was worth taking in the context of the potential benefits of this study, and the committee decided that the proposed procedure was inconsistent with the DHEW guidelines on informed consent.

One aspect of the policy on informed consent is that subjects should be free to drop out of the study at any time, and that they should not be subjected to undue coercion to continue. In one proposed treatment program, each client was to deposit money with the experimenter; these funds would be forfeited if the client did not complete the treatment program. The reviewers felt that this procedure involved excessive pressure on the clients, given the experimental nature of the treatment program. In contrast, a therapeutic approach that had already been carefully evaluated and shown to be effective could include such a deposit. In this latter case, the benefits of the procedure would be known, and they would presumably outweigh the risk of the mild coercion associated with the deposit. In general, it is preferable if the researcher helps the client to understand the implications of his decision to submit a forfeitable deposit. For example, clients could be given an estimate, based on pilot work, of the probability that they would drop out of the program and lose the money. With this additional information, it seems to me that a deposit could be used, even in connection with experimental treatments, because the client would be better informed when giving his consent.

Unobtrusive measures. All the issues relating to informed consent are not as clear-cut as those I have mentioned so far. We are all familiar with the expense involved in measuring ongoing behavior by having an observer score the behavior as it occurs. We are all also aware of the likelihood that the presence of an observer has an effect on the behavior being observed. One way to avoid the expense and interpretive problems of direct observation is to use unobtrusive measures, measures taken of the subject's behavior without his awareness. Unfortunately, using unobtrusive measures involves some thorny ethical questions.

In one proposal, for example, children in a classroom were to be videotaped, without the investigator's obtaining the permission of either the children or their parents. Since the videotape recorder would be hidden, the taping would not affect the children's behavior. But, given the variety of possible uses for the taped material, was it ethical to take these recordings without the children's knowledge?

In another proposal, the researcher planned to use the recently developed technique (McFall and Marston, 1970) in which subjects given assertive training are later telephoned, ostensibly by a salesman who tries to interest them in buying a magazine subscription, but actually by an employee of the researcher who is testing them to see if they are assertive. If the subjects have not, in advance, given their consent to have their privacy interrupted and their behavior evaluated in this way, is it ethical to do so?

In these, as in the other cases I have discussed, the risk-to-benefit ratio needs to be considered. There is no list of proscribed or unethical procedures; rather, procedures have to be evaluated in the context of the entire study and its potential benefits to the subjects involved and to society. While in general it is best to obtain fully informed consent, in some cases the benefits from not doing so are considerable, and the risks are minimal.

What is "informed consent"? As an aside, let me say a few words about the meaning of "informed consent" in the context of applied behavior analysis. The behavioral approach sees the individual's behavior as responsive to environmental contingencies and as a function of his reinforcement history. How, then, can we even talk about "informed consent," when a clever behavior modifier might be able to engineer environmental contingencies in such a way that subjects would consent to the most risky of procedures?

In fact, it does not take a very sophisticated behavioral engineer to design moderately coercive conditions. For example, in many prisons, prisoners are routinely offered inducements such as early parole or special treatment for cooperation with research projects. Also, when it is difficult for clients to pay for therapy, offering them the opportunity of participating in experimental therapy for which there is no charge is another mild form of coercion.

It is important to remember that, in addition to its emphasis on environmental control, the behavioral approach also assumes that people are able to learn behavioral principles and understand how environmental events can control their own behavior (Ulrich, 1967). As behavioral principles are more widely disseminated, it will be possible for an increasing number of people to have access to them. Through the knowledge our potential subjects gain from discussions of behavioral principles in courses, workshops, articles in the public press, television talk shows, and other such sources, they will have a better understanding of their own behavior. As this public awareness increases, the problem of having the subjects' consent engineered by the experimenter becomes less serious. However, until behavioral understanding is more widespread than it is at present, experimenters should be particularly sensitive to the manner they use to describe research and ask for the subjects' cooperation. We should help our subjects by making them aware of variables that may affect their decision.

Reversal designs. Many behavior modification studies use the "reversal" procedure, in which a successful intervention is deliberately stopped, to see if the client then gets worse. If the newly acquired behavior deteriorates when the treatment is stopped and then recovers when it is reintroduced, this suggests that the behavior change was a consequence of the experimental intervention (Baer, Wolf, and Risley, 1968). The use of this sort of experimental design in the study of clinical problems with humans was questioned by the reviewers of one application in my sample. Although peer reviewers apparently do not consider this a serious problem—it was mentioned in only one Summary Statement—I feel it is important to consider, because it goes to the heart of what continues to be the most frequently used experimental design in applied behavior analysis.

The reviewers of this project felt that an experimental design demonstrating the reappearance of undesirable behavior may be defensible with animals, but was questionable with humans. In the reviewers' opinion, the fact that the behavior could be reversed showed that something was lacking in the intervention because, if the client's new behavior really were appropriate, the environment should have taken over the control of that behavior and maintained it with natural consequences. Thus, these reviewers felt that a successful reversal would be a sign of an unsuccessful intervention, one that failed to make use of the reinforcers in the client's environment.

Researchers often justify temporary reversals on the grounds that the literature on reversals in behavior modification generally shows substantial benefit and minimal risk from such an experimental analysis. However, the approach I have been suggesting in this paper is to consider the risk-to-benefit ratio for the individual research project, rather than the general case. The project that elicited the criticism I have described intended to use modeling procedures to try to modify mildly disruptive behaviors in children. Since several children with similar problems were available in the same research setting, and since presumably some of those children would have had a number of undesirable behaviors, a more appropriate alternative would have been a multiple baseline design (Baer, Wolf, and Risley, 1968), a design that does not include the reversal procedure and so is less risky. In planning the research project, the investigator should have weighed the relative risks and benefits from each of these experimental designs, and should have chosen the one that best combined scientific merit and appropriate ethical concerns.

Treatment of the control group. Some studies compare one group of persons who get behavior therapy with another group who get no treatment at all. This experimental design has sometimes been criticized because it does not show an appropriate concern for the needs of the nontreated patients. An evaluation of whether a project appropriately protects the human subjects involved must consider whether the random assignment of subjects to treatment exposes the control or nontreated subjects to risk.

This issue is particularly serious in those biofeedback studies that use subjects with a serious physical disease, such as hypertension or asthma. In general, the review committees have felt that control subjects in such studies should not be kept from treatment for prolonged periods of time, simply for experimental purposes.

One way to avoid the threat of risk to untreated control subjects is to use a different experimental strategy, one in which the control subjects get the standard, accepted therapy for whatever problem is being studied. This latter design not only minimizes the risks to the control subjects, but enables the researcher to assess the relative cost and effectiveness of the experimental and the traditional therapy procedures (Stolz, 1973; O'Leary and Kent, 1973).

Stuart (1973) has developed another way to protect the control subjects. In his procedure, control subjects receiving no treatment are assigned to some activity presumed to have no therapeutic value, but which will bring them periodically into contact with the researcher. At those times, the investigator can determine whether any of the control subjects have changed in such a way as to require immediate treatment, and see to it that they get the treatment. This method seems particularly appropriate when the research population is one that has a high probability of developing personally or socially harmful behavior. The cost of this procedure is that it removes the worst cases in the control group from the study, and so makes it more difficult to show that the experimental treatment was effective.

Use of new therapeutic procedures. Another problem arises when experimental subjects get a treatment that has not yet been proven effective. The possible risk here needs no elaboration. One solution is to permit clients to switch out of the experimental therapy and, if they so desire, into the traditional treatment. Such a provision would be consistent with the requirement discussed earlier in connection with informed consent; i.e., that the subject be free to withdraw from the study at any time.

Unjustified risks. My sample of behavior modification applications includes several in which the procedures seemed to entail a totally unnecessary risk for the subjects. These cases seemed to be examples where the researchers became so involved in setting up feasible projects that they forgot to consider the subjects.

Applied behavior analysis is concerned with socially significant behaviors that are immediately important to the subjects (Baer, Wolf, and Risley, 1968). Yet two applications proposed to use behavioral methods to develop socially inappropriate behavior. The researchers justified this on the grounds that the studies would enable them to understand the variables controlling the undesirable behavior. After the analyses were completed, the investigators proposed to punish or extinguish the undesirable behavior, or otherwise "debrief" the subjects. Since it is debatable whether such studies should be labeled research, perhaps they should not have been included with my sample.

Several other studies, clearly therapeutic in their goals, proposed treatment procedures that review committee members felt were highly likely to aggravate, rather than relieve, the clients' problems. In a study proposing the use of implosive therapy, for example, the researcher apparently had made no provision for offering remedial treatment to the subjects, should the implosive therapy increase their fear. Because this is a risk known to be associated with this sort of treatment (Morganstern, 1973), some such provision is essential. Similarly, in studies proposing the use of biofeedback for hypertension, appropriate medical supervision is necessary if, for example, the patient's reaction to his failure to lower his blood pressure aggravates his hypertension.

In general, when behavior therapists work with procedures such as biofeedback that are used as treatments for serious medical problems, adequate medical supervision is essential. Unforeseen complications are always a possibility in such studies. Investigators lacking a medical background should collaborate with appropriate medical personnel when conducting research on seriously ill clients.

My last example of an unjustified risk concerns a researcher who proposed to use a treatment method that a considerable body of research had shown was likely to aggravate the particular problem he was working on. Here, as in all the examples, the relationship of risk to benefit must be considered. It is conceivable that an investigator might have some pilot work suggesting strongly that the previous body of research had been, say, inappropriately interpreted, and that the treatment method was not, after all, dangerous. If that is the case, such information should, of course, be an integral part of a proposal.

Aversive therapy procedures. I was surprised to find only a single review stating concern about the use of aversive treatments. In that discussion, the reviewers noted that the clients were appropriately protected because they could terminate cooperation in the aversive therapy at any time. There was, however, no general discussion of the use of aversive treatment per se. I would like to go beyond my data base to discuss this issue briefly because it is so often brought up in discussions of ethical problems in applied behavior analysis (see, e.g., Lucero, Vail, and Scherber, 1968).

In the ethical context, the fundamental question is whether aversive methods are by definition inhumane. Krasner has argued that at least some of them are. Speaking of some treatments that he finds severely aversive, he says, "You cannot shape responsible behavior in an individual while at the same time treating him inhumanely. You cannot build a new social environment with any chance of enhancing human dignity based on procedures inducing indignity" (unpublished manuscript, p. 8). The point of view that I have presented in this paper is different, however. I have argued that the decision about whether a procedure is ethical needs to be made on the basis of the risk-to-benefit ratio. In these terms, any proposed procedure, including aversive tech-

253

niques, needs to be evaluated in terms of the risks and benefits associated with a specific use.

Several investigators have used aversive techniques to eliminate children's self-injurious behavior (Bucher, 1969). In such cases, the risk to the child of continuing the self-injurious behavior is serious, alternative treatments appear to be ineffective, and potential benefits to the child from the treatment are great. This is the kind of situation in which the risks from the treatment itself, unexpected side effects, and temporary discomfort, appear to be more than outweighed by the benefits (Baer, 1970). By contrast, it is hard to be sympathetic with a proposal to use severe shocks as a way of facilitating the learning of nonsense syllables, a highly dubious benefit, when the risk looms large in comparison.

Most of the possible uses of aversive treatments fall between these two extremes. It is my opinion that all behavior modification procedures, including aversive control, can be used ethically and with concern for the protection of the subjects involved, or unethically and with insufficient precautions. Aversive methods should not be prohibited simply because they are aversive; rather, when they are used, as when any intervention is used, appropriate measures should be taken to protect the subjects (Begelman, 1971).

CONCLUSION

In this paper I have summarized what I believe to be some of the more important issues related to the protection of human subjects in behavior modification research. For each type of problem I have suggested how the researcher can show appropriate concern for his subjects, by a consideration of the balance between the potential benefit to the subjects that would derive from the study and the potential risk to them from participation in it. While such concern has been imposed on applicants for research grants by virtue of the DHEW guidelines, I hope that a similar concern is felt by all behavior therapists, researchers and clinicians as well. London (1969) has wisely said, "All good people who have power over others, even just a little power and even for just a little while, need access to an ethic that can guide their use of it" (pp. 200-201).

REFERENCES

Baer, D. M. A case for the selective reinforcement of punishment. In Neuringer, C. and Michael, J. S. (eds.), *Behavior modification in clinical psychology*. New York: Appleton-Century-Crofts, 1970.

Baer, D. M., Wolf, M. M., and Risley, T. R. Some current dimensions of applied behavior analysis. *Journal of Applied Behavior Analysis*, 1968, *1*, 91-97.

Bandura, A. *Principles of behavior modification*. New York: Holt, Rinehart and Winston, 1969.

Begelman, D. A. The ethics of behavioral control and a new mythology. *Psychotherapy: Theory, Research and Practice*, 1971, *8*, 165-169.

Begelman, D. A. Ethical issues in behavioral control. *Journal of Nervous and Mental Disease*, 1973, *156*, 412-419.

Bucher, B. Some ethical issues in the therapeutic use of punishment. In Rubin, R. D. and Franks, C. M. (eds.), *Advances in behavior therapy, 1968*. New York: Academic Press, 1969.

Department of Health, Education, and Welfare. *The institutional guide to DHEW policy on protection of human subjects*. DHEW Publication No. (NIH) 72-102. December 1, 1971.

Krasner, L. Behavior control and social responsibility. *American Psychologist*, 1962, *17*, 199-204.

Krasner, L. Applications of token economy in chronic populations. Paper presented at the annual meeting of the American Psychological Association, San Francisco, September, 1968.

Krasner, L. and Ullmann, L. P. *Research in behavior modification*. New York: Holt, Rinehart and Winston, 1965.

London, P. *Behavior control*. New York: Harper and Row, 1969.

Lucero, R. J., Vail, D. J., and Scherber, J. Regulating operant conditioning programs. *Hospital & Community Psychiatry*, 1968, *19*, 53-54.

McFall, R. M. and Marston, A. R. An experimental investigation of behavior rehearsal in assertive training. *Journal of Abnormal Psychology*, 1970, *76*, 295-303.

Miron, N. B. The primary ethical consideration. *Hospital & Community Psychiatry*, 1968, *19*, 226-228.

255

Morganstern, K. P. Implosive therapy and flooding procedures: A critical review. *Psychological Bulletin*, 1973, *79*, 318-334.

O'Leary, K. D. Behavior modification in the classroom: A rejoinder to Winett and Winkler. *Journal of Applied Behavior Analysis*, 1972, *5*, 505-511.

O'Leary, K. D. and Kent, R. Behavior modification for social action: Research tactics and problems. In Hamerlynck, L. A., Handy, L. C., and Mash, E. J. (eds.), *Behavior change: Proceedings of the fourth Banff conference.* Champaign, IL: Research Press, 1973.

Schwitzgebel, R. K. and Kolb, D. A. *Changing human behavior.* New York: McGraw-Hill, 1974.

Stolz, S. B. Overview of NIMH support of research in behavior therapy. *Journal of Applied Behavior Analysis*, 1973, *6*, 509-515.

Stuart, R. B. Notes on the ethics of behavior research and intervention. In Hamerlynck, L. A., Handy, L. C. and Mash, E. J. (eds.), *Behavior change: Proceedings of the fourth Banff conference.* Champaign, IL: Research Press, 1973.

Ulrich, R. Behavior control and public concern. *Psychological Record*, 1967, *17*, 229-234.

Wexler, D. B. Token and taboo: Behavior modification, token economies, and the law. *California Law Review*, 1973, *61*, 81-109.

Wilson, G. T. and Davison, G. C. Behavior therapy and homosexuality: A critical perspective. *Behavior Therapy*, 1974, *5*, 16-28.

Winett, R. A. and Winkler, R. C. Current behavior modification in the classroom: Be still, be quiet, be docile. *Journal of Applied Behavior Analysis*, 1972, *5*, 499-504.

RESPONSE

Stephen C. Bitgood

Dr. Stolz has presented a thought-provoking paper emphasizing the need for us to consider the protection of our clients and subjects in a more serious vein. She has also given us some ethical guidelines for research. As she pointed out, ethical concerns should be applied to all therapeutic situations.

First, it is necessary to determine what the client should be protected from. As I see it, there are three possible dangers which appear to be implied by the ethical guidelines of the American Psychological Association and the Department of Health, Education and Welfare. The first danger is the possible risks involved in the therapeutic program, as well as the possibility that the client will not benefit from the procedures. Dr. Stolz has understandably selected the risk-to-benefit ratio as the primary ethical consideration. It is important to remember that there is a distinction between risks and benefits to the client as well as risks and benefits to society or to the researcher; the benefits to the individual and the benefits to others are often in conflict.

A second danger is that the client may be given insufficient information or misinformation about the procedures and expected outcome. Deceit is rarely desirable and should be avoided whenever possible even in research situations. Lack of information may be as deceiving as misinformation since it often leads to false expectations of the outcome or a misunderstanding of the procedures.

The third danger to clients is involuntary control. Involuntary control includes both coercion to participate in a therapeutic program and excessive pressure to continue after the program has begun. Involuntary control is a thorny issue to define. While some authors have restricted the use of involuntary control to aversive procedures, others have expressed a concern about subtle behavioral control using positive reinforcement procedures. As behavior analysts frequently point out, subtle aspects of control would be greatly diminished if behavioral principles were more widely understood.

Ethical issues and criteria for protecting clients. Table 1 (page 261) shows the three dangers—expressed as criteria for protecting clients. These criteria are listed across the top and the ethical issues down the columns. I have added three issues to Dr. Stolz'. The table summarizes some of the ethical issues that should be considered in therapy. The first issue is the definition of deviance. *Who* has defined the deviant behavior? *What* classes of behaviors have been identified as deviant? *How* has the deviance been defined? Has it been defined in behavioral, cognitive, or psychodynamic terms? This is an issue that should be considered carefully. The first cell in the table shows the risks and benefits associated with defining deviant behaviors. A frequent argument is that intervention, or a specific kind of intervention, may eventually result in harm to the individual or to society, precipitating such things as symptom substitution. It has been argued that if the behavior is changed without modifying the underlying cause, then another symptom, perhaps more severe than the first, may emerge. The evidence for symptom substitution has been overwhelming. However, while new, inappropriate behaviors *may* arise when one class of behaviors is eliminated, the emergence of more acceptable behaviors is at least as likely. Perhaps more important is the fact that a new behavior can be programmed to ensure that it is a desirable one.

A second example of the argument—that intervention may result in harm—is based on the notion that creativity and maladaptive personality traits are causally related. This assumption was apparently the basis of reasoning by one of the review committees described by Dr. Stolz. The review committee criticized a grant application that proposed behavioral treatment for shy, withdrawn children. The committee noted that many shy, introverted children become creative adults and suggested that modifying isolated behaviors may do harm to the individual and society by stifling creative behavior later in life. This speculation suffers from the same logical shortcoming as the argument

258

that smoking marihuana leads to heroin addiction. Any student of introductory logic should recognize this fallacy. Of course there remains the possibility that shyness and creativity are causally related, but it seems to me that this is an empirical question, and that we should not become alarmed until evidence has been provided to prove the hypothesis. The committee may legitimately question whether the benefits of intervention were justified, but using *potential* risks as a criterion seems unjustified in this case.

The potential risks involved in a definition of deviance should be carefully evaluated. The examples of symptom substitution and creativity illustrate how easy it is to speculate about potential risks. We should be wary of the hysterics who see a devil in every corner and a rapist under every bed. I have placed a question mark in the cell representing the possible risks in order to illustrate that they are often debatable and sometimes unjustified.

Informed consent is another debatable issue. As Dr. Stolz pointed out, an element of informed consent is the excessive pressure to continue in a therapeutic program. This element is subsumed under the criterion of involuntary control. The criterion was applied by the review committee that criticized the grant-proposing behavioral contracting, a procedure in which a client deposits money which is returned to him after the conditions of the contract are met. For example, the client may agree to forfeit his deposit in a weight control program if he does not lose weight or if he drops from the program. The reviewers felt that such contracting represented excessive pressure on the client. I strongly question any blanket dismissal of the procedure. If the client understands the procedures, if the terms of the contract are reasonable, if the amount of the deposit is not excessive, and if the client consents to the contract, then it is difficult to understand how "excessive pressure" has been exerted. The client is free to withdraw at any time, and he realizes the consequences of withdrawal from the program. Of course, as with any procedure, it can be misused. But I do not see anything inherently unethical in behavioral contracting.

Deprivation is another debatable issue, and I am surprised that it was not discussed in Dr. Stolz's sample of grant reviews. Lucero, Vail, and Scherber (1968) reported that a Minnesota state hospital workshop recommended that deprivation never be used. Miron (1968) and others have replied that you cannot have reinforcement without deprivation.

And in an attempt to defend their original statement, Lucero and Vail (1968) stated that they were referring to the ordinary, vernacular definition of deprivation, and not to its technical one. Their reply is confusing since the original recommendation that deprivation never be used was a strong, uncategorical statement. It did not distinguish between the vernacular and technical definitions. Cahoon (1968) pointed out that "it is unprecedented in considering professional ethics to insist that a whole class of techniques of proved effectiveness be prohibited because the techniques can be misapplied."

My final comment concerning this table relates to the unethical modifier. I believe that unethical behavior more commonly occurs because of thoughtlessness and lack of training in ethical behaviors than as a result of purposeful design. We do not always ensure that our clients understand the procedures and goals of the therapeutic program. This is unfortunate since, in most cases, the benefits to the client are greater if he understands and cooperates in the therapeutic program. Also, we may unwittingly coerce a client into participating in a program by not explaining the therapeutic alternatives. This danger may be substantially decreased by client involvement in the program's design.

In conclusion, I would like to list some of the recommendations that appear to follow from Dr. Stolz' paper. First, we should consider the protection of our clients more carefully. Second, an informed consent form for all therapeutic programs, including non-research programs, is desirable. Not only would such a form protect the client, but it would also protect the organization conducting therapy. It may also be useful to educate the client in procedures to be followed and the expected outcome. Misunderstandings would be minimized and the role of each person in the program would be clearly defined. Informed consent is probably the most important issue in therapy because it can prevent most of the other issues from becoming problems. A third recommendation is that we train our students to behave ethically. Fourth, we should educate those people who do not understand the behavioral approach. It is often these individuals who unjustly engage in blanket dismissals of behavioral techniques. Behavior modification associations, similar to the one described by Garry Martin at this conference, would be an excellent vehicle for educating the public and minimizing some of the misunderstandings. Fifth, we should encourage ethical review committees in our organizations. However, committee members should understand behavioral principles and techniques in order to avoid another Minnesota hospital workshop incident. Finally, I believe that if we take care in protecting our clients, we will ultimately protect ourselves from unjust public controls.

Criteria for Protecting Clients and Subjects

Issues	Possible Risks and Benefits	Misinformation or Lack of Information	Involuntary Control
Definition of Deviance	?		X
Justification of Intervention	X		
Informed Consent	X	X	X
Reversal Designs	X	X	
Treatment of Control Groups	X	X	
Use of New Therapeutic Procedures	X	X	
Unjustified Risks	X	X	X
Aversive Procedures	X		X
Deprivation	X		X
Unqualified Modifier	X	X	
Unethical Modifier	X	X	X

RESPONSE

William A. Myerson

There is very little concrete data for a discussion of the ethical behavior of behavioral researchers. We have only vague ideas of what is currently accepted practice for the behavioral community, but an accurate appraisal of these practices is critical in any evaluation of ethics for the profession.

Dr. Stolz' paper represents an important step toward explicating the current ethical standards being maintained in human behavioral research. At the same time the paper demonstrates a need for a much more open system so that information on currently acceptable practices can exert control over behaviorists, whether they be researchers or grant reviewers. Similar procedures for evaluating the adequacy of research have already been implemented among behaviorists (e.g., The Division 25 Recorder, *JEAB*, and *JABA* have taken steps to share their "insiders" view of behavioral research by opening up to their readers some of the editorial process).

In evaluating the "ethical problems" discovered by Dr. Stolz in the research she reviewed it should be noted that these researchers were writing to a review committee and were presumably sensitive to issues such as subject risk and informed consent. Thus, to the extent that the current Department of Health, Education and Welfare (DHEW) reviewing policies were known, the data was biased in favor of agreement. It is quite likely that standard practice is somewhat different from this sample.

The effect of public disclosure of DHEW's reviewing policies, as in Dr. Stolz' paper, can profoundly alter both the research of behaviorists and also the criteria for ethical behavior to be used by grant reviewers. The research of people involved with federal funding may be changed by DHEW's collection and presentation of data on types of research which raise "ethical problems" and the way these "problems" were resolved between the researchers and the reviewers.

The systematic evaluation of the decision process should also provide the researcher with some means of reciprocal control by providing him with the means for modifying the ethical standards of the reviewer. For instance, if grants with similar "ethical problems" are continually being submitted and rejected, and this is being monitored, the reviewer is more likely to entertain the possibility that his ethical standards are not in line with those of the research community and to consider changing his standards.

Additional information would be especially valuable to those whose communication with DHEW is limited. The issue of greater publicity and the consequent increase in reciprocal control are especially important. However, I must admit that, as a student, reciprocal control is a process with which I am almost totally unfamiliar.

The impact of the researcher and the practitioner should be strengtened if we are to have a flexible, outcome-oriented definition of ethical practices. The ethical standards of the scientific community are most important since those people are in closest touch with outcome data and with the problems in need of resolution. For instance, some types of traditional therapies are currently considered unethical in many situations, not on the basis of topography and process, but on results of outcome-oriented research currently being conducted.

The availability of public information would make possible empirical research on the effects of changes in DHEW's policies on research practices. It could also provide a place for interested third parties to comment on decisions (e.g., the American Civil Liberties Union or concerned behaviorists).

The concept of a risk-to-benefit ratio has both strengths and weaknesses. Risk-to-benefit analyses make clear that, when research of sufficient importance is being considered, the likelihood of rejection for other reasons is reduced. Such analyses may have the effect of promoting research with more socially important consequences. The use of a risk-to-benefit ratio also makes it clear that we must examine what accounts for an increased judgment of benefit and thus the willingness to accept increased risks. It would appear that the current practices of

DHEW in promoting the subject's "dignity" stand in part because so much of the research they are asked to fund addresses questions with low potential for social benefit. A weakness of a concept such as risk-to-benefit ratio, much like the concept cost-benefit ratio, is that it implies a level of precision which is far from justified.

In summary, Dr. Stolz' paper appears to be important primarily because it presents a data-based analysis of ethics. From this perspective the issue of a risk-to-benefit ratio seems to be less important than the issue of defining what are "ethical problems." The major questions the paper raises are: are the data on ethics being kept in any systematic fashion and are these data given sufficient display both within DHEW and in the concerned scientific community for it to have maximum impact? It seems apparent that the answer to both of these questions is no. Thus, it is clear that Dr. Stolz, as a behaviorist within DHEW, needs to continue her efforts to open up the system.